# Cities and Frontiers in Brazil

# Cities and Frontiers in Brazil:
## Regional Dimensions of Economic Development

## Martin T. Katzman

Harvard University Press
Cambridge, Massachusetts
and London, England
1977

Copyright © 1977 by the President and Fellows of Harvard College
Printed in the United States of America

**Library of Congress Cataloging in Publication Data**
Katzman, Martin T
  Cities and frontiers in Brazil.

  Includes bibliographical references and index.
  1. Regional planning—Brazil.  2. Urbanization—
Brazil. 3. Land settlement—Brazil. 4.  Brazil—
Economic policy. I. Title.
HT395.B7K37        309.2'5'0981        77-23159
ISBN 0-674-13280-7

*À minha luz, Arlene*

# Acknowledgments

Through a Carnegie Field Studies Fellowship I spent an idyllic summer in 1962 with the good villagers of Abrantes, Bahia, who taught me that most lovely accent and kindled my interest in Brazil. Werner Baer, *pai do santo* to many aspiring Brazilianists, facilitated my return in 1970-1972 to teach urban and regional economics at the University of São Paulo, an opportunity that left an indelible mark on my world view. Through the generous logistical support of Stanley Nicholson, Ford Foundation representative in Brazil, I was able to enjoy such experiences as participating in an *umbanda* in Belém, inoculating cattle on the Pantanal, and lecturing in about a dozen capitals around the country. Arriving as a man with roots planted deep in asphalt, I left Brazil with tremendous excitement about the process of frontier settlement, which aroused fantasies and images of the American past, and with an abiding fascination about the many channels by which urban and rural development interact.

During my São Paulo years and since, Milton de Abreu Campanario has been a tireless research aide. Financial support for data processing and typing came from a small emergency grant of the Milton Fund of Harvard University. In the course of writing, I benefited from the encouragement and helpful comments of William Alonso. Without fail Michael Woldenberg clarified the conceptual puzzles and filled the bibliographic gaps I confronted him with. Once again my father, Ira Katzman, lent his creative talents to preparing my maps and figures. Most of all, I owe my comrade-in-arms Edmar Lisboa Bacha for many hours of stimulating debate and painstaking comments, which left his brand on these pages.

Lexington, Massachusetts

# Contents

# Tables

# Figures

# Cities and Frontiers in Brazil

# 1

# Introduction

Economic development has historically been associated with the spatial reorganization of societies. The pioneer clears virgin acreage in hope of leaving a patrimony for his children. His landless brother moves to a nearby small town to obtain a foothold in the world of nonagricultural labor. Young people from farms and villages in stagnant agricultural regions travel to the bustling commercial and industrial emporia where the range of educational, employment, and marriage possibilities is greater, thereby further crowding the slums of the metropolis. The functionary finally saves enough money to purchase a home in the suburbs, where his children are free from the choking industrial pollution.

These examples represent the several levels on which spatial reorganization occurs: *frontier settlement*, the incorporation of empty, resource-rich regions; *regional integration*, an increase in the flow of goods, manpower, private capital, and public funds among the settled regions of a nation; *urbanization*, an increase in the urban share of the population leading to a possible depopulation of some rural areas; *urban system development*, differential rates of urban growth by city size and region as a result of the changing division of labor among cities; and *intrametropolitan* changes in land-use patterns and areal expansion.

While each of these changes is a response to as well as a cause of new opportunities, each also creates complex economic, social, and political problems. The illusion of the limitless frontier may weaken the farmer's resolve to protect his land against erosion and the government's resolve to encourage population control. The integration of formerly isolated regions tends to expand the markets of the dynamic, industrializing center at the cost of destroying cottage handicrafts and the way of life of the less modern periphery. Like interregional migration, urbanization is often associated with the sapping of capital and of the most vigorous workers from the rural periphery, with the flooding of the urban labor market with marginalized workers, and with an overburdening of municipal services and housing. In many countries of the developing world these trends have been associated with what is perceived to be excessive concentration or gigantism of the primate cities and the virtual abandonment of many small towns. Finally, metropolitan growth and land-use specialization tend to overburden public services and to lengthen the supply lines of the city, thereby contributing to congestion and pollution.

Spatial problems on at least one of these levels of analysis are salient in almost every country of the world. At the initial stages of development the problem of creating a dynamic center tends to preoccupy policymakers. As development progresses the issues of regional disparities in growth rates and in per capita income, of overurbanization, and of overconcentration in the primate cities may acquire greater salience. As the economy matures and blatant regional disparities diminish, more attention is paid to the stagnation of older mining and industrial areas, metropolitan land use, congestion, and pollution, or what is now called the "quality of life." That is not to say that large depressed areas are absent in advanced countries or that congestion or pollution is unimportant in developing countries. Such countries as Britain, France, and Australia are obviously concerned with issues of urban overconcentration. The United States is concerned with the urban-rural balance and the creation of growth centers in Appalachia and the Ozarks. Nations do not tend to treat these spatial imbalances as growing pains that will go away automatically; the focus of growth policy seems to vary with the level of development.[1]

By virtue of its size, rapid growth, and regional diversity, Brazil provides a fascinating arena for observing the spatial changes associated with economic development and the evolution of regional and urban growth policy (figure 1). Because of the salience of such processes in the Brazilian context, this book focuses on frontier settlement, regional integration, and urbanization.

Frontier settlement has played an important role in the shaping of many modern nations. The ecological, economic, and political conditions under which such expansion has taken place

**Figure 1.** Brazilian states

are as varied as mankind itself: the southward thrust of Chinese peasants into the tropical forests under the aegis of aspiring warlords, the clandestine flight of Russian serfs to the black soils of Siberia, the Great Trek of the Boers in northward flight from the British, the inward penetration of the "big man's" sheep frontier in Australia, the creation of the wheatlands by tenant farmers and migrant workers on the pampas.[2]

The works of Frederick Jackson Turner have stimulated generations of American scholars to consider the impact of the frontier on our economic, political, and social institutions. His major theses were that the frontier is responsible, even necessary, for the nourishment of our political democracy and of social mobility; that it turns the nation's concerns inward, thereby encouraging the development of a truly indigenous culture; and that it serves as a labor safety valve that discourages class consciousness and revolution among the working class. Subsequent comparative research has suggested that these alleged benefits of the frontier have not been universally enjoyed in other frontier societies or in all parts of the American frontier, of which the slave-holding South was a part. Despite the repudiation of much of the thesis, several Turnerian themes, which Henry Nash Smith calls the "symbol and myth of the frontier," have had considerable impact on public policy in several countries. The theme of turning the nation inward to its own resources and away from foreign influences played no small part in the decisions to construct Ankara, Ciudad Guayana, and Brasília. The theme of the frontier as a safety valve was central to the debates on the great Siberian migration before the Russian Revolution as well as to the Brazilian decision to colonize the Amazon.[3]

As the largest nation in the world still undergoing significant frontier expansion, Brazil provides an opportunity to observe a westward movement under conditions strikingly different from our own in many ways, but similar in others. Modern frontier settlement began in the 1850s with the spread of coffee westward in São Paulo state, weathering the transition from slave to tenant labor after 1888. Although the limits of the best coffee-growing area were reached by the 1950s, the frontier continued westward with the planting of rice and raising of cattle in the vast savanna of the Central West. Until the 1930s frontier expansion took place mainly at the initiative of large landowners and railroad companies. After the 1930s the westward march became an explicit part of nationalist ideology and public policy. Concrete results of this policy have been a planned capital of the state of Goiás in the 1930s, Brasília in the late 1950s, and the Transamazon highway in the early 1970s.

The process of frontier settlement raises a wide range of conceptual and policy issues, some of which are treated here. What determines which frontiers are occupied, when, and at what speed? What impact does the nature of the frontier staple have upon the social relations of production and development prospects of the region? Does the frontier provide poor individuals with an opportunity for social mobility? Does the frontier serve as a safety valve, and hence an alternative to land reform or social revolution in the settled areas? Does its existence unduly inhibit the modernization of agriculture and encourage erosion and soil exhaustion in the settled areas? As a matter of policy, which frontiers ought to be developed and how? Is planned colonization superior to spontaneous migration with respect to efficiency and to provision of opportunity for ownership among the poor? Is it effective to implant growth poles and construct developmental highways to spread economic growth from an urban center throughout a region?

The process of frontier settlement — or extensive agricultural growth — has acquired new salience in the face of the universal perception of an impending food crisis. Given a recognition of the harmful environmental consequences of excessive use of fertilizers and insecticides, the rising prices of these items, and the possible exhaustion of easy technological breakthroughs in grain production, the incorporation of new farmlands will be given greater attention in the future than in the recent past. Since a large share of the world's unutilized farmland lies in Latin America, Brazilian efforts to colonize its savannas and tropical rain forests should be of more than parochial interest.

An increase in the wealth of nations, Adam Smith noted, depends upon the division of labor, which in turn depends upon the extent of the market. This latter varies not only with population and per capita income but also with the facility with which manpower, capital, and commodities can move across space (that is, the friction of distance).

The neoclassical view of the process of regional integration focuses largely on market-directed flows of goods and factors of production. Conditioned by the fact that the United States and Britain were the only societies that have industrialized without major state intervention in the economy, this view takes the action of the state as a given, exogenous to the economic system, and often as a result of the decisions of disinterested statesmen with a benign sense of the general welfare. This framework has an equilibrium bias, such that these market-directed flows lead to long-run equalization in levels of welfare among regions. The lower the friction of distance between regions, the more rapid and more complete the equalization process.

In most developing countries one must take account of the

many ways in which the state intervenes in the market. For instance, in Brazil the state vigorously controls wages and many prices, indirectly channels funds into priority sectors or regions, invests directly in profit-making enterprises as well as in infrastructure, and employs a large bureaucracy, which comprises a considerable market in its own right. While in many cases government investments in energy, transportation, and metallurgical undertakings reinforce private decisions in Brazil, there are striking examples of the government setting its own locational priorities. One such example is the allocation to Brasília of 10 percent of gross capital formation from 1956 to 1962.

In the course of Brazilian economic development, the friction of distance has decreased substantially, thereby facilitating the flow of goods, capital, and labor. Over the past fifty years or so the increasing integration of the Brazilian economy has been associated with the divergence in regional rates of industrial, agricultural, and population growth in favor of the state of São Paulo. This center of Brazilian industrialization has increased its share of industrial production from 17 percent in 1907 to 32 percent in 1920, 36 percent in 1939, and 55 percent by the 1960s.

This concentration of economic activity is occurring in the context of what are likely the worst regional per capita income disparities in the world. For example, in 1939 the Northeast as a whole had a per capita income that was 48 percent of the national average and only 27 percent of São Paulo's. In the next decade the Northeast's relative position worsened, and since then recovery has been so slow that by 1969 its per capita income relative to Brazil and to São Paulo was slightly worse than thirty years earlier.[4]

With about one-third of the Brazilian population, the Northeast is one of the largest depressed areas in the world and has been a preoccupation of policymakers for nearly a century. Despite the enormous injection of federal funds, amounting to 10 percent of the regional income by the 1960s, the region's relative progress has been excruciatingly slow. Its industrialization has absorbed little labor, and the wages of its landless workers have hardly changed in the past two decades.

Public efforts at alleviating regional disparities have been notoriously unsuccessful around the world. The key problems in the Brazilian context are identifying the factors encouraging the continual concentration of industry in São Paulo and identifying the most effective policies for fomenting development in the Northeast.

Like most countries in the developing world, Brazil has been urbanizing rapidly, the urban share of population rising from 25 percent in 1940 to 52 percent in 1970. Again as in other countries, Brazilian policymakers have presumed that the urban population is too large, two symptoms being the labor absorption problem and the perceived breakdown and congestion of urban services.

The labor absorption problem involves the following issues: Why does the urban population grow faster than industrial employment? With the low degree of absorption into the modern industrial sector and the consequent marginalization of the bulk of the urban working class, why does rural-urban migration persist? The labor absorption problem is common to much of the developing world, but it takes a peculiar form in Brazil. As high a share of Brazil's national product is generated in the industrial sector as in such countries as Argentina and Italy (30 percent), but the share of employment in that sector is only 13 percent. The ratio of the employment share to the output share is the lowest in the world.[5]

A different set of concerns is raised by the fascination of many nations with the notion of implanting growth poles in resource frontiers or depressed areas as a method of stimulating regional development. The growth pole is an urban center whose industrial development presumably irradiates the surrounding region. The policy of implanting growth poles, exemplified by the creation of Ciudad Guayana in Venezuela, petrochemical complexes in Lacq, France, and at the heel of the Mezzogiorno, raises the general issue of the role of the city in economic development. Two schools of thought can be distinguished, here called the French and the American, that differ considerably in their policy implications. The French school, whose central figure is Perroux, views the growth pole as the location of a set of tightly interlinked, capital-intensive, large-scale manufacturing enterprises whose product faces a rapid growth of demand. Through the mechanism of interindustry linkages, the growth of these key industries propels the rest of the regional economy. The American school, which has received its form from a large number of scholars, views the city that generates growth as composed of large numbers of small firms, highly specialized quaternary services, and a skilled and diversified labor force.

While the American school maintains that self-sustaining growth is only possible in a highly diversified, small-enterprise city, growth pole policy in most of the world seems to be following the French prescription. Especially in the developing world, the foreign enterprises being established seem to have the characteristics of the ideal-type propulsive industry: highly capital intensive, vertically integrated, high technology. Since few empirical studies have actually tested whether such industrial complexes have in fact generated self-sustaining growth, the Brazilian experience in Amazonia and the Northeast cited here has broader implications.

While the French and American schools focus on industrial development, another line of inquiry focuses upon the impact of urbanization on agricultural modernization. The industrial-urban hypothesis maintains that industrial growth improves the functioning of factor and product markets and that the benefits of these improvements spill over into the agricultural sector. Consequently, those agricultural regions well situated with respect to the loci of rapid industrial growth will become modernized first. Since most of the evidence for this hypothesis is based on the American experience, an understanding of the impact of urbanization on rural development in Brazil is of greater relevance to developing countries.

While this work does not pretend to answer all the questions raised above, these questions suggest the wide range of development problems and policy issues that are played out in the spatial arena.

The conceptual point of departure is location theory, which is a junction between economics and geography. This branch of knowledge has evolved on the basis of the experience of relatively advanced market economies in which the institutions are taken as either given or irrelevant. While location theory and its offshoot, regional science, have normative implications, they have little power to explain policy or have few suggestions on how to improve policy-making capacity other than suggesting the adoption of sophisticated programming techniques. This approach, which ignores institutions and political factors, may be of limited value in understanding a developing country with evolving institutions and characterized by a large state sector that controls the commanding heights of the economy.

The challenge here is to modify the traditional location theory approach by introducing institutional and political factors where essential. The tasks are to understand changes in the spatial organization of the Brazilian economy through synthesis of the relevant works of historians, geographers, anthropologists, and economists; analysis of particular examples of spatial evolution; and testing of hypotheses derived from the experience of advanced countries. As underdeveloped countries usually generate underdeveloped data, these tests are suggestive rather than definitive.

These efforts are guided by two basic questions. What new insights that may be neglected or misunderstood in a sectoral or macroscopic analysis does a spatial analysis cast upon Brazilian economic development? What new insights does Brazilian development experience cast upon orthodox spatial analysis, as conceived and nurtured in advanced capitalist societies?

An appropriate reply to these questions may be a third, "New to whom?" The answer to the first question is addressed to Latin American and North American scholars, journalists, and technocrats, who generate and consume ideas about development, as well as other foreigners interested in the Brazilian model. These are steeped in the unique history of Brazil, versed in varying degrees in some form of economics, but generally unfamiliar with spatial analysis. The answer to the second is addressed to scholars interested in spatial analysis, few of whom specialize in particular developing countries, and to statesmen and practicing planners, who consume, and may wisely neglect to utilize, the ideas these scholars generate.

# 2

# The Brazilian Frontier in Comparative Perspective

In the past century frontier settlement has played a major role in the evolution of not only the new nations of the Western Hemisphere but also the old nations of Eurasia. Most of the English-language research on these frontiers is richly descriptive but not easily amenable to systematic comparison. The Turner theses explored the relationship between land abundance and democracy, so their applicability to such diverse cultures as Latin America, Russia, China, and Burma is not obvious.

On what grounds can such disparate frontier experiences be compared? One point of view holds that comparison is meaningful only where frontiers have many facets in common (such as semiarid grasslands under American, Australian, Argentine, or Soviet institutions). The viewpoint here is that certain questions can be raised of all frontier societies regardless of their physical, political, or cultural environments. Of the many aspects amenable to comparison, three essentially economic ones are considered in this book: What determines which empty regions, if any, are settled? To what extent does the physical environment, as opposed to demographic, technological, or political factors, influence the social relations of production (the establishment of family farms instead of plantations)? To what extent has the existence of the frontier increased wages in the settled regions of the nation, a necessary condition for the functioning of the labor safety valve?

## Frontier Settlement as Extensive Growth

Frontier settlement generally increases the amount of land devoted to agriculture, though this is not necessarily so because new land brought into cultivation may simply offset in area land abandoned in older regions because of soil exhaustion or inherent inferiority. In the tropics the practice of shifting cultivation or slash-and-burn agriculture leads to the abandonment of a cultivated plot for as long as a generation pending regrowth of the forest. This process has been called the hollow frontier by geographer Preston James. Soil exhaustion has not been the driving force behind Brazilian frontier expansion. Indeed, soil exhaustion has been a response to the availability of frontier lands. The phenomenon of abandonment has not been confined to the tropics, for the settlement of western North America has been associated with the decline of farm acreage in the eastern regions.[1]

On balance, frontier expansion in the world has led to an increase in total acreage in farms, in improved acreage, and in crop land. Brazil is the only continental country currently undergoing massive frontier settlement. A crude indicator of the areal extension of agriculture is acreage of crop land (table 1). Of the five nations with roughly three million square miles each, the United States has the largest area of crop land; Australia has the smallest. The rate of growth of crop land began to decelerate after 1900 in

Table 1. Area of crop land, selected countries, millions of acres.

| Year | U.S. | Canada | Australia | China | Argentina | Brazil |
|------|------|--------|-----------|-------|-----------|--------|
| 1850 | 113  | –      | –         | –     | –         | –      |
| 1860 | 163  | –      | 1.2       | –     | –         | –      |
| 1870 | 189  | –      | 2.1       | 201   | 1.4       | –      |
| 1880 | 188  | –      | 4.6       | –     | –         | –      |
| 1890 | 248  | –      | 5.4       | 207   | 2.5       | –      |
| 1900 | 319  | 20     | 8.8       | –     | 18        | –      |
| 1910 | 347  | 36     | 12        | 226   | 46        | –      |
| 1920 | 402  | 50     | 15        | –     | 59        | 16     |
| 1930 | 413  | 58     | 25        | 245   | 67        | –      |
| 1940 | 399  | 56     | 21        | –     | 69        | 46     |
| 1950 | 409  | 62     | 20        | –     | –         | 47     |
| 1960 | 392  | 62     | 29        | 274   | 66        | 71     |
| 1970 | 384  | 69     | 39        | –     | 64        | 84     |

Source: United States Department of Commerce, *Historical Statistics of the United States, Colonial Times to 1970*, vol. 1, p. 433. *Census of Canada, 1961*, Agricultural Bulletin SA-1 and SA-4; *Census of Canada, 1951*, vol. 6, Agriculture, part 1; *Canada Year Book*, 1974. *Official Yearbook of the Commonwealth of Australia*, no. 58, 1972, pp. 742-746. Dwight Perkins, *Agricultural Development in China* (Chicago: Aldine, 1969), pp. 15-18. República Argentina, *Censo nacional agropecuaria*, 1937 and 1960; United Nations, *FAO Yearbook*, 1972, table 1. Brasil, *Censo agrícola*, years indicated.

the United States and after 1920 in Canada, which has experienced a recent upturn. In China crop land has been increasing slowly but steadily at least since the 1800s, but a more important mode of increasing effective area has been through irrigation, which permits multiple cropping. Australia's crop land grew steadily until 1930, declined through the 1950s, and is increasing now. Argentina, with an area one-third that of the other countries, ended its period of rapid expansion by 1920.

The growth of crop area in most of these countries hardly signifies frontier settlement in the sense of the pioneer hoe breaking virgin soil where only animals trod before. Except for China's Manchurian frontier, expansion in these countries has been in long-settled regions.[2] In contrast, the growth of crop land in Brazil shows signs of vigorous expansion. At the same level as Australia and less than one-third the level of Canada and Argentina in 1920, Brazil's crop land had come to exceed these three countries by 1970. Despite repeated prognoses of its imminent demise with the destruction of the last tropical forests, the Brazilian frontier has been expanding into new physiographic zones; wheat and soybeans are grown on the southern prairies and upland rice in the central western savanna.

While Brazil has been consistently increasing its supply of effective crop land, climatic barriers seem to have stifled frontier expansion in other continental countries. These barriers are not absolute, for at some cost irrigation or desalination could extend farming to semiarid zones, such as the American Southwest, or vast greenhouses could combat the cold in the northern Canadian prairies.

Frontier expansion cannot be explained either by the sheer availability of vacant land or by the growth of demand for food. Neither land availability nor climatic barriers would explain why crop land in the United States and Canada has stabilized at 23 and 2 percent of total land area, respectively. Growth of demand does not require an increase in acreage, for output can be increased by greater inputs of labor or fertilizers in a given land area or by technological advances such as improved seed. In North America yield-increasing agrobiological innovation has substituted for the expansion of the frontier. In addition, the diffusion of the internal combustion engine took approximately ninety million acres out of hay production. Despite the growth in total demand for food, technological progress has been rapid enough to decrease the utilization of crop land since the 1930s.[3]

In contrast to North America, the growth of agricultural output in Brazil has largely been due to increase in land area, with little increase in yields and only slight increases in output per man. From the late 1920s to the late 1940s both output and land area rose by 55 percent. From the late 1940s to the early 1960s about 95 percent of the growth in output was due to the expansion of land area, the remainder of the increase due largely to shifts from low-yield to high-yield regions. Largely because of its frontier, Brazil has been able to increase its food supply as fast as demand, in contrast to most other Latin American countries.[4]

An important distinction in understanding the spread of a frontier is between subsistence and commercial economies. While both types may be open to foreign immigration, they differ in their degree of participation in international trade. In the former the value of land for settlement is largely determined by site factors (climate, fertility, or relief). In the latter the situation of land with respect to roads or ports predominates as a determinant of land values.

A subsistence economy is generally one that is too distant from the market or whose production possibilities are too similar to those of its potential trading partners to engage in interregional commerce. While there are few economies that engage in no exchange whatsoever, examples of subsistence frontier expansion are suggested by the *habitant's* penetration of the Saint Lawrence and Saguenay valleys until the middle of the eighteenth century, the Boer societies of South Africa from about 1650 to 1850, and the southward penetration of the Chinese until they encountered the European imperialists in Indochina.[5] The differences among these experiences are too obvious to detail, especially in the social relations of production they involved: the *habitant* as the Turnerian family farmer in fact, although in law a vassal; the farmer-rancher Boer as *baas* to quasi-slave Bantu; the Chinese peasant as tenant on a newly formed estate.

Despite these differences, land abundance generates two similar responses. Suppose that land is so abundant that if each unit of production, be it a family or a gang of slaves, cultivated as much land as it could, there would still be plenty of good land left over. First, agriculture is undertaken on an extensive basis, wasteful of land, which is not scarce by assumption. In the temperate zone extensive agriculture may take the form of field rotation with long fallow periods; in the tropics it is exemplified by shifting cultivation. Although extensive agriculture may seem primitive and low yielding on a per acre basis, it does maximize returns to labor.[6]

Second, high labor productivity leads to improved nutrition, which in turn may increase fertility and reduce mortality. In the land-abundant environment the adaptive advantage of cultural sanctions on birth control are minimal. Consequently, the population may grow rapidly and the parent group maintains its customary allotment of land per worker simply by sending its children off to settle new virgin lands.

These conditions held in southern Brazil in the early nineteenth century, when modern European immigration began. Italian and German colonists were brought to the states of Rio Grande do Sul and Santa Catarina in hope that they would introduce the more advanced agricultural techniques of their homelands. Despite their background in intensive farming, the immigrants readily adopted the extensive, slash-and-burn techniques of the natives, even abandoning the plow for the digging stick. This behavior is easily understood in economic terms: the natural resources of the region were not so propitious that the settlers could compete for world markets in the production of any staples. Thus in this region the demand for land was low and its price cheap. Concentrating on production for their own use, the immigrants practiced extensive agriculture because land was cheap, fertilizers expensive, and plows impossible to use in slash-and-burn agriculture.[7]

The settlement and deforestation of Brazil's southern highlands have been almost entirely due to the rapid growth of this immigrant population. Diminishing returns eventually limit perpetual expansion in this mode. As the highlands are now largely occupied, migrants from this region have been forced to utilize the less fertile savannas of Mato Grosso. At the same time a road system from São Paulo has been penetrating this subsistence frontier. The possibilities for marketing wrought profound changes in the behavior of the descendants of the European immigrants: their techniques are becoming more modernized or less extensive and their harvests contain a higher proportion of commercial crops. This process also invited the encroachment of powerful interlopers who wrested much of the land from the erstwhile subsistence farmers. As Barraclough and Domike warn, "In many cases, lands opened for cultivation are reclaimed by their owners as soon as they begin to have a commercial value, which pushes the colonizer into a latifundia system . . . or else obliges him to migrate further into the backlands."[8]

Factors that explain commercial frontier expansion are the capability of the land to produce a commodity for which there is a growing export demand, a labor force that can be attracted to or compelled to immigrate to the frontier, and a marketing system that can move the staple to market. Whether or not a particular piece of new land is incorporated into the agricultural economy is a matter of comparative costs. The money return of spending additional dollars on bringing more land into cultivation is compared to that of spending on other farm inputs (labor, machinery, fertilizers), and the return on dollars spent in increasing agricultural output is compared to that of spending on other sectors of the economy.

Let us now consider the settlement of an empty region exceptionally well endowed for the production of some staple highly valued in foreign markets. Suppose that all exports and imports are traded at an entrepôt on the coast of the frontier region.

The exploitation of frontier lands is not costless. Migration to the frontier requires heavy direct expenditures in the transportation of people and belongings and in losses of income while traveling and acclimating to the new environment, not to mention the emotional burden of broken ties. Second, land must often be cleared, fenced, and otherwise improved before cultivation can begin.[9] Such costs are also incurred in subsistence frontier settlement. Crucial in export-propelled settlement, increased distance from the market requires greater transportation outlays in exporting the staple and importing the consumer goods and farm implements. Such long hauls may justify massive investments in railroads, highways, or port facilities.

One offsetting benefit to frontier expansion may be the encounter of superior soils or climatic conditions. If the superiority merely reflects the natural stock of fertility locked in the virgin soil, this advantage will be quickly dissipated. It is clearly fortuitous whether ecological conditions on the frontier surpass those in the established regions. While the American Corn Belt or Canadian prairies, for example, were more fertile than regions farther to the east, penetration of the high plains, the Australian outback, Manchuria, and the Brazilian Central West represented movement to less favorable conditions. Even though the settlement of the Corn Belt represented a shift of agricultural production to superior soils, the growth of American grain output in the nineteenth century was due less to an increase in acreage or fertility than to technological advances and mechanization that increased yields and output per man.[10]

When a population of fixed size, a closed population, undergoes export-propelled frontier settlement, the increase in the supply of land per man raises labor productivity, a necessary condition for the functioning of the labor safety valve. Land area per worker may not increase, however, if frontier settlement is accompanied by equally rapid natural population growth or immigration from abroad.

The Great Siberian Migration and the Great Trek in South Africa were undertaken by a closed population from more densely settled regions of the same nation. The settlement of the Great Plains and São Paulo, on the other hand, were accompanied by massive immigration from abroad. The movement of Scandinavians to the Plains and Italians to São Paulo dampened the wage-enhancing effect of frontier expansion for the earlier settlers of North America and Brazil, respectively. This is not to imply that frontier expansion-cum-immigration has no benefits. The question is for whom? The movement of people from low-productivity regions abroad to a high-productivity frontier certainly raises migrants' incomes, increases world output, and lowers the price for consumers of the frontier staple. The opening up of São Paulo, however, provided more of a safety valve for Italy than for the Northeast of Brazil.[11]

What are the limits to export-propelled frontier settlement? More important than ecological constraints are the costs of transporting the staple to market. At some distance from the entrepôt, which can be called the pioneer fringe, the prices received net of transport costs are so low that commercial production is not profitable. Beyond this fringe, land will be utilized only by subsistence farmers. Interactions between yields, commodity prices, labor costs, and transport costs and their influence on frontier expansion are explained graphically and algebraically in the appendix.

### The Physical Environment and Social Relations of Production

It is tempting to assume that the social relations of production on the frontier are determined externally by legal norms and political power in the metropolis rather than determined internally. For example, in commenting on the nature of latifundia in Latin America, Barraclough and Domike aver, "These land tenure institutions are a product of the power structure." The powerful classes surrounding the Crown presumably shaped these institutions to maximize their self-interest, which included extra- and even antieconomic objectives. In addition, Barraclough and Domike assert, "The fundamental difference between this migration toward the frontier in Latin America and the settlement of American frontier land in the last century is that in the United States . . . these lands belonged to no one, while in Latin America almost all land already has an owner."[12]

Experience in both the United States and Brazil suggests that this is not a sufficient difference. First, it is difficult to find much difference in the motivations, pretensions, and world view of the aristocrats who organized the settlement of these nations. With the exception of the Puritans in New England, the colonizers sought huge land grants in order to replicate a feudal order that was already moribund in England. The headright system of land grants employed in the middle and southern colonies encouraged the latifundia-minifundia pattern of land distribution common in Latin America. Despite the similarity of interests of colonizing companies, family farms emerged as the dominant form of tenure in the North; plantations based upon slave labor predominated in the South. As Griswold notes, the family farm was hardly a typical English institution.[13]

Second, although the Homestead Act of 1862 provided free land to those satisfying certain residency requirements, the major waves of pioneering preceded the act. Prior to 1862 public land was available in plots of 640 and later 320 acres at a minimum price of $1.25 per acre at an auction or a flat $1.25 under preemption. Free or low-priced land, however, can also be effectively worthless if it is too arid, too distant from transport facilities, or too difficult to clear. Most farmers purchased land at higher prices per acre from canal or railroad companies who provided both financing and transport facilities, from speculators who subdivided sections into smaller plots, and from professional pioneers who took the risks of preparing and testing the land.[14]

Third, self-interest of the ruling class is a poor predictor of the ultimate tenure form. In both the subsistence frontier of Rio Grande do Sul and the commercial frontier of northern Paraná, family farms were carved out of large properties held by the original grantees and by British financiers, respectively. In Rio Grande do Sul, the land had little value in staple production; therefore, landlords had little inducement to undertake direct commercial exploitation. Great capital gains could be reaped, however, by subdividing these lands for family plots and reinvesting the profits in lands farther west.

In contrast to theories of institutional inertia, two economic models attempt to explain the social relations of production on the frontier by characteristics of the physical environment: *technological determinism* and the *factor endowments* approach, of which the Turner thesis is an exemplar. Technological determinism attempts to deduce the social relations of production from the technological conditions under which the regional staple is produced. Family farming is most likely when there are no significant economies of scale (the optimum size farm is small), the crop is land intensive rather than capital intensive or labor intensive, and capital can be easily substituted for labor if wages rise. A farmer needs little capital or labor to produce efficiently; furthermore, as general progress raises wages, the small rural proletariat is displaced by machines.[15]

Under tropical conditions, it is alleged, economies of scale are quite important because of gains to the specialization of labor, huge capital outlays required for production and processing, or the superiority of large farms in developing new breeds. Technological imperatives thus dictate large-scale organization with the vast majority of workers in dependent status.

It should be emphasized that this approach is completely ahistorical. Regardless of the institutions or cultural traditions under which the frontier society was formed, market forces will determine which crop will be produced in a given region and hence the viable social relations of production.

These conditions for the establishment of family farming may be necessary but not sufficient. If land is owned by a large landlord and there are legal or financial barriers to small land purchases, family farmers may remain in a dependent status as tenants. For example, as is effectively true in Brazil, mortgages for land purchase may simply be unavailable through the formal banking system.

Considerable empirical evidence suggests that family farm and plantation crops cannot easily be distinguished on the basis of economies of scale or labor intensity. Scale economies in wheat production and processing are of the same order as in sugar production and processing; moreover, wheat is considerably more capital intensive than cane, cotton, or other plantation crops. Within the tropics one may observe a given crop being grown under a wide range of tenure forms.[16]

The factor endowments approach looks at the effect of the man/land ratio on the social relations of production. Suppose a densely settled region comes under the control of a ruling class that bases its wealth and power on the ownership of land or at least upon the ability to tax land. A high man/land endowment implies that the marginal productivity of land is very high and that of labor is very low. Consequently, landlords can extract very high land rents with no particular advantage to the imposition of any restrictions on labor mobility.

Next suppose that a frontier is opened up whose lands are also granted to big landlords. Frontier landlords can extract rents from their land only if labor is expended. Since labor on the frontier is scarce, wages are high and land rents are so low that many landlords may not even bother to enforce their claim.

High wages on the frontier may attract laborers from the settled regions, where wages would tend to rise and rents to fall, a necessary condition for the functioning of Turner's labor safety valve. Where land is monopolized by the few, however, Domar suggests that it is also possible that labor dependency increases in both regions. If labor were free to migrate, the opening of the frontier would force landlords to compete more intensively for a fixed labor supply, forcing down rents. The imposition of serfdom, which restricts the movement from one estate to another, prevents competition in the labor market and enables the landlords to keep wages down and rents up despite the existence of the frontier. While serfdom on the frontier forces wages below and rents above their competitive levels, it does not alleviate the frontier landlords' labor shortage. In the absence of voluntary migration, slavery is a mechanism for increasing the man/land endowment.[17]

The linkage between the man/land endowment and the social relations of production depends upon whether the landlords can offset labor's market power with their own political power to enforce serfdom. Turner tended to emphasize examples where the market power of labor overwhelmed the landlords' political power. As a counterexample Domar traces the revival of Russian serfdom in the sixteenth century to the opening up of new lands in the Ukraine. It is also obvious that the revival of slavery in Western civilization followed the discovery of empty staple-producing lands in the American tropics and subtropics.

The social relations of production are of special interest to the extent that they affect agricultural land use. There is substantial evidence from such diverse circumstances as Czarist Russia and the Brazilian Northeast that the greater the area of operating units, the lesser the intensity of land use, even when land quality is held constant.[18] One reason is that the few local landowners who effectively monopolize the land can maximize their profits by restricting the access of labor to their land. Another reason is that landowners find the cost of recruiting and managing a labor force more costly the larger the operating unit. Finally, a permanent class of farm workers may eventually claim vested rights in the land, seriously weakening the landlord's power. This last reason explains the unwillingness of Argentine cattle barons to provide anything but short-term leases to wheat farmers, who were thus discouraged from planting fruit trees or building barns. Landlords in the interior of the Brazilian Northeast offer short-term sharecropping arrangements out of similar fears.[19] Were family farms to replace large holdings worked by day laborers or sharecroppers, agricultural land use would be more intense, rural population densities higher, and the viability of urban centers in rural areas enhanced. Since greater production would now flow from a smaller land area, the commercial frontier would be less extensive.

### The Economic Significance of the Brazilian Frontier

Frontier settlement has played a major role in fixing the political boundaries of Brazil. Although the popes attempted to divide

the Western Hemisphere fairly between the Spanish and Portu-
guese Crowns by setting boundary lines westward from the
Azores, the ultimate boundaries were determined by the doctrine
of *uti possidetis*, which granted sovereignty to those effectively
occupying the land. While Brazilian Indian hunters, traders, and
other fortune seekers, the romantic *bandeirantes*, penetrated
deeply into the interior of South America in the seventeenth century, effective and permanent occupation began with the
discovery of gold in Minas Gerais and to a lesser extent in Goiás
and Mato Grosso at the end of the eighteenth century. The brief
gold cycle from 1720 to 1770 had national repercussions. Besides
attracting an influx of slaves from the decadent northeastern
littoral, cattle raising in the semiarid interior of the Northeast
and especially in the grasslands of the far south were stimulated
to provide meat and work animals to the miners. With the decline of gold, the great center of South America remained effectively occupied by the Brazilians and their cattle.[20]

Agricultural frontier settlement is a relatively modern
phenomenon. Despite the Crown's attempts to settle Azorean
freeholders in the far south as a bulwark against Spanish penetration, the preponderance of the Brazilian population remained
heavily concentrated on the more fertile stretches of littoral between São Paulo and Pernambuco until well into the nineteenth
century.

Modern expansion of the agricultural frontier began around
1850 with the production of coffee for world markets. In the
earlier part of the nineteenth century the West Indies and Java
dominated world coffee production; but Brazil's share of world
output rose from 20 percent in the 1820s to 52 percent in the
1850s, 57 percent in the 1880s, and 75 percent after the turn of
the century. The redistribution of world coffee production in favor of Brazil took place in the context of a tremendous expansion
in world demand, especially after 1850. This expansion was due
largely to the newly acquired taste for this brew by the rapidly
growing and increasingly affluent masses in Europe and the United States.[21]

Coffee grows under rather strict climatic constraints. Arabica,
one of the more palatable varieties, cannot tolerate repeated
frosts; excessive heat, aridity, or humidity; or uneven rainfall.
Within the acceptable climatic zone there is a wide variety of
relief, soil structure, and fertility. There are consequently few

areas in the world where arabica thrives, notably the volcanic soils of the tropical highlands. Introduced into the Amazon Basin in the early eighteenth century, coffee shifted to the lowlands around Rio de Janeiro around 1770, to the Paraíba Valley between Rio and the Paulista capital by the 1850s and then to the highlands northwest of the capital after the 1860s. Coffee culture today is well within the optimal zone, which comprises most of the São Paulo plateau and adjacent portions of southern Minas Gerais and northern Paraná.[22]

This century-long migration of coffee stimulated cattle raising in Goiás and Mato Grosso beyond the agricultural frontier. In the 1940s Goiás began to partake in the expansion of the agricultural frontier as a rice-producing region followed by Mato Grosso in the 1950s. The spread of the agricultural frontier into the neighboring states has been associated with the decline of coffee production in São Paulo state. The history of the coffee frontier illustrates the interplay of demand, the availability of the labor force, natural resources, the marketing system, agricultural technology, and patterns of land ownership.

As in Argentina and Australia, pioneering in São Paulo was clearly a "big man's" game. Little land remained in the public domain for free distribution, most having been given or sold to courtiers to the emperor, who became a large land-owning class. Land originally held in dubious title by small holders or squatters and that later acquired value was rapidly annexed to large estates by influential men who were able to manipulate the law in their own behalf.[23]

The coffee elite directed the settlement of São Paulo through the control of public policy in several crucial areas: the development of a railroad system that lowered intraregional transport costs, the recruitment of a labor force that made their empty lands productive, and after 1900 through stockpiling schemes that guaranteed high coffee prices.

Through public loan guarantees the coffee planters were able to induce British capitalists to construct a railroad that connected the port of Santos to the coffee-producing highlands by 1867. Once the profitability of the railroad concept was proven, groups of landowners in several sections of the state banded together to construct feeder lines to the Santos road.

The recruitment of a labor force posed a serious problem because Brazil was still a slave-holding country at the beginning of the coffee boom. Although Stein shows that a majority of slaves were transferred to the south of Brazil at the time of abolition (1888), the cessation of the slave trade by the British limited the potential supply of slave labor to a level considerably below the coffee planters' demands. As a slave-holding country Brazil offered little attraction to free labor. The São Paulo planters reasoned correctly that the abolition of slavery would facilitate the recruitment of immigrant labor from Europe. Subsidized by the state, foreign immigration to São Paulo, which averaged eighteen thousand per year from 1881 to 1890, soared to seventy-five thousand per year in the following decade.[24]

The importation of free immigrants, however, did not alter the hierarchical relations of production. In order to supply themselves with a dependent work force the planters permitted the immigrants to purchase only the most inaccessible, infertile, or exhausted lands.[25]

The São Paulo coffee frontier was hardly a labor safety valve for the rest of Brazil. It might have been so had the plantations recruited workers from the densely populated, low-wage Northeast. The draining off of excess northeastern labor would have improved that region's endowment of land per man, raised the productivity of labor, and probably improved the bargaining power of peasants against landlords. Those who migrated from the Northeast to the south would have probably enjoyed much higher wages. Why the Paulistas recruited Italians instead of northeasterners is a moot point. Fernandes suggests that ex-slaves and free whites from all regions were temperamentally unsuited to performing plantation tasks, which had the connotation of slave work. Perhaps ideologists of "whitening" preferred to attract a labor force with Mediterranean physiognomy rather than mestizo and mulatto northeasterners. Perhaps restrictions on emigration, enforced by northeastern plantation owners, such as artificially high fares on coastal steamers, were crucial.[26]

The existence of the frontier encourages extensive agricultural practices that exhaust the soil. When a plantation owner moved on to new lands, he frequently subdivided and sold his old property to the workers, many of whom had been saving for such a purchase. In the absence of the Paraná frontier beyond São

Paulo, such a filtration process may have been less likely. The collapse of world coffee prices around the First World War accelerated the fragmentation of plantations by forcing the sale either to the workers or to coffee merchants to whom the planters were heavily indebted. Perhaps equally important, the opportunities to invest in industrial-urban growth since the 1930s may have further contributed to the willingness of landowners to liquidate their rural holdings.[27] Such fragmentation notwithstanding, the social relations of production in the São Paulo coffee region retain the hierarchical character established at the outset.

In the early phases of the coffee frontier the spatial distribution of the market for foodstuffs was more or less identical with that of the rural labor force. The urban population was relatively small, fulfilling largely marketing and service functions for the coffee hinterland. For example, the capital comprised only 4 and 11 percent of São Paulo state's population in 1872 and 1900, respectively.

Initially, most of the rural food supply seems to have been produced within the coffee region itself. In the period between planting and the first harvest of the coffee tree, foodstuffs have been traditionally planted between the rows of trees by the resident workers. Since the food crops compete with the trees for nutrients, folk agronomy dictated shifting food production to separate plots once the trees began to yield. Until the collapse of the world coffee market in 1929 the output of foodstuffs in São Paulo varied inversely with coffee exports. This indicates that during boom periods less land was devoted to food production while food imports increased.[28]

Prior to the Depression the dominant crop in all commercialized areas of São Paulo state was coffee. Interspersed with coffee was the cultivation of foodstuffs, although pockets of subsistence farming on infertile or inaccessible lands existed. Beyond the coffee frontier lay a pastoral region that provided the coffee planters with work animals and meat. The pace of frontier expansion was largely dominated by the vagaries of foreign demand for coffee.

Entering the twentieth century as an entrepôt for its coffee-producing hinterland, the city of São Paulo (the state capital) has been transformed into the locus of Brazilian industrialization. The share of state income originating in the agricultural sector has fallen from 23 percent in 1939 to 12 percent in 1969. Although there are no detailed state income statistics before 1939, the weight of the agricultural sector was clearly higher then.[29]

Associated with industrialization has been an urbanization of the state population, from 40 percent in 1940 to 78 percent by 1970. There has been an enormous increase in the population of the capital, which has accounted for about half the state's manufacturing output during this century and which currently employs 28 percent of all industrial workers in the country. The capital, which contained 11 percent of the state's population in 1900, increased its share to 13 percent in 1920, 18 percent in 1940, and 33 percent in 1970.[30]

The industrialization-urbanization of São Paulo has profoundly altered the forces affecting frontier expansion and land use in south central Brazil. Unlike foreign demand, which was focused upon coffee, domestic demand is for a wide range of perishables, nonperishable foodstuffs, and industrial raw materials, particularly cotton. Second, domestic demand is no longer dispersed like the rural labor force but is heavily concentrated in a single metropolitan area and its satellites.

The effect of this increasingly important domestic demand can be traced by focusing on the supply area of this industrial complex, which includes the peripheral states of Paraná, Goiás, and Mato Grosso in addition to São Paulo itself. The three peripheral states ship the overwhelming share of their food exports to São Paulo.

Since the 1930s crop land in São Paulo has remained fairly stable at 4 to 5 million hectares, but it rose from 1.3 million to 7.1 million hectares in the three peripheral states by 1970. Almost all of the expansion in the four states combined has been devoted to noncoffee crops. Indeed, coffee area in these states has remained stable at about 2 million hectares.

In the period since the 1930s the westward march of coffee continued until it reached its climatic limits in northern Paraná. Although this movement has been interpreted as a hollow frontier created by soil exhaustion in the older zones, the evidence indicates that coffee was outbid for the land by other crops. Rather than being abandoned, land in the environs of metropolitan São Paulo has become specialized in the production of fruits, vegetables, milk, and eggs, all perishable and bulky commodities that cannot bear transportation over long distances. In the regions beyond the coffee frontier, especially in Mato Grosso and Goiás, agriculture has become specialized in high-value, nonperishable foodstuffs like rice.[31]

The rapid growth and concentration of the national textile industry in metropolitan São Paulo played a role in the expansion of the state's cotton acreage after the 1930s. Cotton compensated to some extent for the disastrous losses in coffee during the Depression and the location of cotton culture in the state helped overcome bottlenecks in supply caused by the inferior quality and uncertain quantity of this raw material from the Northeast, the traditional source. State-financed research encouraged by the local industrialists generated higher yielding and longer fiber cotton. Like coffee, however, cotton has been ejected toward Paraná, especially since the 1950s. Although the Northeast has adopted the Paulista cotton seed, south central Brazil still accounts for half of the national acreage. Although cotton acreage was only 10 percent of coffee acreage in the 1930s, it has remained 50 percent of coffee acreage since the 1960s.[32]

The increasing specialization and areal extension of agriculture in south central Brazil reflects the changing pattern of demand, commodity prices, and transportation costs. These prices and costs can hardly be considered given or even market determined. As was true in the nineteenth century, the state has intervened significantly in their formulation, especially since the 1930s.[33]

The most venerable and important form of intervention has been in setting coffee prices. In order to forestall a possible decline in international prices at the turn of the century, several coffee-producing states initiated a stockpiling scheme. Since Brazil was the major coffee producer, the withholding of stocks effectively raised coffee prices. Later assumed by the federal government, the scheme raised internal coffee prices above market-clearing levels. A similar effect was achieved via an overvaluation of the exchange rate, which also discouraged the export of products in which Brazil had no such monopoly. After 1947, when the power of the coffee planters was considerably diluted, the government undertook a policy of exchange confiscation that effectively taxed away half the earnings of the coffee sales. Consequently, in the 1950s the relative price of coffee fell about 59 percent, while that of rice and beans rose somewhat. Nevertheless, internal coffee prices were high enough to stimulate considerable overproduction. The accumulation of stocks in the 1950s cost the government about 1 percent of the gross national product each year.

A second form of intevention has been the application of the exportable surplus doctrine to foodstuffs. In order to lower the cost of food for the urban working class, the populist governments of the 1950s embargoed the export of many foodstuffs on the grounds that they were needed by the Brazilian population. This doctrine effectively reduced the prices of many commodities to half the international levels. This doctrine has not been totally repudiated and the government embargoes noncoffee farm exports from time to time.

Third, the government has imposed price floors and ceilings on various agricultural commodities. In the 1950s minimum prices were generally set below the market-clearing level and consequently had little impact on the food supply. Price ceilings have generally been applied to meat and dairy products with the effect of creating shortages and discouraging the expansion of milksheds around the metropolitan areas.

Fourth, the government has at times granted preferential tariffs and interest rebates for fertilizer purchases. A cost-benefit analysis of these programs suggests that Brazil has been underconsuming fertilizer. This implies that agriculture is not intensive enough and thus frontier settlement excessive.

Fifth, the marketing system has been improved by conscious and unconscious public action. In the 1950s federal, state, and municipal governments undertook a massive road construction program. Trucking costs from Goiás to São Paulo fell to one-quarter of the 1948 level by 1965; costs for farm to local market shipments fell to about one-third. Besides reducing transport costs directly the road system indirectly increased the competitiveness of the marketing system. Marketing on the pioneer fringe was originally dominated by a few firms that earned great middlemen's profits on the basis of their monopoly power. In contrast to a railroad system, where the carrier tends to be a large enterprise, a highway system is open to anyone's cargo. Large numbers of truckdrivers therefore became middlemen, buying directly from the farmers and delivering to retailers in São Paulo.

In further support of competition the government constructed considerable warehousing capacity. As a result of increased competition, marketing margins on the major frontiers have declined markedly since 1950. For example, the ratio of rice prices in Goiânia relative to São Paulo rose from 0.71 in the late 1930s, to 0.83 in the early 1950s, and to 0.87 in the late 1960s.

It should be noted in passing that postwar import substitution policies have had little effect on the demand for local as opposed to foreign foodstuffs. Although tariffs and exchange rates have been biased against the importation of consumer nondurables, the share of foodstuffs in total imports by value has remained in the range of 10 to 15 percent from 1940 to 1970. Furthermore, food actually imported during this period hardly competes with tropical or subtropical output, for roughly one-half of these imports consists of wheat and flour.

Questions have been raised whether frontier settlement has adverse technological and environmental consequences. Preston James argues that the existence of the frontier is responsible for a self-defeating lack of modernity in Brazilian agriculture, as defined by low levels of mechanization and limited use of improved seeds and fertilizers. The existence of the frontier, he continues, leads to the "mining" of the soils and the practically irreversible destruction of the forests, which overlay the best soils in the tropics. Paiva and Nicholls counter that given the high cost of modern inputs it is more rational to use traditional extensive techniques than to modernize for its own sake. When transportation costs become excessive, when the ecological limits of traditional agriculture are reached, or when the costs of fertilizer or improved seed become low enough, farmers will modernize.[34]

These arguments about technology are essentially static. There is considerable evidence that innovations are induced by scarcities in factors of production. Hayami and Ruttan note that yield-increasing innovations were not introduced into the United States until the 1930s, when the cost of fertilizers fell and the federal government placed acreage restrictions on farmers. Agrobiological innovation occurred much earlier in Japan because more severe land supply constraints were reached sooner. Brazil's innovations in cotton seed since the 1930s seem to have responded to the demands of the textile industry, while improvements in coffee yields since the 1950s can be traced to governmental restrictions on plantings.[35]

The argument that traditional frontier expansion causes irreversible destruction is less easily resolvable. These arguments
have been heatedly raised about the deforestation in Amazonia
associated with recent development efforts. While there is
evidence that some tropical soils turn to concrete after deforestation and exposure to air, the area of such soils seems to be small.
There is little evidence of such irreversible destruction from previous frontier settlement in Brazil. As in the eastern part of the
United States, older agricultural zones of inferior quality have
undergone reforestation or have been shifted to the production
of perishables. An example is Vassouras, which was severely de-
forested and largely abandoned in the nineteenth century. This
old coffee county now provides metropolitan São Paulo and Rio
de Janeiro with tomatoes, milk, and beef raised on improved
grasses.[36]

The generality of the Brazilian frontier settlement process can
be surmised by reverting to the basic questions raised above.
Which frontiers are settled? Much of the interior of Brazil was effectively occupied by a subsistence-oriented cattle economy
dating from the eighteenth century. While the cattle economy
served the geopolitical function of legitimizing Brazilian sovereignty, significant sedentary population began to settle the interior as recently as the mid-nineteenth century. Although the
settlement of the interior of south central Brazil was initially propelled by the international demand for coffee, it has become increasingly influenced by internal demand for foodstuffs and fiber
originating from industrial urban development in São Paulo.

What is the impact of the physical environment on the social
relations of production on the frontier? Brazil hardly provides
confirmation of any simplistic theories relating the abundance of
land to rural social structure. Some frontiers have fairly democratic social structures; others, hierarchial ones, thus providing
counterexamples to both the Turner and Domar theses. Democratic and hierarchical coffee regions coexist, invalidating any
simple technological determinism that links the technology of
production to social relations. The impact of the frontier on the
social relations of production is clearly mediated by a large
number of factors, such as initial political power, and perhaps by
financial institutions. The importance of the latter factor is
suggested by the apparent decline of the democratic social struc-

ture in Paraná. Such complexity implies that all frontiers are unique, generalization is hazardous, and historical explanation is necessary.

To what extent does frontier settlement raise wages in the older areas of the nation? The role of the frontier as a safety valve has been perceived in at least three major nations: the United States, Brazil, and Russia. Wages are most likely to rise when the frontier is closed to foreign immigration, so that surplus population from settled regions of the nation can be absorbed.

# 3

# Growth Poles and Developmental Highways in Goiás

One of the fastest growing states in Brazil during this century has been sparsely settled Goiás, located in the Central West region of the country (figure 2). The state's share of national population has doubled in the last fifty years (from 1.7 percent in 1920 to 3.2 percent in 1970) and has nearly doubled in the last thirty years if one includes the population of the new Federal District located within its borders. Expressed another way Goiás's growth rate has been roughly 60 percent each decade since 1940, about twice the national rate. Since 1900 Goiás's growth rate has been surpassed only by that of Paraná in the south and equaled by Mato Grosso, Goiás's western neighbor (table 2).

The rapid growth of Goiás is of considerable satisfaction to Brazilian policymakers, for the *marcha para o oeste,* akin to the Manifest Destiny of the United States, has been a nationalistic theme for some time. In part western settlement is viewed as legitimizing Brazilian territorial claims, especially to neighbors with expansionist ambitions. In part the western regions are presumed to have untold natural resources that guarantee high returns to investment.

The attraction of Goiás to immigrants is not obvious, since its per capita income is roughly half the national average. As the only state with below-average income attracting net migration, Goiás is a striking anomaly.[1] Moreover, associated with net migration has been a slight gain in relative per capita income, again an exception. This implies that the settlement of Goiás does not represent the spreading of fixed sums of fabulous opportunities over a larger number of people but rather a growth in opportunities faster than a growth in population.

Considerable public investment has been poured into the state in the last forty years and especially in the last twenty to acceler-

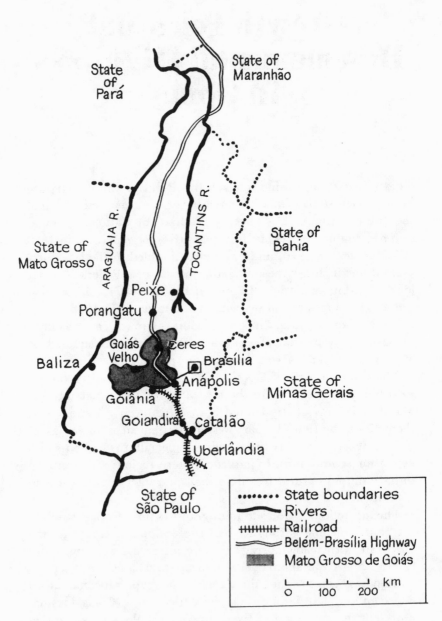

**Figure 2.** Goiás

**Table 2.** Population (in thousands), central western states, 1872 – 1970.

| Year | Goiás | Mato Grosso | Federal District | Total region | Percentage of national population, total region |
|------|-------|-------------|------------------|--------------|--------------------------------------------------|
| 1872 | 160   | 60          | –                | 220          | 2.2 |
| 1890 | 228   | 93          | –                | 320          | 2.2 |
| 1900 | 255   | 118         | –                | 373          | 2.1 |
| 1920 | 512   | 247         | –                | 759          | 2.5 |
| 1940 | 826   | 432         | –                | 1,259        | 3.1 |
| 1950 | 1,215 | 522         | –                | 1,737        | 3.3 |
| 1960 | 1,955 | 910         | 142              | 3,007        | 4.2 |
| 1970 | 2,998 | 1,475       | 545              | 5,009        | 5.8 |

Source: Brasil, *Sinopse preliminar do censo demográfico,* 1970, table 2.

ate its settlement. Projects include the extension of national railways into the state from the 1910s; a new state. capital, Goiânia, in the late 1930s; a new national capital, Brasília, in the late 1950s; and the nation's first major interregional developmental highway, the Belém-Brasília, also in the late 1950s. Less spectacular, but of great significance, has been the continual extension of the state's network of all-weather roads as well as roads to southern markets.

Goiás has historically been peripheral to Brazilian economic life. Penetrated and explored as early as the eighteenth century, the region has not until recently sustained a large permanent population integrated into national markets.[2] During the eighteenth-century gold cycle in neighboring Minas Gerais prospectors penetrated the region from the south on the Paranaíba River and its tributaries but found little to induce permanent settlement after the meager supply of ore was extracted. The human residue of the mines remained engaged in subsistence farming and cattle raising, the latter activity facilitated by the state's extensive natural pasture, a savanna broken by low bushes.

With so much virgin land closer to market and better suited for the production of the major staples (coffee and sugar), there was little public inducement to invest in transport facilities until the beginning of the twentieth century. The modern era in Goiás began with the extension of the railroad lines from São Paulo and Belo Horizonte into the state in the 1910s and 1920s. The railroads and the connecting feeder highways helped integrate Goiás into the great markets of south central Brazil. As a result, there has been a continual expansion of exports, 70 percent of which are beef cattle and rice.[3]

Simultaneously with the construction of Goiânia a network of roads linking the new capital to other market towns in the fertile Mato Grosso de Goiás subregion was begun. The growth in road mileage in the 1930s was truly spectacular. The number of kilometers doubled from 1930 to 1937, nearly doubled again by 1939, and increased by another 33 percent by 1943. It was not until the construction of Brasília in the late 1950s that road construction again approximated these rates. By 1940 the number of kilometers of road per square kilometer of land was at the national average, while the length of road per person was second in the nation.[4]

While there was no logical reason why this road network could not have been constructed without a transference of the capital and why it could not have focused on the old capital, the federal government's interest in making Goiânia a showcase provided the incentive to make these complementary investments that were necessary for its success. This pattern repeated itself with the initiation of a national system of highways radiating from Brasília. Whether or not these road investments were economically sensible, they might not have elicited the attention and support of national policymakers in the absence of such showcase projects.

## Conceptual Framework

At one level the impact of planned urbanization or developmental highways on rural development is easily understood. An increase in urban demand or a decrease in transportation costs raises the prices received by farmers on the frontier. Commercial agriculture consequently becomes profitable farther from the market center and the pioneer fringe pushes outward.

Merely extensive growth is far from what is considered economic development defined as a sustained increase in productivity and income of the farm population. A growth pole like Brasília is supposed to perform the function of diffusing modernization and development toward its hinterland. Unfortunately, most discussions of growth poles abound with mystical concepts that are neither observable nor easily translatable into conventional economics. The mechanisms by which a growth pole performs its function must be spelled out rigorously.

Two complementary conceptual schemes provide a means of grasping the interrelations between urbanization, transportation improvement, and agricultural modernization. These are the neoclassical theory of rents and the industrial-urban hypothesis. In contrast to the common belief that farmers in developing countries are irrationally traditional, both paradigms view the farmer as responsive to price incentives.[5]

The neoclassical model of agricultural modernization can be presented with great precision mathematically, as has been done elsewhere.[6] In essence, this paradigm views the farmer as a rational profit maximizer who chooses a mix of land, labor, and capital on the basis of their relative prices. Where land is relatively cheap, say near the pioneer fringe, applications of labor and capital per hectare are low and consequently yields are low. Conversely, near the market center or in especially fertile areas the valuable land is used more intensively, with heavier applications of labor and capital. As a result agriculture near the urban center obtains high crop yields and appears more modern.

The creation of a growth pole raises urban food demand, improves transportation to market, lowers the cost of diffusing modern technologies, and helps absorb a portion of the natural increase of the rural labor force. The effect of these changes on agricultural modernization and rural incomes depends upon the elasticity of the labor supply. For a frontier region like Goiás it is reasonable to assume that the supply of immigrants is highly responsive to small changes in wages. Consider now the effect of each change individually.

An increase in urban demand for food, due to increasing population or per capita income, raises food prices at the market center. As shown in the appendix, increased prices at the center translate into an upward shift in the rent-bid gradient in the entire region and hence an extension of the frontier. At any distance from the market the increase in prices received by farmers increases the value of the land and hence encourages its more intensive use (by greater use of fertilizer, improved seed, and insecticide, for example). Because each farmer now has somewhat more land to work with and because prices received at any location are higher than before, farm wages rise. Consequently, the food supply increases as a result of both the extension of the frontier and the more intensive use of land within the pioneer fringe.

The effect of transportation improvements and innovations on farm wages depends upon the price-elasticity of demand for food. While this elasticity is generally less than unitary for the market as a whole, the demand facing a small region like Goiás is relatively elastic. This means that any increases in supply from Goiás can be absorbed with only a slight decline in the market price.

Within a small region improvements in transportation flatten the rent-bid gradient, encourage frontier expansion, and induce more intensive land use within the pioneer fringe. Yield-increasing or land-saving innovations, such as improved seed, better techniques of rotation, and mechanical weeders, result in a decreased demand for land and a retraction of the frontier. While such innovations may result in wage increases, labor-saving innovations such as mechanical harvesters and plows decrease the demand for labor. Were transportation improvements and agricultural innovations to occur in the entire food supply area of south central Brazil simultaneously, the increase in supply would lead to drastic decreases in prices and hence farm wages.

In light of these dynamic factors, what is the impact of industrialization-urbanization upon rural modernization and farm wages? Industrialization-urbanization encourages modernization, raises rural wages as the demand for food increases, and prevents further deterioration of these wages by the absorption of labor from the growing rural population. To the extent that industrialization-urbanization is responsible for the diffusion of a transportation network and agricultural innovations, it may lead to a deterioration in farm wages.

What have been the actual parameter shifts in south central Brazil in recent decades? Urban food demand has increased and the marketing system has improved, but technological progress has been slow. While an increase in demand tends to increase food prices, an improvement in the marketing system tends to lower them by bringing more land into cultivation and therby increasing the food supply. The agricultural price index has remained stable relative to nonagricultural prices, so the shift in demand seems to have roughly offset an equivalent shift in supply.

The impact of these changes on agricultural wages depends upon whether the land supply has increased faster or slower than the farm labor supply. This is somewhat difficult to determine since published data refer to all land in farms, whether or not commercially exploitable, or to all crop land, which employs most but not all rural labor. In the period from 1940 to 1970 the ratio of farm labor to crop land decreased in São Paulo and Goiás and increased in Paraná and Mato Grosso. More significantly, there has been a decline in agricultural wages in these states during the 1950s and 1960s.[7] In other words, industrialization-urbanization in south central Brazil has not resulted in development from the point of view of the mass of rural population.

While the neoclassical paradigm assumes that markets function perfectly, the industrial-urban hypothesis focuses on the evolution of market institutions. The hypothesis maintains the following propositions: economic development is normally uneven in space, development originates in industrial-urban centers, markets are more differentiated and more competitive in the more highly developed industrial-urban centers, and agricultural areas benefit from these markets in proportion to their proximity to industrial-urban centers. The markets of greatest relevance are for labor, capital, intermediate inputs, and agricultural commodities.[8]

Industrialization causes the demand for labor to grow faster than the supply in urban areas relative to rural areas, an effect magnified by the more rapid rural natural increase. This disproportionality between supply and demand raises urban wages relative to rural wages in the short run. Suppose that rural wages were initially invariant regionally. Potential migrants from rural areas will weigh the lifetime gain in earnings from rural-to-urban migration against its economic and psychic costs. The farther a rural area is from the urban opportunities, the higher the costs of migrating and acquiring information about these opportunities. Consequently, at equilibrium the disparity between urban and rural incomes will increase with distance from urban centers.

In addition, if industrial opportunities arise within a rural area, farm families located closer to the new urban center will be better able to avail themselves of them. Marginal farmers may abandon farming altogether or may supplement their income with city work. Secondary farm workers, notably children and women, are more likely to work in the urban center on a part-time or off-season basis the lower their commuting costs. Since specialized educational facilities are likely to be located in the urban center, farm children within commuting range are more likely to take advantage of them. All of these channels draw labor out of the farm sector, raising its marginal productivity. Finally, low-income urban workers may be recruited for seasonal farm work, thereby lowering the cost of harvesting.[9]

The capital markets may function more perfectly closer to the industrial-urban core because large cities have more banks, which thereby suffer greater competition, and large cities attract more savings both because they are more competitive and because more savings are generated there. Because small loans are hard to obtain from beyond the local area due to information and transaction costs, farms in less industrial-urban areas face higher capital costs.

In the markets for intermediate inputs and farm commodities the more industrial-urban region tends to have better transportation infrastructure and marketing facilities for assembling and disposing of farm products, distributing agricultural inputs, and distributing goods and services consumed by farm families. Partly because of the better transportation system, the service area of the marketing firms is larger, permitting them to enjoy internal economies of scale. Moreover, the larger service areas can support larger numbers of marketing establishments, making them more competitive as well as more specialized than those existing in isolated small towns. The better marketing system in the industrial-urban region means that farmers receive higher prices for their products and pay lower prices for their intermediate inputs and consumer goods.

The predictions of the neoclassical and industrial-urban paradigms are generally similar. Closer to the industrial-urban center, land is more intensively used with greater applications of capital and intermediate inputs per hectare. Yields and labor productivity are correspondingly higher; rural populations are denser and more prosperous. It should be noted that the relationship between rural development and urbanization is reciprocal. The more prosperous and dense the rural population, the larger the urban population it can support in providing services for the hinterland.

In order to determine whether Brasília and the Belém-Brasília Highway had their anticipated effects, it is important to establish a baseline. Does the spatial structure of Goiás conform to the predictions of the two paradigms in the period from 1940 to 1960, before these projects were completed?

The mechanisms postulated by the neoclassical and industrial-urban paradigms can be distinguished empirically. According to the neoclassical view, the major influence on land use is the distance of the farm from that market center at which supply and demand are equilibrated, the size of the local market being basically irrelevant. According to the industrial-urban hypothesis, even localized industrialization can have modernizing effects on the surrounding countryside.

Although there are several marketing centers in this Texas-size state (642,000 square kilometers), the two major ones are close enough together (50 kilometers) to be viewed as one. While Goiânia and its twin, Anápolis, are the largest industrial cities in the state by employment and value added, neither is primarily industrial and manufacturing is widely scattered throughout the state. Because it is the largest city and state capital, Goiânia is chosen as the market center for statistical purposes. Industrialization-urbanization is measured by manufacturing wage bill per capita. The effects of distance from Goiânia and industrialization-urbanization can be distinguished because they are not very highly correlated on a county basis ($r = -0.2$ in 1940 and 1970).

To control for natural resource variations, Goiás can be readily partitioned into an infertile savanna, comprising 80 percent of its surface; the fertile Mato Grosso de Goiás, comprising about 10 percent; and a northern equatorial forest zone, where the extraction of forest products is the predominant activity. For statistical purposes fertility is represented by a dummy variable, with counties in the Mato Grosso de Goiás assigned a value of 1, all others a value of 0.

Regressions of county farm characteristics against distance from Goiânia, fertility, and industrialization-urbanization indicate that the spatial structure of Goiás in the baseline period conforms to expectation (table 3). The amount of total land area

**Table 3.** Spatial structure of agriculture, Goiás, 1940-1960: regression coefficients (standard errors).

| Dependent variable | 1940 | | | 1950 | | | 1960 | | |
|---|---|---|---|---|---|---|---|---|---|
| | Distance | Fertility | Industrial urbanism | Distance | Fertility | Industrial urbanism | Distance | Fertility | Industrial urbanism |
| Percentage land area in farms | $-.100^a$ (.020) | .085 (.232) $R^2 = .36$ | — — | $-.089^a$ (.018) | 0.57 (.205) $R^2 = .37$ | — — | $-.072^a$ (.014) | .161 (.160) $R^2 = .42$ | — — |
| Percentage farmland in crops | $-.003$ (.003) | $.815^a$ (.321) $R^2 = .13$ | — — | $-.070^a$ (.030) | $1.178^a$ (.307) $R^2 = .41$ | — — | $-.060^a$ (.027) | $1.579^a$ (.321) $R^2 = .47$ | — — |
| \$ machinery, vehicles per ha. | $-.009^a$ (.004) | $1.100^a$ (.468) $R^2 = .28$ | $.397^a$ (.227) | $-.012^a$ (.002) | $.747^a$ (.286) $R^2 = .55$ | $.090^a$ (.036) | $-.023^a$ (.004) | .565 (.473) $R^2 = .56$ | $.017^a$ (.009) |
| \$ fertilizer, etc. per ha. | $-.013^a$ (.006) | .354 (.761) $R^2 = .05$ | .407 (.370) | $-.241^a$ (.127) | 2.539 (15.89) $R^2 = .03$ | $-2.147$ (2.015) | $-2.866$ (2.015) | $-271.$ (230.) $R^2 = .05$ | 5.34 (4.51) |
| \$ machinery, vehicles per worker | $-.009^a$ (.003) | .028 (.432) $R^2 = .16$ | $.319^a$ (.210) | $-.009^a$ (.001) | $-.413^a$ (.162) $R^2 = .55$ | $.038^a$ (.021) | $-.021^a$ (.003) | $-.167$ (.396) $R^2 = .57$ | $.015^a$ (.008) |

| | | | | | | | | |
|---|---|---|---|---|---|---|---|---|
| $ fertilizer, etc. per worker | .002[a] (.001) | −.061 (.088) $R^2 = .13$ | .073[a] (.043) | −.047[a] (.025) | −.213 (3.143) $R^2 = .02$ | −.436 (.399) | −.569[a] (.238) | −20.507 (30.13) $R^2 = .08$ | .318 (.591) |
| Crop output per ha. | −.002 (.003) | −.218 (.321) $R^2 = .04$ | .075 (.156) | — — | — — | — — | −.007[a] (.003) | 1.412[a] (0.166) $R^2 = .41$ | .0002[a] (.00001) |
| Crop output per worker | −.002 (.002) | −.126 (.280) $R^2 = .00$ | .149 (.136) | — — | — — | — — | −.011[a] (.002) | 0.323[a] (.104) $R^2 = 35$ | 9.567[a] (3.034) |

Source: Martin T. Katzman, "The von Thuenen Paradigm, the Industrial-Urban Hypothesis, and the Spatial Structure of Agriculture," *American Journal of Agricultural Economics* 56 (Nov. 1974): tables 5-7. Yield and productivity regressions for 1970 are from David Garlow, "Comment," *American Journal of Agricultural Economics* 57 (Nov. 1975): table 2; these are indicated in column for 1960. Data for counties in 1950 and 1960 are aggregated to conform to the 1940 boundaries.
[a]Significance .05 (one-tail); n = 52.

absorbed in farms and of farmland devoted to crops decreases with distance from the market and increases with fertility. The use of capital (machinery) and intermediate inputs (fertilizers, seeds, and insecticides) decreases with distance from market and increases somewhat with industrialization-urbanization. While information on output is sparse, there is a tendency for output per hectare and per worker to decline with distance from the market and to increase with industrialization-urbanization. While this tendency was weak in 1940, it was clearly significant by 1970.

These farm characteristics have implications for population patterns (table 4). The gradients of land incorporated into farms and of crop land imply that the farm labor force per square kilometer varies inversely with distance from market and is higher in the fertile zone. While rural population densities tend to vary with those of the farm labor force, they also vary independently with distance from the market. This result is clearly consistent with the industrial-urban hypothesis: closer to the market center a larger proportion of children attend school full time and a larger proportion of the rural labor force engages in off-farm jobs. Consequently, labor dependency rates are higher closer to the market center.

Since the vitality of small service centers depends upon the density of rural population, it is not surprising that the urban population per square kilometer in a county varies directly with rural population density. Total population density, then, can be related to distance from the market and fertility.

### Brasília

Transferring the capital of Brazil to the Goiás plateau has been an aim ritualistically inscribed in all constitutions since the end of the nineteenth century, an idea attributed to the revolutionary pronouncements of Tiradentes in the eighteenth century. The rationales for such a transfer were many: shifting the face of the country away from the coast, which represents links to the colonial past, toward the geographical center of the country; creating a new indigenous urban form; and implanting a growth pole that would accelerate the march to the west, allegedly launched by Goiânia. To Juscelino Kubitschek, Brazil's first avowedly development-minded president, the new capital would be

**Table 4.**  Densities of farm labor force, rural, urban, and total population, Goiás, 1940-1960: regression coefficients (standard errors).

| | 1940 | | 1950 | | 1960 | |
|---|---|---|---|---|---|---|
| | Distance | Fertility | Distance | Fertility | Distance | Fertility |
| Farm labor force/km² | -.0103[a] (.0032) | .8095[a] (.3666) $R^2 = .32$ | -.0125[a] (.0028) | .8607[a] (.3248) $R^2 = .44$ | -.0076[a] (.0023) | 1.1637[a] (.2582) $R^2 = .50$ |
| | Distance | Farm labor force | Distance | Farm labor force | Distance | Farm labor force |
| Rural pop./km² | -.0026[a] (.0013) | .8589[a] (.0523) $R^2 = .89$ | -.0020[a] (.0012) | .7990[a] (.0505) $R^2 = .90$ | -.0024[a] (.0009) | .8789[a] (.0434) $R^2 = .93$ |
| | Distance | Rural pop./km² | Distance | Rural pop./km² | Distance | Rural pop./km² |
| Urban pop./km² | -.0044[a] (.0027) | .7647[a] (.1116) $R^2 = .64$ | .0000 (.0023) | 1.2227[a] (.1035) $R^2 = .82$ | -.0029 (.0029) | 1.1818[a] (.1433) $R^2 = .71$ |
| | Distance | Fertility | Distance | Fertility | Distance | Fertility |
| Total pop./km² | -.0116[a] (.0030) | .7262[a] (.3375) $R^2 = .37$ | -.0119[a] (.0025) | .995[a] (.288) $R^2 = .51$ | -.0101[a] (.0022) | 1.2877[a] (.2560) $R^2 = .59$ |

Source: Martin T. Katzman, "Regional Development Policy in Brazil," *Economic Development and Cultural Change* 24 (Oct. 1975): table 5.
[a]Significance .05 (one-tail); n = 52.

the "key to a process of development that would transform the Brazilian archipelago into an integrated economic continent."[10]

Fearing that his successor might not continue the project, Kubitschek directed a round-the-clock effort that left the major buildings and infrastructure in place by the completion of his term. The cost of this effort was about 2 percent of the GNP per annum from 1956 to 1962, about as much as was devoted to Amazonia or the Northeast. As the country was undergoing high rates of growth because of its import substitution policy, Brasília strained the nation's resource  capacity, accelerating inflation from 10 to 33 percent during the Kubitschek years, 1956 to 1961.[11]

The transference of the national capital from Rio de Janeiro to the Goiás plateau adds to the state's economic base the export of federal services to the rest of the nation. The presence of an ultimate population of six hundred thousand or more in the new Federal District was expected to induce economic development in Goiás through forward and backward linkages.

The probability that Brasília will induce substantial industrial growth in Goiás does not seem high in the foreseeable future. Because the size of the market is too small to support much manufacturing, consumer goods, office furniture, paper, and business machines will continue to be imported from São Paulo, Belo Horizonte, and Rio. Perhaps the transference of the capital will induce the relocation of financial and consulting enterprises that require face-to-face contact with politicians and bureaucrats; however, the major impact of Brasília is most likely to be felt in the agricultural sector.

The transference of the national capital also brings a potential market of six hundred thousand or more consumers about a thousand kilometers closer to the frontier. The impact of this new market on the production of export staples must be distinguished from the impact on foodstuffs that are never exported because of their perishability and bulk.[12]

Recall that the price of the frontier staple is determined at the entrepôt where aggregate supply and demand are equilibrated. This market price is diffused throughout the urban hierarchy down to the farmers, and at any point in the urban hierarchy the price of the staple equals the market price less transport costs to the entrepôt.

Whether originating in the entrepôt or in some other city, any increase in market demand will lead to an expansion of the frontier. The growth of Brasília, however, creates little increased demand for the staple but mostly shifts it locus from Rio de Janeiro, which already consumes this staple. Because of lower transportation costs, rice is 30 percent cheaper in Brasília than in Rio. With a price-elasticity of demand for rice on the order of $-0.1$ or $-0.2$, civil servants moving from Rio to Brasília will consume about 3 to 6 percent more rice.[13] Consequently, about 95 percent of the rice supplied to Brasília reflects a reduction of rice exports to Rio and only about 5 percent reflects new demand. The case is different for nonexport foodstuffs. In the environs of Brasília the production of export crops decreases as a green belt producing perishable and bulky foodstuffs arises.

As in most Brazilian cities, about 40 percent of average family expenditures in Brasília is on food. Among the most important items in the food budget are beef (15 percent) and rice (10 percent), the major staples of Goiás. Consumption patterns in Brasília are similar to those in Rio except that less rice and more fish and oranges are consumed in the former capital, a reflection of price differentials.

In terms of value, about 80 percent of Brasília's food is supplied by Goiás and the Federal District itself.[14] Not surprisingly, these two sources predominate in supplying meat and fowl, cereals, and perishable vegetables. The supply area is especially constricted for low-value crops such as manioc and perishables like lettuce, most of which are produced in the Federal District.

Food-processing industries are forward linked to some agricultural activities. In Brasília the most important such industries by percentage of sales are bakeries (31 percent), meat and poultry packing (23 percent), and flour milling (12 percent). In terms of markets, nearly all food-processing industries except meat and poultry packing are oriented to the local market.

On the average, for every dollar value of sales of these industries seventy-five cents represents raw materials purchases. By no means are all the indirect demands of these industries met by local suppliers. About 50 percent of both raw materials purchased (such as sugar cane, wheat, and unpolished rice) and services consumed (such as freight and insurance) result in payments outside the region.

What is the total impact of the demand for food in Brasília on employment and population in Goiás? A partial impact may be estimated by looking at the three large counties surrounding Brasília, parts of which were dismembered to form the Federal District. The residuals for these counties were calculated for the period from 1920 to 1970 from population density-distance regressions. Throughout the period under consideration the densities of these counties were slightly less than expected, although not significantly so, and there has been no tendency for these residuals to become more positive since 1960.

Although Brasília apparently has had no impact on settlement in the three counties that market their food there, it may have an impact on the rest of Goiás, the source of over half its food. A back-of-the-envelope calculation is possible if one assumes that the impact of demand on Goiás is proportional to the impact in the Federal District itself.

Approximately 3 percent of the labor force in the Federal District is engaged in agriculture, and an additional 0.5 percent is employed in food-processing industries. On the assumption that rural and urban dependency rates are similar, roughly 3.5 percent of the population of the Federal District (or twenty-one thousand persons) is supported by food-supplying activities. Since Goiás supplies Brasília with about four or five times as much food by value as the District supplies itself, perhaps an additional eighty to a hundred thousand persons of that state are supported by supplying food to the new capital.

Since there are approximately two urban dwellers for every three rural inhabitants in Goiás, the roughly ninety thousand farm population may engage indirectly perhaps an additional sixty thousand people in commerce, industry, and public administration. This brings the total impact of Brasília on Goiás to a hundred and fifty thousand persons, just 5 percent of the state's total and only about 15 percent of its growth from 1960 to 1970.

As to order of magnitude, these calculations are consistent with direct evidence of Goiás's exports. In 1962 less than 1 percent of the state's exports by value went to Brasília, a figure that rose to about 8 percent by the end of the decade.[15] These figures suggest that the place of Brasília in Goiás's markets is marginal rather than decisive.

These estimates of Brasília's impact are biased upward substantially, for it is incorrect to conclude that the population currently engaged, directly and indirectly, in supplying food to Brasília necessarily comprises a net addition to the Goiás population. If Brasília did not exist, most of the farmers currently producing lettuce and milk would be growing rice and beans. The net impact of Brasília on Goiás would seem to be proportional to the additional labor absorbed by these labor-intensive perishables and the slightly higher rice consumption of the transferred civil servants.

### Belém-Brasília Highway

Linked to the construction of Brasília was a national transportation plan that envisioned eight highways radiating from the new capital in the major directions of the compass. Two of these radial axes, the roads to São Paulo and to Rio, were largely upgraded versions of existing roads. The most dramatic highway to be built in the late 1950s was the Belém-Brasília, a two-thousand-kilometer road that completed the overland link between the industrial southeast—which includes São Paulo, Guanabara-Rio, and Minas Gerais—and the major entrepôt of Amazonia.

To construct the road an executive group, RODOBRAS, was established in 1958 under the jurisdiction of the Amazonian development agency SPVEA, as northern Goiás was included in Amazonia for planning purposes. Construction began before an ideal route was surveyed, the surveyors preceding the bulldozers by only a few kilometers. Nevertheless the actual and the subsequently traced, ideal trajectories did not diverge much. The road was constructed between 1958 and 1960 at a cost of roughly $50 million. Not being paved, the road required considerable maintenance and was only partially usable during the rainy season. In 1961, when the new president took power, RODOBRAS was abolished and maintenance ceased for about a year, leading to the deterioration of about 40 percent of the road bed. In 1963 RODOBRAS was revived in order to continue with the maintenance and upgrading of the road, which was paved in its entirety by 1973.[16]

Until the construction of the Belém-Brasília Highway the state of Goiás could not be considered economically integrated. The northern counties were linked to the Belém market by the Araguaia and Tocantins River systems. The Tocantins, with its headwaters near Brasília, has four major cataracts and is navigable as far south as Peixe on the first cataract only during the rainy season. The Araguaia is navigable to Baliza in the southern part of the state, where the road network was just beginning to reach. Because of the high costs of river travel and the absence of roads, northern settlement had clustered in the wedge where the two big rivers meet. The central part of the state, below Peixe and above the southern road network before the 1950s, was practically uninhabited.

The impact of the highway on settlement may be measured in several ways. On the most aggregate level, the percentage of total state population residing in the northern counties of Goiás has remained low and fairly constant in the last fifty years (table 5).[17] In the period from 1960 to 1970, after the completion of the road, the northern region grew 60 percent as opposed to 52 percent in the rest of the state, thus raising its share from 14 to 16 percent of the total population. If we assume that all the state's regions would have grown proportionately in the absence of the highway, as they did before 1960, then only eight points of the decadal growth in the north is due to the highway.

Next, the density of the northern counties can be compared to the predictions on the basis of distance from Goiânia. The residuals for five northern, riparian counties, taken as a group, are slightly larger than expected from 1920 to 1970 but not significantly so in any period. Within the northern subregion, the residuals become more positive as one moves from south to north, suggestive of the influence of accessiblity to Belém. To test this influence, distance from Belém is added as a variable to the original density-distance relationship for nine counties more than six hundred kilometers to the north of Goiânia and the five of these counties located along the rivers. Access to Belém raised density significantly in all periods since 1940 in the first formulation and since 1960 in the second. Traditionally oriented towards the Belém market, the northern counties have become more so as transport costs to this center have fallen (table 6).

Leaving the borders of Goiás, the northern third of the highway passes through the states of Maranhão and Pará. The former had the slowest decadal growth (22 percent) of the three states on the highway; however, a disaggregation of the data reveals that the microregion of Imperatriz, on the highway, grew by 126

**Table 5.**  Subregional distribution of Goiás population, percentages, 1920 – 1970.

| Subregion | 1920 | 1940 | 1950 | 1960 | 1970 |
|---|---|---|---|---|---|
| Mato Grosso de Goiás[a] | 15 | 24 | 32 | 37 | 40 |
| (Goiânia) | (2) | (6) | (6) | (9) | (16) |
| (MGG less Goiânia) | (13) | (18) | (26) | (28) | (24) |
| Northern riparian[b] | 14 | 15 | 14 | 14 | 16 |
| Paranaíba forest[c] | 13 | 12 | 11 | 12 | 11 |
| Southern savanna | 58 | 49 | 43 | 37 | 33 |
| Total | 100 | 100 | 100 | 100 | 100 |

Source: Brasil, *Censo demográfico, Goiás,* indicated years.

[a]Anicuns, Anápolis, Goiânia – Trinidade, Itaberaí, Goiás, Jaraguá (1920 county boundaries).

[b]Boa Vista Tocantins, Couto Magalhães, Pedro Affonso, Peixe, Pôrto Nacional (1920 county boundaries).

[c]Buriti Alegre, Catalão, Rio Verde, Santa Rita Paranaíba (1920 county boundaries).

percent, while the adjacent Chapada Sul Maranhense, off the highway, grew only 11 percent. In this case some of the growth of Imperatriz comprises population drained from its neighboring microregion.

Population trends in the state of Pará, at the end of the highway, are less conclusive. While growing more slowly than Goiás (42 as opposed to 53 percent), Pará underwent a more striking population redistribution from 1960 to 1970. The older, more densely populated areas along the Belém-Bragança highway, the Bragantine microregion, grew at about one-third of the statewide rate, while the more southerly zones grew at explosive rates. The explanation is that the exhausted and intensively worked soils in the Bragantine microregion were suffering from rapidly diminishing returns, while the virgin, albeit less accessible, soils to the south offered higher physical returns. Hence the Guajarine microregion, which straddles the southernmost portion of the Belém-Brasília in Pará, grew at a rate of 77 percent, which is faster than corresponding counties in Goiás. Paradoxically, two southern microregions that grew even faster (Araguaia Paraense, 246 percent and Tomé-Açu, 81 percent) are not on the highway. Ad hoc explanations for these anomalies are the fiscal incentives for cattle raising in Amazonia, which are benefiting the former,

**Table 6.** Population densities, Goiás, 1920 – 1970, as a function of distance from Goiânia and Belém and soil fertility: regression coefficients.

| Independent variable | 1920 | 1940 | 1950 | 1960 | 1970 |
|---|---|---|---|---|---|
| Distance from Goiânia | − .010[a] | − .015[a] | − .016[a] | − .016[a] | − .016[a] |
| Fertility | .499 | .829[a] | 1.080[a] | 1.316[a] | 1.318[a] |
| Distance from Belém[b] | .001 | − .003 | − .004 | − .007[a] | − .008[a] |

Source: Martin T. Katzman, "Regional Development Policy in Brazil," *Economic Development and Cultural Change* 24 (Oct. 1975): table 10. Data for counties are aggregated to conform to 1920 boundaries.
[a]Significance .05 (one – tail); n = 48.
[b]Variable entered only for northern counties over 600 km. from Goiânia.

and the boom in pepper exports, which are grown by Japanese colonists in the latter.

The range of the impact of the highway in Goiás can be estimated by assuming that all population growth in northern Goiás or alternatively all population growth in excess of the growth rate of the rest of the state is due to the highway. Under the first assumption the Belém-Brasília Highway induced 185,000 new settlers, under the second, 60,000. In Pará the highway induced 65,000 settlers under the first assumption and 35,000 under the second. In Maranhão the highway induced 80,000 settlers under the first assumption and 66,000 under the second. One is not too far off in concluding that the Belém-Brasília Highway is responsible for between 160,000 and 320,000 pioneers. This conclusion conflicts with the official claim of two million pioneers, which has been repeated in the scholarly literature.[18]

Per capita income in the north of Goiás rose by over 106 percent from 1950 to 1960, while the average increase in Goiás and Brazil was about 41 and 36 percent, respectively.[19] For natives of Goiás, the extra growth in per capita income may measure highway benefits; but for immigrants from other states, one would have to know what their income would have been had they stayed behind.

The rapid population growth of Goiás, accompanied by a slight increase in its relative per capita income, has been associated with spectacular public investments in two planned capitals and a two thousand-kilometer interregional highway. To what extent are these investments responsible for the state's growth?

The growth of Goiás predates these projects by several decades. Largely as a result of the improved inter- and intraregional transportation system, Goiás has become a major supplier of rice and beef to metropolitan São Paulo, its principal source of demand. Extensive growth has been accompanied by rural modernization, which is more intense closer to Goiânia, the regional entrepôt, and near local industrial centers. Rather than proving decisive, Brasília and the Belém-Brasília Highway have reinforced these trends.

Brasília now channels a portion of Goiás's food exports away from Rio and São Paulo. While perhaps ninety thousand Goianos and their families are engaged in supplying the new capital with food, it is likely that had the capital remained at Rio, most of them would be producing rice and beef rather than fruits and vegetables.

The Belém-Brasília Highway has had more far-reaching consequences on Goiás and beyond. While its impact on interregional trade between Amazonia and the south has been ignored here, it appears that the road attracted at most 320,000 settlers, 185,000 of them to Goiás.

Together, Brasília and the Highway may have attracted at most (90 + 185 = ) 275,000, but more likely (90 + 60 = ) 150,000 migrants to Goiás in the decade from 1960 to 1970. During this period the state's population grew by about one million, of which perhaps 570,000 reflects natural increase. Of the remainder, nearly one-half million, or one-third to one-half of the growth, can be attributed to these projects.

# 4

# Colonization and Rural Democracy in Northern Paraná

Colonization, or the planned settlement of agricultural frontiers, has been attempted by almost all land-abundant nations of Latin America. Colonization has been justified geopolitically as a means of effectively occupying the national territory, as an alternative to a politically impossible land reform, and as a profitable investment. Efforts at colonization have been notably failure prone. Because they rarely repay their costs, these schemes are often abandoned before completion, despite their professed geopolitical or income-redistribution justification.[1]

What is perhaps the most successful example of regional development planning in Latin America occurred in northern Paraná beginning in 1923 and continuing into the 1950s. This experience has been heralded as implanting a middle-class island in a sea of latifundia. The planners clearly defined their goals, specified the interrelated means of obtaining these goals, coordinated and phased appropriate programs, and carefully evaluated the results of their actions throughout the process. What is remarkable is that an area of twelve thousand square kilometers, roughly the area of Connecticut, was developed within a space of about twenty-five years not by the Brazilian government but by private enterprise, a British enterprise at that.

The Paraná experience was in many ways unique, but it sheds light on some of the preconditions for successful rural development, on the role of the frontier as a labor safety valve, and hence on the possibilities of substituting colonization for land reform.

### The Tradition of Colonization

Land development schemes occurred in Brazil prior to the northern Paraná adventure, under both public and private auspices. In the sixteenth century the Crown divided the entire eastern coast among twelve private citizens on condition that they attract settlers to produce an export staple that would provide revenues for the state. Except for small amounts of land brought under cultivation, these grants lapsed sixteen years later. In the following three centuries huge tracts were granted on similar conditions to wealthy individuals. Those holdings not exploited because they were infertile or inaccessible eventually reverted to the Crown and after the Republican revolution of 1889 to the states.[2]

After 1820 the Crown attempted to import Europeans as colonists with the aim of filling the demographic vacuum on the nation's frontiers, of generating tax revenues, and perhaps most important, of providing Brazilians with models of modern agricultural practices. Most public colonization schemes in the nineteenth century failed in the latter two objectives because of the political conflict between the interests of the state and existing latifundia. While the Crown wished to establish a tax-paying class of small freeholders, large landowners in the coffee-producing areas were more interested in a steady supply of dependent laborers. During the latter part of the nineteenth century colonists were either established as sharecroppers on the plantations or relegated to lands so sterile and inaccessible that they would be irrelevant to the booming commercial sector of the economy.

Some of the more successful regional development schemes have been undertaken by railroad companies that wished to realize the capital gain on lands through which their lines were constructed. Like their North American counterparts, Brazilian railroads acquired vast tracts of virgin land for ultimate resale to small farmers, who would generate the traffic. After 1910 the publicly owned São Paulo-Rio Grande Company, which linked São Paulo to Pôrto Alegre, sold its lands to large-scale subdividers, who attracted freeholders from the more heavily populated areas of the south. While the financial terms on which land was sold are obscure, these lands never became populous because of the relative sterility of the soils. The Paulista Railroad Company, which passed through the potentially rich lands of Marília, sold lands directly to small holders during the 1930s for a 50 percent down payment. This region became the leading edge of the coffee frontier thanks to the favorable combination of fertility and transportation.[3]

The experience of the National Agricultural Colony of Goiás at a site optimistically named Ceres, not far from a newly constructed railway terminus, is illustrative of the problems of official schemes. In order to provide a model for rational agricultural development in what was hitherto essentially a cattle region, the federal government selected lands in Mato Grosso de Goiás and provided a staff of agronomists as administrators. Each peasant was allotted a fifty-hectare farm, about a quarter of which was to remain a forest reserve. In addition, free housing, implements, and technical assistance were provided. A study of Ceres and a private colony in Goiás found that settlers neither expected nor experienced much increase in income over their place of origin, where most were landless. Their major motivation to migrate was a desire to free themselves from their dependency. Despite clear public ownership of the land, the delivery of title to the colonists was delayed, in many cases for decades, so that colonists could not mortgage or sell their land. Annoyed by such delays, many moved on to virgin land farther west.[4]

In order to generate income and tax revenues the government of Paraná began to sell its vast public domain in the northern and western parts of the state after 1919. These objectives threatened no major interest group in the state. At this time the economic center of Paraná lay in the capital city, Curitiba, located in a prairie that served as a resting place for the cattle that marched from Rio Grande do Sul to São Paulo. Not only did the Curitiba elite welcome the revenues that land development in the north would bring, but the westward march of agriculture has been generally viewed as a desirable geopolitical goal by all articulate segments of the population. After years of inept public effort at colonization, the state elite felt that the task could be best undertaken by private enterprise, thus saving public revenues for other activities.[5]

In the 1920s northern Paraná lay well beyond the coffee frontier that circumscribed the most dynamic area of Brazil. In the years 1923 and 1924 Simon Fraser, Lord Lovat, who had helped organize the Gezira cotton scheme in the Sudan, was actively seeking new opportunities for land development in Brazil. Following careful analysis of soils and climate, Lovat convinced some London investors to finance Companhia de Terras Norte do

Paraná, which would implement the development plans for the lands he had selected.

Northern Paraná has been characterized as an area of merged superlatives. The rainfall is evenly distributed throughout the year, the humidity is not excessive, and the temperature is mild. The *terra roxa* soils are formed of basaltic parent matter, which offers a friable and adequately water-retentive structure with considerable natural fertility. The relief is somewhat hilly, providing adequate drainage and substantial variation in microclimate for the cultivation of a wide range of crops. The care, or perhaps luck, with which Lovat selected lands within northern Paraná is impressive. His boundaries lie just above the northern limit of the normal frost line, twenty-four degrees south, below which coffee is a precarious enterprise. Just to the west of his boundaries, the soils become sandier, less water retentive, and hence less suitable for a wide variety of annuals.

After purchasing roughly 2.5 million acres (6.25 million hectares) at fifty cents per acre, the company spent two years clearing title to the land, often paying off multiple holders of dubious claims. This step was critical as land tenure for small holders is most precarious in Brazil and land would acquire more value were the owner assured of his title. Other companies in the area did not engage in this practice, to the distress of many small purchasers. In contrast the purchaser of company land who took a mortgage could receive title in no more than four years.

Without transportation facilities the land would be of value only to subsistence farmers. To guarantee linkages to national and world markets, the company purchased in 1928 the railway and rolling stock of the thirty-kilometer line built by landowners between Ourinhos and Cambará. Lying on the São Paulo-Paraná border, Ourinhos was linked by rail to the great coffee port of Santos. The company immediately began extending the line from Cambará, which was about 130 kilometers from the property's eastern border. By 1935 the railroad reached Londrina, the administrative capital of the property on the eastern border; by 1942 Apucarana, a planned center with a company hydroelectric plant; and by 1954 Maringá, near the middle of the property (figure 3).

To ensure that each property was adequately served by

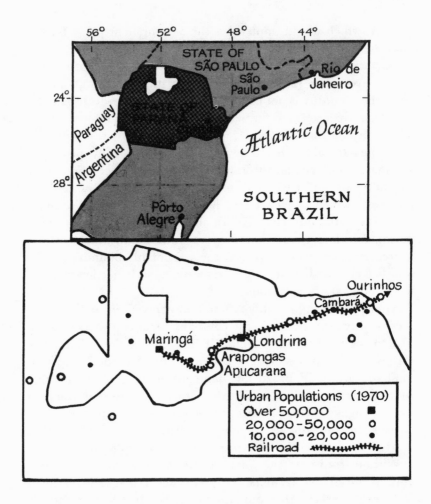

**Figure 3.** Northern Paraná

transportation facilities, the company surveyed properties so that each would have access to a feeder road built on the interstream divides as well as to the streams themselves. The company built one thousand kilometers of road by 1940, three thousand by 1950, and five thousand by 1967. In order to finance the construction of these roads and to capitalize on the value they created, the company sold only those lands in which the roads were installed. The state and counties later assumed the maintenance of the roads.

The company's marketing strategy was to tap the small and medium buyer, who had hitherto been excluded from the land market by lack of mortgage institutions. In the absence of mortgages only those with considerable savings could afford to purchase fertile and accessible plots. When large plantation owners sold lands to their workers under the duress of repeated financial crises in the coffee economy, these plots were generally small and exhausted. Although not opposed to selling plots to large purchasers, the company offered no quantity discounts.

The establishment of small and medium farmers, which has been a goal of all official colonization schemes, can be interpreted as profit-maximizing behavior on the part of the company: land values equal the capitalized value of the stream of rents, discounted at an appropriate rate. The rent an individual can offer for land equals the value of the output less variable production costs, largely labor in the context of the Brazilian coffee economy. If there were substantial economies of scale in agriculture, large landowners employing considerable labor could outbid family farmers for the use of land. In the coffee economy, however, there is no statistical evidence for scale economies, and the customary unit of operation is a group of trees tended by a family.[6] The wage a large landowner has to pay generally exceeds the wage someone imputes to working for himself. Why then do not family farmers outbid large landowners for coffee land? Or why do not large landowners sell the land to workers rather than hiring them, thereby destroying the latifundium by market forces? A partial answer lies in imperfections in the financial markets. For lack of mortgage institutions, poor farmers must rely on their meager savings to purchase land. Because of lack of developed securities markets, landowners have few alternative financial instruments in which their wealth can be invested, with such security against inflation.

The company attempted to reach the small buyer by selling plots in small units and offering two- to four-year mortgages. Farm lots were platted in twelve-hectare units. While suburban plots could be purchased in such a size, rural lots were generally sold in bundles of two to four units (in twenty-four to forty-eight-hectare plots). Urban lots were sold in units of five hundred to six hundred square meters.

The Paulista Railroad sold lands for 50 percent down in the

1920s but the company offered land on somewhat easier terms. Urban lots were sold for 40 percent down and 30 percent in each of the following two years. Farm lots were sold for 30 percent down, 10 percent for the next year, and 20 percent for the next three years. An explicit interest rate of 8 percent, later increased to offset inflation, was applied to the unpaid balance. The term of these mortgages may seem short for such a long-lived capital good as land, but these were clearly the best financial terms on which land was ever sold to a small holder in Brazilian history.[7]

Smaller farmers in the interior of Brazil would traditionally market their produce and buy essentials through a large landowner on whom they were dependent. Both to increase the income of the farmer, and hence the amount he would be willing to pay for the land, and to capture some of the gains from marketing, the company planned a series of urban centers along the railroad. Towns were planned at fifteen-kilometer intervals, the regional centers lying thirty to forty-five kilometers apart. The company eventually subdivided and built the urban infrastructure for six major towns, two of which surpassed one hundred thousand inhabitants by the 1960s.

Other colonization companies operated in northern Paraná during the 1930s and 1940s. Most of these operated under traditional forms of subdivision whereby large landholders supplied privately owned access roads, warehouses, processing plants, and stores and the land was allotted to workers in various forms of dependent status (such as crop sharing, work sharing, and wage labor).[8]

### Evaluating the Company Plan

The company was not an immediate success because the Depression disrupted the world coffee market. By 1935 the company had sold only 4.6 percent of its property; by 1939 it had sold another 6.5 percent. In the 1940s sales spurted: 23.3 percent was sold from 1940 to 1944 and another 38.7 percent was sold from 1945 to 1950. Most of the remaining land was sold in the 1950s.[9]

Northern Paraná was essentially uninhabited west of Cambará in 1920. By 1940 company lands contained 100,000 inhabitants, by 1950 about 400,000, and by 1965 about a million. Lands in the north outside the company boundaries grew a bit slower: from 240,000 in 1940 to 1.7 million in 1965, but rapidly nonetheless.

As indicated by population density, the growth of northern Paraná from 1940 to 1960 was considerably faster than that of New York, Illinois, and Ohio during a comparable phase of frontier settlement. During that period Paraná grew faster than any state in Brazilian history, raising its share of the national population from 3 to 6 percent.[10]

Population growth is an inadequate indicator of the success of development policy or a guide to planning. Two objectives of the company were profits and the establishment of small farmers, which objectives, it can be argued, were mutually supportive. In evaluating the company as a development institution, the relevant criterion is whether the social rate of return on capital exceeded the cost of capital (the interest rate). Since the social costs, usually funded by government, were undertaken by the company (from title search to road building) and since the company realized the benefits of these expenditures through land sales, the company's rate of return on investment provides a minimum estimate of social returns.

It is known that land purchased for fifty cents per acre near Londrina in the 1920s sold for about $4.50 in 1940 and $35 in 1950. On all company holdings real land values per acre increased more than sevenfold in the 1940s and another 30 percent in the 1950s. In noncompany lands in northern Paraná values increased only fourfold and 10 percent in the same two decades. In 1940 company lands were 15 percent more valuable than noncompany lands; in 1950 they were 100 percent more valuable; and by 1960 they were 150 percent more valuable.[11]

These data suggest that company policy clearly increased the value of the land. Unfortunately, it is not clear what net capital gain remained after the company's investment costs are subtracted, and no published studies have calculated the private rate of return on investment. Indirect evidence, however, suggests that the operation was clearly profitable. First, although the steps of road construction, surveying, and financing were coordinated, development proceeded incrementally. In other words, the whole railroad or road system was not completed as a prerequisite to development; they were completed at the same pace as land sales, one period's sales financing the next period's development. If the operation were proving unprofitable, the company could have stopped at any point and sold the unimproved land for more than the purchase price. Second, the company was forcibly sold to Brazilian investors during the Second World War as part of a worldwide liquidation of British overseas investments. Not only is it unlikely that an unprofitable operation would be forcibly purchased, since most of the value of the project lay in the conception not in the land, it is also unlikely that the successor company would have continued its predecessor's policy unchanged, as was the case.

If the concept were so profitable, why was it not imitated by other private land development companies in Brazil? In order to undertake such long-term planning, an entrepreneur must have the funds to purchase large blocks of land and to finance the surveys, the infrastructure, and the mortgages. The preparation time between Lovat's conception and the first land sales was about a decade. In the absence of such financial capacity and willingness to wait, a land developer could utilize secondary securities markets in which he could sell his stock. Such markets are only beginning to develop in Brazil.

In view of the failures of Brazilian private enterprise to undertake such activities, why has the government not filled the gap? In the 1920s and 1930s the dominant coffee planters had no particular interest in seeing funds expended on projects of this sort. Not only did their laissez faire ideology limit the role of the state to maintaining coffee prices, but colonization schemes could not help solve their labor supply problem. During the Depression the most salient problem was disposing of huge coffee surpluses, not creating new agricultural capacity. In the 1940s and 1950s the increasingly activist state viewed industry rather than agriculture as the source of economic development and agriculture was relatively slighted in receiving investment funds. Since 1950 agricultural policy has involved improving the marketing of agricultural produce within the given distribution of land ownership.[12] Although sporadic attempts at colonization were undertaken, they lacked the scale and term of commitment of the company. Only in the 1970s has a strategy of the type described here been adopted by the Brazilian government in Amazonia.

Did the company effectively establish a rural middle class in the midst of a latifundia-minifundia complex? The rural middle class connotes the ideal-type family farmer who is an owner-operator. In order to answer this question, several characteristics of agriculture in company lands and in several control regions were measured for 1940, 1950, and 1960. Characteristics that indicate average farm size are mean hectares per farm, mean hectares per worker, and mean workers per farm. For census purposes farms are defined as operating units not ownership units, therefore these measures may understate the average size of holdings. Characteristics that indicate the equality of rural social structure include Gini coefficient of size distribution of farms, tenure of farm operator (owner, administrator, renter, squatter), and status of the labor force (owner's family, wage laborer, sharecropper). The control regions include lands in northwestern Paraná outside of the company boundaries (noncompany lands) with some similarity in soils and climate; Marília, some of whose coffee lands were developed by the Paulista Railroad; Ribeirão Prêto, coffee lands developed in the 1880s by large landowners; Mato Grosso de Goiás, a pioneer rice-producing zone settled at the same time as northern Paraná, largely through private subdivision; and the Northeast, a nine-state region that epitomizes the latifundia-minifundia complex.

Over the years the average sale by the company measured forty hectares, which is relatively low for a coffee region. Consequently, the mean hectares per farm is smaller on company lands than in any other region. Although farm size is not much smaller than in Marília, it is considerably smaller than in noncompany lands and in Ribeirão Prêto. The small mean farm size on company lands and in Marília indicates that small farmers can outbid larger ones for land when equal access to mortgage financing is available. It is noteworthy that in all regions except Ribeirão Prêto the mean size of operating units fell between 1940 and 1960. Rather than indicating increasing opportunities for independent small holding, it reflects a rising dependency of the labor force.

When farm size is measured by mean workers per farm, the differences between company lands and other regions become less pronounced. Except for Ribeirão Prêto, all regions employ about five workers (about two families) per farm. Given the smaller than average farm size and about average number of workers per farm on company lands, there are fewer hectares per worker there (table 7).

Mean ratios disguise the size distribution of holdings. Com-

Table 7.    Intensity of agriculture, selected Brazilian regions, 1940-1960.

| Year | Company | Non-company North Paraná | Marília | Ribeirão Prêto | Mato Grosso de Goiás | North-east |
|---|---|---|---|---|---|---|
| Mean ha./farm | | | | | | |
| 1940 | 74 | 100 | 53 | 149 | 154 | 58 |
| 1950 | 56 | 73 | 68 | 205 | 155 | 69 |
| 1960 | 27 | 37 | 28 | 170 | 108 | 45 |
| Mean workers/farm | | | | | | |
| 1940 | 6.0 | 10.0 | 7.2 | 16.9 | 4.4 | 5.9 |
| 1950 | 7.8 | 12.0 | 8.2 | 17.8 | 5.3 | 5.1 |
| 1960 | 5.7 | 5.2 | 4.9 | 12.6 | 4.7 | 4.7 |
| Mean ha./worker | | | | | | |
| 1940 | 12.4 | 10.0 | 7.3 | 8.8 | 34.8 | 9.8 |
| 1950 | 7.2 | 6.1 | 8.3 | 11.5 | 29.4 | 13.5 |
| 1960 | 4.7 | 7.1 | 5.7 | 13.5 | 22.9 | 9.5 |

Source: State volumes, *Censo agrícola,* 1940, tables 29, 31, 36, 57; *Censo agrícola,* 1950, tables 22, 25, 30, 31; *Censo agrícola,* 1960, tables 10, 12, 14, 16. Figures for company and noncompany regions are from Emilio Willems, "The Rise of a Rural Middle Class in a Frontier Society," in Riordan Roett, ed., *Brazil in the Sixties* (Nashville: Vanderbilt University Press, 1972), pp. 325-344.

paring the number of establishments and amount of area in the various size classes of farms provides a Gini coefficient of inequality, which can vary theoretically from 0 to unity, the latter signifying complete inequality. In 1940 company lands were not noticeably more equally distributed than noncompany lands; in 1950 they were less equally distributed; and in 1960 the two were about the same. All land in northern Paraná is more equally distributed than in Marília and in Ribeirão Prêto, which compares to the Northeast in inequality of holdings.

The patterns of land tenure and labor force status, however, tend to dispel the image of company lands as comprising an egalitarian, middle-class society. In 1940 company lands tended to be managed by owners, but not much more so than non-company lands or Ribeirão Prêto. By 1960 the percentage of farms managed by owners tended to be smaller than in Ribeirão Prêto, Mato Grosso de Goiás, and the Northeast. Both company lands and those in Marília have undergone a rise in tenancy.

On company lands the share of the labor force composed of farm operators (only some of whom are owners) was about 60 percent in 1940, but only 50 percent in 1960. By 1960 a higher share of farm laborers was in some dependent status (as wage earners or sharecroppers) in company lands than on noncompany lands or even in the Northeast.

Perhaps the most telling indicator is the share of the labor force composed of the owner-operator family. This share has been declining in all regions, indicative of the growing dependency of the rural labor force throughout Brazil. Company land had a higher share of owner-operator workers than any other region except Mato Grosso de Goiás in 1940, but this share was less than in noncompany lands and in the Northeast by 1960 (table 8).

Measures of equality of holdings, of tenure, and of labor force composition indicate that the company's financing policies had no long-term effect in establishing a middle-class society. Not only is a minority of farms on company lands operated by family owners, but company lands are not much different from noncompany lands in this respect. Although the company created a more middle-class society than the plantation owners of Ribeirão Prêto, the former society is less middle-class than Mato Grosso de Goiás, which was also developed by the voluntary subdivision of large estates.

It should be emphasized that while company lands were more equally distributed and more family-owned, -operated, and -worked than those of other coffee zones in 1940, all such zones became less middle class by 1960. What factors seem to bring these different zones into line with each other? Surely not the technology of coffee production, since there are considerable differences in scale and in land per worker between Ribeirão Prêto and the other coffee zones.

A major influence results from the increasing necessity of farmers to purchase fertilizer as the virgin soils become exhausted. Large landowners, with political connections, prestige, and excellent collateral, have better access to credit than small farmers.[13] One reason banks prefer dealing with large borrowers is that the time and energy involved in transacting a large loan is not much more than that in transacting a small one, but the larg-

**Table 8.** Equality of rural social structure, selected Brazilian regions, 1940-1960.

| Year | Company | Non-company North Paraná | Marília | Ribeirão Prêto | Mato Grosso de Goiás | North-east |
|---|---|---|---|---|---|---|
| Gini coefficient | | | | | | |
| 1940 | .69 | .74 | .69 | .79 | .74 | .80 |
| 1950 | .89 | .79 | .73 | .78 | .68 | .83 |
| 1960 | .60 | .62 | .75 | .89 | .68 | .83 |
| % managed by owners | | | | | | |
| 1940 | 78 | 71 | 61 | 75 | 67 | — |
| 1950 | 76 | 76 | 58 | 75 | 65 | 72 |
| 1960 | 52 | 50 | 30 | 74 | 76 | 63 |
| % labor force operator family | | | | | | |
| 1940 | 50 | 34 | 15 | 17 | 72 | — |
| 1950 | 46 | 45 | 34 | 17 | 63 | 57 |
| 1960 | 52 | 65 | 60 | 19 | 64 | 64 |
| % labor force owner – operator family | | | | | | |
| 1940 | 47 | 28 | 9 | 12 | 50 | — |
| 1950 | 35 | 34 | 21 | 13 | 41 | 41 |
| 1960 | 27 | 32 | 18 | 14 | 48 | 40 |

Source: State volumes, *Censo agrícola,* 1940, tables 29, 31, 36, 57; *Censo agrícola,* 1950, tables 22, 25, 30, 31; *Censo agrícola,* 1960, tables 10, 12, 14, 16. Figures for company and noncompany regions are from Emilio Willems, "The Rise of a Rural Middle Class in a Frontier Society," in Riordan Roett, ed., *Brazil in the Sixties* (Nashville: Vanderbilt University Press, 1972), pp. 325-344.

er loan yields greater profits. Regardless of the private rationality of such behavior on the part of the bank, this bias encourages the concentration of land and the proletarianization of the labor force throughout Brazil. Another factor accounting for the decline of the middle-class society may have been the inability of the owners to sell their lands to dependent workers because of the continuing lack of land mortgage institutions and of alternative opportunities for middle-size investors.

The long-term effects of the company's policy are most visible in land-use patterns. In comparison with noncompany lands, mean hectares per farm are lower and land values higher on company lands. Higher land values in turn encourage lower land/man ratios and hence higher rural densities. As can be seen in figure 3 company lands are better served by urban places, which stimulate and are stimulated in turn by the more intensive rural land use.

An issue related to the establishment of family farms is whether these lands served as a means of providing social mobility to the lowest echelons of Brazilian society. The attractiveness of company land to the poor depends upon the relationship between the annual amortization and interest payments and their income. In order to purchase a lot of about six hectares in 1950 an individual had to pay forty-eight monthly installments, each of which equaled the official minimum salary in São Paulo, which was considerably above the rural wage. Company land was out of reach of most landless workers in São Paulo and even farther out of reach of workers in poorer states. The minimum salary in Paraná was half that in São Paulo.[14]

This analysis does not imply that company policy failed to improve the social status of the poor. The immigration of landless workers into northern Paraná undoubtedly led to an improvement in their material levels. Their basic dependency, however, remains. In the 1960s in northern Paraná net family income of owner-operators was $763, of sharecroppers $715, and of renters about $600. Thus dependency of those who share in production decisions is not accompanied by extreme poverty. On the other hand, nonresident wage laborers, who make up about 30 percent of the labor force, earned about $200.[15]

The frontier of Paraná served the labor safety valve function better than that of São Paulo. A larger share of the settlers in Paraná were native Brazilians than in São Paulo, where foreign immigrants predominated. The existence of Paraná may indirectly have increased the willingness of Paulista planters to subdivide and sell their exhausted lands to their tenants.

The importance of secure tenure in northern Paraná as a contributor to the well-being of the small holder cannot be underestimated. In southwestern Paraná, for example, the descendants of European colonists from Rio Grande do Sul began penetrating as subsistence farmers in the 1950s. Although these lands were originally in the public domain, they eventually acquired at least one owner of dubious legitimacy, usually an absentee with political connections to the state governor. So long as these lands remained isolated, these claims were not worth enforcing. As roads began to penetrate this subsistence frontier, the legitimate owners began pressing their claims. After some violence in the mid-1960s, most of these immigrants were ultimately ejected from the land or reduced to dependency as plantation workers.[16]

In comparison with other Latin American colonization schemes, northern Paraná succeeded in being completed as planned, in returning a profit above costs, and in creating a somewhat more middle-class society than the Brazilian norm, at least initially. How can this relative success be accounted for? What lesson can be drawn from this success?

Both the political environment and the formal planning process must be considered in answering these questions. First and foremost, there were no political obstacles in the way of the company's plans. In the 1920s, when the project was conceived, these lands were far enough ahead of the coffee frontier that Paulista planters did not perceive them as a magnet drawing away their labor supply. In the 1930s, when settlement began in earnest, the coffee planters were in disarray as a result of the Depression. Some planters turned to Paraná when coffee plantings were restricted in São Paulo as part of the government's efforts to maintain high prices. They could have hardly found the will or means to fight the company that was building a railroad to open up this region.

The planning process in northern Paraná can be characterized as incremental, comprehensive, market oriented, and long term. Rather than tying up huge amounts of capital in establishing prerequisites for development, the company paced its investment in land surveys, transportation links, and urban centers in accordance with land sales, thereby minimizing front-end risks for the investors. In planning comprehensively, the company internalized all the external benefits of urban, rural, and transportation investments. Consequently, returns were maximized as funds for the next phase of investment were obtained.

Market orientation has three components. First, the company raised its funds through the market rather than by legislative appropriation. Profit-and-loss accounting serves as a great incentive for efficiency. Second, the product was tailored to the demands of the customer rather than to professional standards. Many public colonization schemes provided model housing, education, medical care, and agricultural extension services far above the prevailing rural standard and ability to pay. Consequently, projects are usually unable to remain self-financing, are undersubscribed, abandoned, and too costly to repeat. Third, the company was able to increase the demand for its product by perfecting the capital market (by offering farm mortgages on unprecedented terms). Finally, the self-financing nature of the project meant that a long-term planning effort could be maintained so long as the investment proved profitable.

The company took a longer view of the development process than any Brazilian government could have taken. As Hirschman has aptly noted, if a president does not complete a project within his administration, it is unlikely to be completed by his successor.[17] The conceptualization of the Paraná project and preparatory surveying alone took longer than a presidential term. Finally, the company was operating in a unique phase of Brazilian development in which an extraordinarily fertile area with reasonable accessibility to market was about to acquire value because of industrialization-urbanization in São Paulo. In terms of fertility and accessibility, there are probably no more northern Paranás left in Brazil, or anywhere else in Latin America for that matter.

Since the conditions in northern Paraná were so propitious, would settlement have not occurred anyway in the absence of comprehensive planning on the part of the company? Indeed, settlement would have occurred but at a somewhat slower pace and at an ultimately lower level of intensity. Because investments in railroads, feeder roads, and urban infrastructure create external economies that are realized in land values, the lack of comprehensive planning would have meant that the investor in such infrastructure could not capture all the returns. By integrating these investments with real estate operations, the company achieved higher returns from more intense development. The proof of this hypothesis lies in the lower intensity of land use, the more widely spaced cities, and the lower land values in noncompany lands in northern Paraná.

Another difference the company made was in providing greater opportunities for family farming than in any other coffee frontier. Although initially a region of small holders, northern Paraná is experiencing increasing labor dependency, mainly because of the biases of the Brazilian farm credit system. The lesson here is that a formalistically well-planned project cannot sustain itself unless its operating requirements can be met by the broader society of which it is a part.

# 5

# Planning for a Demographic Vacuum: Amazonia

To a world that intermittently has seen itself as running out of natural resources and living space the six-million-square-kilometer Amazon Basin has appeared as the ultimate reserve. Brazilian policymakers have consequently dealt with their 70 percent of the basin with considerable ambivalence. On the one hand, this lush equatorial forest is seen as freeing the nation from the Malthusian specter. On the other hand, less well endowed powers are seen as constantly challenging, often surreptitiously, Brazilian sovereignty over half of its national territory.[1]

Brazilian efforts to develop Amazonia have been initially in response to geopolitical challenges from abroad and only recently to perceived opportunities for solving internal problems. In the thirty years that policymakers have paid any serious attention to the region, the definition of development has changed from protecting the decadent rubber sector, to creating employment opportunities for the natives, to serving as a labor safety valve for the densely populated Northeast, and finally to exploiting the region's mineral resources. The emphasis has oscillated between what regional economists call people prosperity and place prosperity, and in fact the accelerated resource extraction of recent years has led to the deterioration in the well-being of many inhabitants of the region.

Paraná benefited from superb natural resources; easily established transportation linkages to market; and a relatively abundant, educated, and healthy labor force, but Amazonia enjoys few of these boons. Paraná would have developed spontaneously without the efforts of the company — albeit at a slower pace, in a pattern of larger holdings, and with less intensive land use — but Amazonia has experienced little development of any sort despite massive public effort. If Paraná is a planner's dream of success, then Amazonia is his nightmare.

### The Era of Laissez Faire

The inventions of vulcanization in 1839 and of the pneumatic tire in 1888 and then the rise of the electrical and automotive industries around the turn of the century made rubber the raw material facing the fastest growing demand in international markets. The world's greatest source of natural rubber lies in the Amazon Basin, a virtually uninhabited and uninterrupted expanse of forest penetrated by a gigantic river system. One might suspect that this untamed environment would make an ideal setting for a frontier of ruggedly independent rubber gatherers and traders, a lucky few making a fortune. Nothing could be further from the truth. By grace of the physical environment and the institutions by which it was exploited, Amazonia was to be a "big man's" frontier.[2]

Although the vast Brazilian Amazon was settled by only a few hundred thousand Indians at the inception of the rubber boom around 1870, it was not unclaimed. Almost all the exploitable territory was under title (and often under several titles of dubious value), and whatever valuable land remained was rapidly claimed by men rich and powerful enough to control the land by force of arms and to consummate the tortuous process of land registration.

The rubber trees were useless until workers could be recruited to tap them. The gatherers originally came to the region at the beginning of the rubber boom, mostly from Ceará in the Northeast. Some were brought by their landlords to work under a stringent form of debt-peonage. Others were transported by government ships as refugees from the devastating drought of 1877-1878. As a result of the boom Amazonia's population rose from 333,000 in 1872, to 700,000 in 1900, and to 1,144,000 in 1920, and thus from 3 percent to 5 percent of the national population during the fifty-year period.[3]

Like all equatorial forests, the Amazon is an intermixture of many species of trees, and hence rubber trees are widely scattered.[4] A rubber tapper must consequently range widely, at a considerable expense in time and energy, in order to collect his latex. Productivity was correspondingly low, a factor favoring the shift of rubber to regions where plantations existed.

In 1876 a British subject smuggled some seedlings from Amazonia, which were raised in Kew Gardens in London and later established in great plantations in Malaya, which began exporting around 1912. Using cheaper labor and taking advantage of the more compact plantation, Malayan producers drove the price of rubber down from 12 shillings per pound in 1910, to 7 shillings in 1921, to 1.6 pence in 1932. Although its volume of production has not declined much since 1912, Brazil's share of world supply practically vanished, turning the nation into a net importer of rubber.[5]

If plantations were the solution to the productivity problem, why could they not be tried in their native soil? That epitome of Yankee optimism and ingenuity, Henry Ford, attempted to develop rubber plantations in the late 1920s on a huge concession at the edge of a tributary of the Amazon to provide materials for his tire plants. To discourage worker turnover, Ford built housing, hospitals, and mess halls. Unfortunately, the clustering of Amazonian rubber trees in a plantation hastened the spread of a deadly blight, which could be palliated by a grafting technique. The costs of providing worker amenities and combating blight rendered Amazonian rubber noncompetitive by the late 1930s. Thus the most serious attempt up to this time to expoit Amazonia using modern technology failed.[6]

Because of the sparseness of the population and the minuteness of the market in the major urban centers, further attenuated by the highly unequal distribution of income, few profits from the rubber boom were reinvested in self-sustaining economic activity. With the decline of rubber, the descendants of the northeastern gatherers became a basically stranded population engaged in hunting, subsistence agriculture, and the extraction of nuts and rubber on a reduced level. At least since the 1940s they have been moving to the cities, making Amazonia the most urbanized region outside Brazil's industrial Southeast.

Since the collapse of the rubber boom, the per capita income of Amazonia has remained at roughly 60 percent of the national average, but rising absolutely from about $100 in 1939, to $150 in 1950, to about $250 in 1970.[7] Because of the unequal income distribution, these figures overstate the income level of the population engaged in extraction. Their net income was far less than the value of the rubber gathered. First, they owed a share to the landlord. Second, the rubber had to be marketed and essentials imported, notably, food, clothing, kerosene, and ammunition.

The sparseness of the population and the tremendous distances of the trees from Belém, the entrepôt at the mouth of the Amazon, dictated a hierarchical commercialization system. At the local level, a trading post owner sent canoes out to the shacks of the gatherers, bringing a few essentials and collecting the balls of latex the gatherer prepared. The former were debited, the latter credited to the gatherer's account at the post. As the trader was generally the only buyer and seller with whom the gatherer dealt (a monopoly relationship reinforced by paternalistic ties and intimations of force), the gatherer received low prices for his rubber and paid high prices for his imports. His nearly constant indebtedness to the trader reinforced his peonage and weakened his bargaining power.

The small trader had a similar relationship with a larger distributor who plied the tributaries of the Amazon in larger boats, always dealing on a credit basis. The collection and distribution hierarchy culminated with the great import-export houses in Belém, which sent the rubber abroad in exchange for the essentials that made their way down the hierarchy. This system, which was developed for rubber trade, has also generalized to other extractive products, such as Brazil nuts.[8]

Perhaps the most lasting consequence of the rubber cycle was geopolitical. In the 1890s the search for rubber trees led the Brazilians to the upper Amazonian territory of Acre, which was nominally Bolivian. De facto occupation and the threat of superior force led to the peaceful transfer of this territory from Bolivia to Brazil, which paid a minor indemnity.

The difficulty of developing an agricultural export base to compensate for the decline of rubber may seem puzzling in a region of such impressive verdure, interlaced by an excellent fluvial transportation system. Despite the exuberance of the forest, the overwhelming share of the basin's surface is sterile and provides the most precarious base for sedentary agriculture.

Like the rivers of the ancient hydraulic civilizations, the Amazon annually deposits a layer of silt on its floodplain, renewing the fertility and permitting the perpetuation of sedentary agriculture. Consequently, the preponderance of the region's rural population congregates on the 2 percent of the region comprised of floodplain.

The remaining 98 percent of the area, the terra firma, is never inundated but is constantly battered by the rains. The huge Amazonian trees grow figuratively upon the soil in a fragile balance with the elements. The nutrients for the trees are extracted from the forest litter, whose rate of decomposition is slowed by the shade from these very trees. The destruction of the trees under traditional slash-and-burn agriculture hastens the decomposition of the humus and the leaching of the soil, which must be abandoned after one or two seasons.

The first major attempt at colonizing the terra firma was undertaken by the state of Pará through the 1883 to 1905 extension of a railroad eastward from Belém through an area known as the Bragantine strip. The European colonists, who were expected to bring advanced agronomic techniques, soon abandoned the area because of the poverty of the environment. In their place came tens of thousands who were escaping the recurrent droughts of the Northeast. The sterility of the soils conspired with their technological backwardness to yield the northeasterners little marketable produce. The resulting low volume of freight forced the railroad to cease operation in 1936.

In the 1920s the Japanese government signed a contract with Brazil to send colonists to various parts of the nation. While most went to São Paulo, where they began producing cotton for export to the mother country, some went to Amazonia. Under the auspices of a private Japanese company, the colony of Tomé-Açu was established about two hundred kilometers south of Belém on a concession granted by the state of Pará. The company provided transportation to the colony, some technical assistance, schooling, and marketing facilities, as well as financing for the first few years. Initial attempts at planting cashews, rice, and other familiar crops failed, leading to the consequent abandonment of the project by the company and emigration of most of the settlers.

In contrast to the Brazilian settlers in the Bragantine strip, the Japanese of Tomé-Açu were literate and included individuals with broader experience in tropical agriculture, having been drawn from the diaspora of overseas Japanese. Perhaps the Japanese had greater aspirations and patience than the Brazilians and more confidence in their ability to conquer the Amazon, for those staying behind undertook experiments with a wide range of crops. One immigrant from Singapore brought the black pepper plant, which ultimately proved to be the staple of the colony. An immigrant to another part of Amazonia, near Manaus, introduced jute as a second modern regional staple.[9]

The first major successful example of agriculture on the terra firma, Tomé-Açu is now responsible for about 80 percent of the total Brazilian pepper supply. Even the successes of the Japanese suggest the difficulties of turning Amazonia into a great food-producing region of the world. It is unlikely that the world pepper market could sustain much expansion of pepper production from Amazonia, as Brazil is currently the fifth largest supplier. Viable terra firma agriculture will depend upon either new techniques or new crops.

### The Rise of Public Initiative

During World War II the United States attempted to compensate for the loss of Malayan rubber with that from Amazonia. In order to stimulate production, the federal government established the Rubber Credit Bank in 1942 to provide credit for those engaged in the rubber trade. A definitive study of this bank has not been written, but it is clear that little of the credit filtered below the highest middlemen, who were freed from paying the enormous interest charges to their superordinates in the hierarchy. The minimum prices guaranteed by the bank and the credit hardly affected the welfare of the gatherer. Indeed, the wartime program may have even strengthened the traditional system, as it was utilized to distribute antimalarial drugs and consumer goods to the gatherers. Because of the shortage of labor and the sparseness of the trees, not much rubber was forthcoming despite these policies.

Several events increased Brazilian awareness of foreign interest in their natural resources. The history of *uti possidetis* in Acre, the rhetoric of *lebensraum* in two world wars, and the creation of the International Institute of the Hileia Amazonia to study the utilization of this demographic vacuum for the benefit of mankind rekindled fears of internationalization of the region.[10] As a result, the new constitution of 1946 earmarked 3 percent of all federal revenues for the development of Amazonia.

It was not until 1953 that enabling legislation was passed establishing the Superintendency of the Plan to Valorize the Economy of Amazonia (SPVEA). This agency was charged with nothing less than raising the standard of living of the people of Amazonia and developing the region's resources. Linked directly to the presidency, SPVEA was granted the right to exempt private enterprises from 50 percent of their tax burdens for ten years; to provide financing for these projects; to implant an infrastructure of energy, transportation, and urban utilities in the region; and to receive 3 percent of state and municipal revenues within its jurisdiction. To give SPVEA additional financial clout, the Rubber Credit Bank was transformed into the Amazonian Credit Bank, a change in name meant to signify a broadening of its mandate. The credit bank and its successor were to receive 10 percent of all funds earmarked for SPVEA. Although these funds were supposed to be applied to investment projects consistent with SPVEA's development strategy, the bank remained a provider of short-term commercial credit rather than long-term loans.[11]

In its twelve-year history (1953 to 1965) SPVEA rarely received its authorized 3 percent of federal revenues and never received the 3 percent of state and municipal revenues. Nevertheless, the agency received more funds per capita than any other regional development agency. For example, in the 1960s SPVEA received as much money as SUDENE, the northeastern development agency that served nine times as many people. Such transfers amounted to about 5 percent of Amazonian income.

SPVEA's strategy was to select sixteen growth poles into which public and private investments would be poured. In view of the contemporary ideology of creating prerequisites for development, the bulk of SPVEA's funds was spent on energy, port improvements, and water supply in the designated growth poles. With no prior analysis of the region's potential comparative advantage, SPVEA had no rigorous criteria for choosing among investment projects.

In 1964 the revolutionary government investigated SPVEA and found misappropriation of funds, poor accounting, technical incompetence, and employment of supernumeraries. Policymakers' consensus was that little permanent benefit resulted from its projects.[12]

A fair evaluation of SPVEA has yet to be written and perhaps can never be because records were haphazardly kept. While such criticisms can be leveled against many development agencies, in this case they may reflect the frustrations of attempting to develop a region where there is little potential for response. Nevertheless, SPVEA was replaced by the Superintendency for the Development of Amazonia (SUDAM) and the credit bank by the Bank of Amazonia (BASA) in 1965. The region's earmarked funds fell from 3 percent to 2 percent of the federal budget, and greater reliance was placed on fiscal incentives.

In 1963 the Amazonian Credit Bank became the depository of private funds obtained by SPVEA under the new fiscal incentive system. Under the system that ultimately evolved, any corporation could deduct up to 50 percent of its federal income tax liability by depositing such funds in a blocked account. These funds became available as short- and long-term loan capital for entrepreneurs whose projects were approved by SPVEA, and later SUDAM. Originally the investor had to put up one dollar of his own resources for every two received though this fiscal incentive system. The investor's equity requirement was eventually reduced to 25 percent of the total cost of the project. In addition, existing Amazonian firms were granted 50 percent income tax exemption until 1982; new firms received a 100 percent exemption.

In contrast to a direct federal grant, a fiscal incentive has several additional functions. First, it makes the payment of income taxes by corporations less painful because their deposits in the bank become negotiable five years after the completion of the project. Second, by offering capital on easy terms in a capital-scarce economy, investments in neglected areas like Amazonia become more attractive. Third, because several other regions and sectors are favored by fiscal incentive programs, planners in Amazonia have to convince depositors of the inherent profitability of the potential projects in the region. SPVEA-SUDAM attracted a considerable share of fiscal incentive funds at first, about 20 percent from 1963 to 1965; then it lost ground to the Northeast, falling to 15 percent in 1966; finally, it regained its 20 percent in the early 1970s. On a per capita basis the inflow of capital to Amazonia through this mechanism is about three times higher than to the Northeast.

The process of project approval should theoretically heighten the rationality of investment decisions, as the private investor, the holder of fiscal incentive deposits, and SPVEA have to convince themselves and each other of the project's viability. In fact, the process of project review was rather perfunctory because the supply of fiscal incentive deposits was greater than the demand.[13]

With respect to the objective of developing Amazonia by creating industry and employment, a tentative evaluation of the fiscal incentive system is possible. In the period from 1967 to 1971 SUDAM approved projects involving approximately $1 billion worth of investment, creating forty-five thousand jobs. Sectorally, about 10 percent of the investments were in services and the remainder was equally divided between agriculture and industry. Almost all the agricultural projects were in fact cattle ranches, which invest about $32,000 per worker, mostly in livestock. The extreme capital intensity and low labor absorption of cattle projects is emphasized by comparisons with investment per worker in industrial projects in the Northeast ($12,000), colonization projects ($3,000), and traditional agriculture ($300). In other words, the huge inflow of capital into the Amazonian countryside has generated few jobs.[14]

Projects in the industrial sector have been more diversified: from traditional food and textile industries to modern chemicals. An increasingly important form of industrial activity is mining, reflecting Amazonia's rich deposits of iron, manganese, and tin. The rate of labor absorption of these projects, about 9,000 jobs per year, may seem disappointingly low in comparison to the Amazonian labor force growth of 30,000 per year. In comparison with SUDENE in the Northeast, this rate of job creation is spectacular. In the longer period of 1964 to 1970 SUDENE approved projects providing 120,000 jobs, of which half were in modernization proposals. In contrast about 10 percent of SPVEA-SUDAM projects were in modernization.[15] As modernization projects generally lay off workers, the net contribution of SUDENE must have been considerably less than 120,000 and that of SUDAM not much less than 45,000. As the labor force of the Northeast is about nine times larger than that of Amazonia, the impact of SUDAM is more formidable than that of SUDENE on their respective regions.

It may be argued that cattle ranching and mining also generate indirect employment in services and in backward-linked industries; however, past performance of the mining sector, in particular, provides little basis for this belief. Commencing in the early 1950s, a consortium including Bethlehem Steel began exploiting the manganese deposits of Amapá Territory near Belém. The consortium built a railroad from the mines to the port that it also constructed and turned Brazil into one of the great manganese exporting countries in the world by 1956. In 1959 tin mining began in Rondônia Territory in western Amazonia. Unlike the Amapá case, exploitation began with individual placer miners. Such practices were forbidden as wasteful in 1971 and rationalization of the industry called for highly capital-intensive mechanization, which led to substantial unemployment.

Throughout the 1950s and 1960s these two mining territories approximately tripled their populations, from 37,000 to 120,000 each. It is unlikely that this population reflects the creation of much of a new economic base for Amazonia as a whole; this growth probably reflects instead a shuffling of an existing marginalized population.

The enclave nature of the mining economy is illustrated by comparing the growth of Amazonian output before and after mining began. Throughout the 1947-1956 period the region's output grew about 3.8 percent per annum, about two points below the national rate and only slightly higher than the Amazonian population growth rate. After 1956 growth spurted and began to exceed the national rate through 1963. If the value of mineral exports is subtracted from the post-1956 growth curve, the old trend line continues. If manganese or tin mining had significant multiplier effects, the subtraction of mineral exports would have left additional generated output above the old trend line. Imports of food and manufactures into the two territories confirm more directly the enclave nature of mining, which is a nearly universal phenomenon.[16]

In the late 1950s the problem of the Brazilian Northeast became salient because of the social upheavals triggered by the drought in 1958 and a political awakening of the plantation workers in the littoral. An official government analysis of the Northeast identified rural poverty and landlessness as fundamental problems that could be solved by measures such as emigration to the nearby Amazonian forests. To this latter end the state of Maranhão, a transitional area between Amazonia and the semiarid zone of the Northeast, granted SUDENE three million hectares for colonization of ultimately a million people.

SUDENE transported one thousand families at a cost of $18,000 per family to seventeen colonies by 1964, when the program was quietly abandoned.[17] Because of the lack of roads and marketing facilities, the colonists lapsed into subsistence. Although this experiment failed, the notion of Amazonia as a labor safety valve acquired the mystique of embodying a single solution to two sets of problems at once: reducing poverty without land reform in the Northeast and asserting Brazilian sovereignty over Amazonia.

The latest phase of Amazonian development policy was triggered by the northeastern drought of 1970, the first to be witnessed personally by a Brazilian president. In a surprise move that has been called an "emotional accident,"[18] President Médici announced the National Integration Program, which reiterated the importance of Amazonia as a labor safety valve.

A subsequent apologia for these programs makes the following type of argument: technological imperatives dictate that modern agriculture, especially northeastern cotton and sugar production, must be organized on a large scale with the majority of the labor force as wage earners rather than owner-operators. Defined as mechanization, continual modernization will reduce the ability of agriculture to absorb labor. Therefore the aspirations of the landless in the Northeast cannot be satisfied if agriculture is to modernize. Migration from the rural Northeast to the cities only produces a marginalized mass that cannot be usefully absorbed in the urban economy (by industry). Such a mass is a potentially explosive social force whose living standards must be repressed if the nation is to develop (to grow at the maximum aggregate rate). Since Amazonia contains boundless resources, the aspirations for land ownership on the part of the rural lower class can be satisfied without attenuating development in the settled areas.[19]

The National Integration Program consisted of three elements: the construction of the Transamazon and Cuiabá-Santarém Highways, the colonization of lands within ten kilometers of either side of these highways, and irrigation of the Northeast. The Transamazon links Recife, the largest northeastern city, to the Peruvian border in western Amazonia; the other highway connects the middle Amazon to the southern cities.

When colonization schemes in Latin America fail, it is gener-

ally because the soils chosen are infertile or inaccessible or the
settlers are underfinanced. In the face of these problems, the
National Integration Program borrowed elements from the
northern Paraná scheme. The National Institute of Colonization
and Agrarian Reform, INCRA, planned to pay the farmers'
migration and setting-up costs, to provide credit for the first year
and mortgage money for the purchase of a 100-hectare plot, and
to establish an urban infrastructure (schools, banks, hospitals).
At 7-kilometer intervals along the highway was to be an *agrovila*
containing schools, a welfare post, and a general store; at 20-kilo-
meter intervals there was to be an *agropolis* with extension services, warehouses, and repair shops; and at 140-kilometer intervals there would be a *ruropolis,* a small industrial center with an
airport, hospital, and technical school.

To finance these activities, 30 percent of all fiscal incentives
was to be transferred to the program from 1971 to 1974. No su-
perordinate administrative agency was established to implement
the program: the Ministry of Transportation was to construct
the highways and INCRA to settle the immigrants.

The National Integration Program was greeted by a noticeable
lack of enthusiasm by politicians in both the Northeast and Amazonia, mainly because it diluted the fiscal incentives program
that had effectively increased capital formation in these regions.
Providing an alternative outlet for northeastern migrants was
more popular in the industrializing Southeast, where northeasterners were being blamed for all the urban ills. Some policymakers on the Right attacked the program as a retrocession in planning competence. No prior analysis suggested that the Transamazon was a critical highway, for it had been omitted from the
recently published national transportation plan. Experience on
the Belém-Brasília indicated that an unpaved road through a
rain forest was often unpassable during the rainy season and required costly maintenance. Not only were the soils through which
it passed of dubious quality, but the distance of the colonies from
the market would require guaranteeing the farmers minimum
prices at levels that would force the government to subsidize the
freight. Although muffled, the Left considered colonization an
unsatisfactory substitute for land reform.[20]

Falling back somewhat from this criticism, the government
claimed that the highway could not be evaluated solely on narrow

economic grounds but that national security was a major objective. To emphasize the point about national security, the government commenced construction of the Northern Perimeter Road, which skirts the crescent of nations bordering western Amazonia. If, as Brazilians joke, the Transamazon links misery to nothing, then the perimeter road links nothing to nothing.

Progress in colonization was considerably slower than planned. Hoping to settle one hundred thousand families in the 1971-1974 period, INCRA had succeeded in fixing a total of only thirty-seven hundred by mid-1973.[21] By mid-1974 the colonization scheme was virtually abandoned as a failure.

Despite the avowed goal of settling the Amazon, there is considerable evidence that the Brazilian government perceives people as an obstacle rather than an asset for development. The fiscal incentives and road-building programs have often brought outside modern entrepreneurs in conflict with traditional populations. Many cattle companies attracted by fiscal incentives found what they consider their lands occupied by squatters of long-standing whose claims are invariably overridden by the government. Cattle companies entering the rubber regions have cleared the trees, expelling the workers. The entry of multinational mining corporations into Rondônia has deprived thousands of placer miners of a livelihood. Finally, the government has answered critics of road building through reservations by arguing that Indians cannot stand in the way of development.[22]

### Agricultural Prospects

In light of the apparent failure of the latest colonization scheme and shift toward corporate mining and ranching, what are Amazonia's prospects as an agricultural region? Geographers have generally been skeptical about the possibilities of viable field crop agriculture on the terra firma. The profession, however, has underestimated the viability of Brazilian agriculture in the past. For example, it failed to anticipate the rise of pepper cultivation in Amazonia and stable rice cultivation on the savanna. The fact that pepper is a tall vine suggests that a successful terra firma crop must shade the soil to permit the recycling of its nutrients and to suppress weeds. The destruction of the forest for cattle raising and the consequent growth of scrub savanna may cause an irretrievable loss of these nutrients.[23]

The success of pepper also suggests that successful terra firma agriculture cannot result from the wholesale adoption of varieties from other parts of the world. The discovery of pepper resulted from years of scientific experimentation under indigenous conditions. The tremendous variations in soil conditions under what appears to the untrained eye as a monotonously uniform forest indicates that even indigenous agrobiological innovations cannot be diffused throughout the region without adaptation to local conditions.

Because of its relative fertility and accessibility, the Amazonian floodplain is more likely to support a stable agricultural population than the terra firma in the near future. Although the floodplain is only about sixty-five thousand square kilometers, roughly one-third the area of Iowa, it is physically capable of producing an enormous amount of rice or jute under existing techniques. Assuming that all of the floodplain were devoted to rice production, that double cropping yielded sixty-six hundred kilos per hectare, and that per capita consumption were one hundred kilos,[24] Amazonia could furnish rice for, although not necessarily feed, two hundred million people. The risk of exceptional flooding that destroys the crop on the average of once every four years and the immense costs of commercializing production in the intricate river system would undoubtedly reduce economically viable production; however, the potential of the floodplain is still impressive.

Developing the floodplain would require constructing protective dikes, creating an integrated fluvial transportation system, delivering credit to innumerable small farmers, and disseminating some new agronomic techniques. Such development could not only provide a basis for "people prosperity" within the region but enable Amazonia to make a significant contribution to the world food supply. Whereas the potential lies on the floodplain, recent Brazilian development policy has focused on integrating the terra firma, where agricultural potential is minimal.

More than any other region, Amazonia has been out of the mainstream of Brazilian life, except for the period of the rubber boom. Until after World War II the government had no policy toward the region whatsoever, and there was little reason to have one. The population was small, remote, and invisible to the literate elite in the southeastern section of the nation. Although the luxuriant forest has evoked contrary images of green hell and a boundless treasure chest, in practice, investments in the region did not seem to produce any lasting benefit. With such inviting prospects still to be exploited in Paraná and Goiás, Amazonia was to remain a low-priority region.

Brazilian policymakers' response to the Amazonian problem confirms several hypotheses of Albert Hirschman.[25] First, policy-makers are strongly biased against programs that involve techno-logical uncertainties. Specifically, the agrobiological process of the equatorial rain forests of the world are not so well known as those of temperate regions, and hence ready-made farming tech-niques cannot be imported from advanced countries. With so much more accessible and hospitable land available in the Cen-tral West, the inducements for indigenous agrobiological innova-tions are weak. At the polar extreme, mining processes are prac-tically universal, while cattle-raising techniques of the tropical highlands of Brazil can be transferred with some modification to the equatorial lowlands. On simply technological grounds, the odds of success for colonization schemes are lower than for min-ing or cattle-raising schemes.

Second, administrative costs of establishing a few mining or cattle enterprises are less than costs of settling hundreds of thou-sands of farmers. Unless they have strong ideological biases to-ward mobilization of the masses, planners prefer to avoid projects that involve the political and psychological problems of dealing with large numbers of people. Brazilian public policy hardly shares this bias.

These technological and administrative obstacles aside, it is unlikely that in the near future Amazonia will produce much food for export markets or absorb much labor from the North-east. On the grounds of its isolation, Amazonia's comparative advantage seems to lie in activities producing high value per unit weight or enjoying low transportation costs. Such activities as mining, cattle raising, lumbering, or spice production absorb little labor.

# 6

# The Process
# of Regional Integration

Economic development and regional integration have long been viewed as interrelated processes. In the course of development the friction of distance tends to decline, facilitating the flows of commodities and factors of production. While regional integration has been espoused as a goal in almost every nation, it does not uniformly affect all groups. Relatively diversified and self-sufficient regions begin to specialize along particular lines of activity, while dispersed rural workshops staffed with artisans are supplanted by urban factories manned by an industrial proletariat. Manufactures often become concentrated in a single metropolitan area. The orthodox neoclassical analysis views these symptoms as leading to long-term equalization of wages, interest rates, and possibly per capita incomes among regions; but the polarization paradigm views regional integration as the means by which the dynamic center exploits the periphery.

The concept of region has been defined in many ways. In the analysis of industrialization-urbanization and frontier settlement the concept of an area polarized around an entrepôt, namely metropolitan São Paulo, was utilized. A more useful concept for studying the process of integration comes from international trade: a region is an economic space within whose boundaries factors of production flow freely but across which they do not. Within a nation with a well-developed transportation system and capital market, such as the United States, the region in this sense has arbitrary boundaries, for the facility with which labor and capital flow across space declines continuously with distance between any two points, not abruptly at well-defined boundaries, such as state lines. Brazil, on the other hand, had been likened to an archipelago in the 1956-1961 Target Plan. While this term had largely rhetorical purposes, there were, in fact, no all-weather road connections linking the three great macroregions of the nation — Amazonia, the Northeast, and the Central South — until the 1950s. Because most Brazilian economic statistics are published on a state basis, that unit serves as the operational definition of region and the building block for macroregions.

The barriers that have Balkanized the Brazilian market have been declining rapidly at least since the 1940s, largely through the action of the federal government. First, interstate fiscal barriers have been reduced. States levied taxes on interstate imports and exports until President Vargas abolished the taxes in 1937. How effective this abolition was is not clear since tax evasion was then an accomplished art form. Second, a hierarchical system of national, regional, and state development banks has been created. One purpose of the regional banks is to serve as a depository of fiscal incentives, which has made the cost of financing lower in Amazonia and the Northeast than in the Central South, at least for a limited number of large firms. Third, import substitution policies, particularly tariffs and quotas, have increased the cost of foreign manufactures relative to domestic. A potential effect is to divert demand away from foreign goods toward domestic ones, thereby increasing interregional trade.[1]

The most important force reducing the friction of distance has been improvements in the transportation system. A tentacular road system centering on São Paulo, and on Rio to a lesser extent, has been expanding at a rapid rate, first integrating the immediate hinterlands of these capitals, then thrusting into the empty agricultural frontiers of the Central West and Paraná, and finally linking the industrial Southeast to the population centers of the Northeast and Amazonia. From 1952 to 1965 the mileage of federal (largely interstate) highway and county feeder roads increased by 200 percent and that of state roads by 100 percent. In the decade since 1965 the mileage of federal and state roads increased by another 100 percent. The mileage of paved roads of all jurisdictions increased even faster.

Road construction, the creation of a domestic truck and bus industry, and fuel import subsidies have cheapened the movement of both people and goods. Although a time series for transportation costs in general is unavailable, fragmentary evidence suggests a striking decrease in trucking costs. In São Paulo, the state responsible for about 50 percent of all interstate exports, costs per ton-mile on laterite roads fell by two-thirds from 1940 to

1960. In terms of overall accessibility (density of road network, type of surface) transport costs fell by more than that. For the Goiás-Brasília region trucking costs fell roughly by two-thirds as well for farm-to-market, local market-to-regional market, and regional market-to-national market journeys.[2]

In the 1948-1966 period labor productivity in the railroad sector apparently rose 60 percent and freight rates fell by the same amount. Despite heavy railroad subsidies, trucking costs fell even faster, and the share of ton-mileage carried by railroads fell from 29 to 16 percent from 1950 to 1963, a share that has held steadily through 1972.[3]

## Polarizing and Equilibrating Effects of Integration

The declining friction of distance facilitates the flow of factors of production and commodities. The ultimate consequences of increased integration are viewed differently by two conceptual schemes: the polarization paradigm and the orthodox neoclassical or equilibrium paradigm. The latter includes the industrial-urban hypothesis analyzed in chapter 3. While the equilibrium approach views integration as a means of improving the well-being of all regions, sectors, and classes in the long run, the polarization approach maintains that the development of one region causes the underdevelopment of another.[4]

The distinction between these approaches is best illustrated by dividing the space-economy into a center, which is relatively prosperous, industrial, and growing, and a periphery, which is relatively poor, rural, and stagnant. The growth of the center is left unexplained, as the result of some random shock such as exceptional natural transportation facilities, fertile soils, or a fortuitous invention. The basic difference between the two approaches lies in an analysis of how the facilitation of the following flows between the center and the periphery affects the latter: trade, migration, capital, technology, fiscal transfers, and other public policies. While the equilibrium approach focuses almost completely upon market-mediated transfers, the polarization approach places a major emphasis on the interests and resultant policies of the peripheral elite.

Prior to integration the center and the periphery are relatively diversified and largely self-sufficient in food, raw materials, and manufactures. Industrial activity is closely linked to the natural resource base and heavily weighted toward subsistence crafts (such as spinning and food milling), the beneficiation of agricultural products for exports (such as ginning and coffee roasting), and the manufacture of low-quality, mass-consumption necessities (such as food and apparel). In 1919 industrial output reported in the Brazilian census reflected this pattern typical of low-income countries: food (33 percent), textiles (27 percent), beverages (5 percent), tobacco and lumber (4 percent each). Industries forward linked to the above contributed another 9 percent of total industrial output: apparel (8 percent), furniture (1 percent). Under these conditions industry tends to be highly dispersed in a manner roughly predictable by the location of the agricultural populace.

A decrease in transportation costs enhances comparative cost differences between locally produced and imported commodities. The equilibrium approach focuses on how differences in comparative advantage generate mutually beneficial interregional specialization and trade. In the long run, however, the existence of significant agglomeration economies brings additional consequences. The center, by virtue of its larger volume of production, may have an absolute advantage in all industrial activities and will tend to attract mobile factors of production from the periphery. To the extent that agglomeration economies are internal to the firm, average firm size increases and the number of firms may decline. To the extent that the agglomeration economies are external to the firm, the number of firms located at the major production center increases.

The obverse of the concentration of production in larger firms is the destruction of cottage industry and rural handicrafts. The cheapness of industrialized goods, due to economies of scale that more than outweigh greater collection and distribution costs, usually leads to an increased specialization of rural families in agricultural production. To the extent that rural handicrafts are more labor intensive than agriculture, the declining demand for these crafts will lower wages and increase the rents of landowners.

Through trade there are other forces that may lead to divergences in growth patterns between the center and the periphery. The center produces manufactures for which there are high price- and income-elasticities of demand, while the periphery produces primary products for which there are low corresponding elasticities. Because of the income-elasticities, growth in income will shift the terms of trade (the price ratio of manufactures/primary products) against the periphery. Because of the price-elasticities, technological progress in the center will lead to a slight drop in price and a great expansion in demand while that in the periphery leads to a great drop in price and a tiny increase in demand. Consequently, the periphery suffers immiserizing growth through trade. The equilibrium paradigm, nevertheless, maintains that the periphery is still better off trading than not. The terms of trade need not turn against the periphery if the elasticity of supply for its products is lower than that for products of the center.[5]

The equilibrium approach views migration as a mechanism for increasing the welfare of both the migrant and the population that remains behind. Integration with the industrial-urban center improves the efficiency of the labor market in the periphery in proportion to its proximity. When the industrial-urban center is quite close, primary and secondary workers in rural families have access to part-time urban employment and children have a better chance of obtaining education. Whether the movement of labor represents long-term migration or daily commuting, the draining of surplus farm labor raises its marginal productivity.

The polarization approach focuses on the selectivity of migration. The center extracts the most vigorous and educated workers from the periphery, leaving behind those too old or young to work and the least educated and least entrepreneurial. While individual migrants may have benefited, the residue in the periphery does not, it is argued.

The integration of capital markets may accelerate the flow from the periphery to the center, where returns to all factors of production are higher, because of economies of scale, more rapid technological progress, or superior natural resources. The equilibrium approach views such capital transfers with equanimity, since returns to scarce capital are thereby maximized. In the long run, when the agglomeration economies in the center are exhausted and returns on capital drop, the periphery may enjoy a net capital inflow.

The polarization approach focuses considerable attention on the origins of the capital that flows from the periphery to the center. Although a small fraction of capital outflow represents savings deposits of residents of the periphery, the bulk of the outflow is viewed as literal booty plundered from the masses on the periphery. Through the monopoly over the marketing system the middlemen of the center extract a large share of the wealth generated by raw materials producers on the periphery. The possibility of eventual net inflows of capital to the periphery in generally discounted.

Both paradigms view the center, by virtue of its wealth and diversified economic base, as the generator of inventions and incubator of innovations. The equilibrium approach does not contain a well-developed model of the spatial diffusion of innovation; however, it tends to view technology as a public good that can be easily adopted in the periphery either in its disembodied form or embodied in new investment. Although the diffusion of innovation is not instantaneous, the periphery will eventually benefit from the center's technological achievements.

The polarization approach sees the center's technological progress as a mechanism for perpetuating the high returns to capital and skilled labor, further draining the periphery of these resources. Because of patents and other monopolistic restrictions, technology does not freely diffuse to the periphery. One mechanism of diffusion is the sale of patents, which have zero opportunity costs to the center firms, to enterprises on the periphery, thereby contributing to capital exports. Another mechanism of diffusion is the establishment of a branch plant if the local market is large enough to warrant one. In either case, this technology was developed for the labor-scarce and capital-rich center, while the periphery is capital scarce and labor abundant. The openness of the periphery to the introduction of technology from the center preempts the possibilities of developing an indigenous technology more appropriate to factor endowments in the periphery. Finally, the technological superiority of the center results in the competitive destruction of indigenous businesses and hence local sources of entrepreneurship.

The equilibrium approach has a poorly developed behavioral theory of government. An essentially neutral entity, the government may choose to invest its resources so to maximize aggregate income of its citizens over the long run or to redistribute income to the poor. In any event, the preferences of all citizens are taken into account equally in the formulation of collective choice. In the polarization approach the government is an expression of the interests of the ruling class and is another mechanism by which the center exploits the periphery. By reducing interregional tariff and transportation barriers, which protect the industry of the periphery, the state benefits that of the center. Second, the state may tax the periphery for the benefit of the center. Third, by virtue of its being the center of power, the center will be additionally favored as an industrial location where entrepreneurs will attempt to influence the state to act in their favor.

A more sophisticated model is proposed by Albert Hirschman, who argues that the government's behavior can be predicted by the structure of the problems it faces.[6] At the initial stages of development state policy favors the center, where the returns on investment are highest, at the expense of the periphery. When economic development at the center has become self-sustaining and the problem of regional disparities becomes more salient and politically less tolerable, the periphery may enjoy favors and net inflows of public funds.

The polarization approach maintains that even with the influx of public funds the periphery is unlikely to develop because the elite in the periphery has a stake in its underdevelopment. Their interests lie in exporting raw materials, using cheap labor, and purchasing inexpensive manufactures from the center. Any industrialization on the periphery that creates countervailing industrial groups or that raises wages, educational levels, or taxes is opposed.[7]

In summary, the polarization approach predicts that levels of industrialization, wages, and per capita income between the center and periphery will continually diverge. While the equilibrium approach recognizes the forces leading to spatial agglomeration, it tends to view differences in wages as self-liquidating in the long run. Hirschman suggests that both polarizing and equilibrating tendencies are continually operating and that the former tend to predominate at the onset of development while the latter finally offset them at a turning point after which regional disparities tend to decline. The exhaustive empirical analysis of Williamson tends to confirm this view, although the process of convergence has taken longer than a century in the United States, for example.[8]

## Concentration and Disparities

Without question, Brazilian states are becoming more specialized, especially since 1949. The indices of dissimilarity of state shares of national agricultural versus industrial income have been rising: .35 in 1939, .33 in 1949, .43 in 1959, and .49 in 1968. When employment is disaggregated into twenty-five commercial and industrial sectors, the results are similar, with states tending to diverge from the national sectoral pattern.[9]

There has been a slow redistribution of income and population from the Northeast to the South and Central West, largely because of industrialization in São Paulo and the rise of the Paraná and Goiás frontiers. Per capita income disparities have been fairly stable in the 1939-1969 period, although there have been minor short-run shifts (table 9).

Total income, manufacturing, and population are tending to concentrate in the Rio-São Paulo axis, located in the Southeast. The magnitude of this tendency is not visible on the macroregional level, since the Southeast includes the relatively declining states of Minas Gerais and Espírito Santo.

Accounting for interstate differences in per capita income is a common goal of regional economics. The technique generally involves determining whether regional differences in wages exist when industrial structure and labor force quality (age, experience, and education) are held constant. If not, then regional per capita income disparities are reducible to differences in industrial composition, labor force participation, and the age-sex-education distribution of the labor force.

While such analysis has not been performed with Brazilian data, two studies provide a rough approximation. The first classified industrial firms by sector, number of employees, city size, and state. About one-half of the variation in mean wages per firm was explainable by sectoral differences in wages, about one-quarter by wage differences associated with firm size, and the rest by unexplained state differences. In other words, about three-quarters of interfirm wage disparities can be explained by industrial sector and firm size.[10]

Using a similar approach, the second study attempted to explain variations in individual incomes by labor force participation, sex, age, education, and region. About one-third of the in-

**Table 9.** Regional percentages of national income and population, 1939-1970.

| Region | 1939 – 40 | 1949 – 51 | 1959 – 61 | 1968 – 70 |
|---|---|---|---|---|
| Percentage of income | | | | |
| Amazonia[a] | 2.6 | 1.8 | 2.2 | 2.1 |
| Northeast[b] | 16.7 | 14.1 | 14.4 | 14.1 |
| Southeast[c] | 63.2 | 65.9 | 63.0 | 62.9 |
| South[d] | 15.3 | 16.1 | 17.6 | 17.3 |
| Central West[e] | 2.1 | 1.9 | 2.7 | 3.3 |
| Percentage of population | | | | |
| Amazonia | 3.6 | 3.5 | 3.7 | 3.4 |
| Northeast | 35.0 | 34.6 | 31.6 | 30.3 |
| Southeast | 44.5 | 43.4 | 43.8 | 42.7 |
| South | 13.9 | 15.2 | 16.9 | 17.7 |
| Central West | 3.1 | 3.3 | 4.2 | 5.8 |
| Relative per capita income | | | | |
| Amazonia | .72 | .51 | .59 | .62 |
| Northeast | .48 | .42 | .46 | .47 |
| Southeast | 1.42 | 1.52 | 1.44 | 1.47 |
| South | 1.10 | 1.06 | 1.04 | .98 |
| Central West | .68 | .58 | .64 | .57 |
| Index of dissimilarity | | | | |
| Macroregions | .20 | .23 | .20 | .20 |
| States | .25 | .34 | .26 | .26 |

Source: *Conjuntura econômica* 24 (June 1970): 89 – 106; Brasil, *Censo demográfico,* 1970.
[a]Amazonas, Para, Acre, Roraima, Rondônia, Amapá.
[b]Maranhão, Piaui, Ceará, Rio Grande do Norte, Paraíba, Pernambuco, Alagoas, Sergipe, Bahia.
[c]Minas Gerais, Espírito Santo, Guanabara – Rio, São Paulo.
[d]Paraná, Santa Catarina, Rio Grande do Sul.
[e]Mato Grosso, Goiás, Federal District.
The Central South includes the Southeast, the South, and the Central West.

equality in personal income is explained by educational differences and about one-fifth by sector of employment (agriculture-
industry-services). Holding these factors constant, only about
one-tenth of the inequality is traced to unexplainable regional
factors. In other words, regions where income is low have a disproportion of population that is poorly educated and employed
in agriculture.[11]

It is difficult to draw inferences from these statistical associations unless one concedes that interregional differences in industrial composition, firm size, educational levels, and age distribu-

tion are natural or exogenous to the development process. All of these factors are clearly consequences of development as well: higher incomes lead to a disproportionate growth of industrial and service employment, as well as expanded educational opportunities; the extension of the market facilitates the growth of firm size; and industrialization-urbanization alters fertility and mortality rates and hence the age distribution of the labor force. These reciprocal relationships are not completely deterministic, for public policy can affect the supply of educational facilities, the incomes of small farmers, and possibly the age-sex composition of the labor force.

### Interregional Flows

Of the various interregional flows, migration has received the greatest attention in Brazil and elsewhere, mainly because of the availability of data. The most extensive research on interregional migration has been undertaken by Douglas Graham and Sérgio Buarque de Hollanda Filho. Using the forward-cohort survival technique, they have painstakingly reconstructed net migration to and from each Brazilian state for all intercensal periods. Since 1872 the southeastern states have been net recipients of internal migrants, the northeastern states, net generators. Only during the rubber boom at the turn of the century has Amazonia been a net importer of population.

As a percentage of population at the beginning of the decade, interstate migration involved less than 2 percent of the population between 1900 and 1920, accelerating to over 5 percent between 1950 and 1960, declining about one point in the succeeding decade. The stock of migrants, however, has been increasing from about 3 percent in 1940 to about 11 percent in 1970.[12]

These data on flows and stocks are insufficient to indicate trends in the geographic mobility of the Brazilian population (the responsiveness of migration flows to interregional differences in opportunity). Actual flows should reflect both the friction of distance, which has been declining historically, and interregional disparities in per capita income, which increased in the 1940s, declined in the 1950s, and remained stable in the 1960s. The rate of flow increased in the 1950s over the previous decade, which suggests that the facilitating decline in transportation costs more than outweighed the damping effect of the convergence in per capita income. Surprisingly, in the 1960s the rate of migration declined despite the stability of the income disparities and the further decline of transportation costs.

What has been the role of internal migration in increasing or reducing interregional disparities in per capita income? It is clear that migration is selective, as the younger and more educated tend to be more mobile. In terms of educational characteristics, migrants tend to have more schooling than the average resident of regions of net outflow and somewhat less than residents of regions of net inflow. While the movement of educated, prime-aged workers may possibly reduce income averages in the region of origin, the question of greatest interest is whether their departure improves the opportunities of those left behind.[13]

From 1940 to 1950 the magnitude of net immigration as a percentage of 1940 population was unrelated to state per capita income, relative to the national average. Changes in relative state per capita income, moreover, were unrelated to the magnitude of net migration. From 1950 to 1960, however, the rate of net immigration was directly related to state per capita income: high-income states attracted and low-income states generated migrants. Furthermore during this period relative income gains were inversely related to the rate of net immigration: receiving states grew slower in per capita income, generating states grew faster. A similar pattern was visible between 1960 and 1970. These findings suggest that migration was insufficient to offset the forces leading to divergence in the 1940s, such as the tremendous industrial growth in high-income São Paulo and Rio, as well as the frontier opportunities in Paraná, adjacent to these prosperous states. Since 1950 migration has seemed to reduce regional per capita income disparities.[14]

The cohort-survival technique does not discriminate among emigrants by state of destination or immigrants by state of origin. Using 1950 census data on place of birth versus place of residence, Sahota constructed matrices of lifetime migration for two age cohorts. For both cohorts the stock of migration between any pair of states increased with their income differences and decreased with the distance between them. Not only did migrants tend to move to higher income states from lower income ones, but the rate of immigration itself had a dampening effect on wages in the recipient state. These findings lend further support to the notion of migration as an equilibrating force in Brazil.[15]

Longitudinal evidence on fiscal transfers in Brazil are inadequate to test precisely Hirschman's hypothesis that net transfers favor the center at the onset of industrialization but swing in favor of the periphery after the process has become well established and regional disparities intolerable. It should be noted that Hirschman's own study of the Northeast shows that the occurrence of a drought increased the fiscal inflows to that region, which suggests that the determinants of fiscal flows are more complicated than simply the level of industrialization.[16]

A study of fiscal transfers would ideally consider the changing patterns of fiscal federalism — the division of powers among federal, state, and municipal governments and the evolution of the tax bases at each level of government — income, wealth, consumption, and user taxes and the degree of interregional tax shifting. In the absence of such a study, only some crude tests of the Hirschman hypothesis are possible.

POLITICAL BACKGROUND.     The Republican Revolution of 1889 overthrew a centralized government and devolved considerable fiscal powers to the states. From 1889 to 1930 Brazil was effectively a federation of states dominated by São Paulo and Minas Gerais. While the federation raised its revenues mostly through foreign import and export taxes, the states had the power to tax the incomes of corporations and individuals within their borders and to charge duties on goods exported to other states and abroad. An important role of the federation was the sustaining of coffee prices, which basically benefited São Paulo and Minas, the great coffee exporting states.

The Depression and the collapse of coffee brought the revolution of 1930, led by men from the periphery, that resulted in a recentralization of power, which presumably weakened the fiscal autonomy of São Paulo. A coup in 1945 weakened the central government and strengthened the states; the revolution of 1964 caused a recentralization of power but a new pattern of administrative decentralization through revenue sharing.

The Hirschman hypothesis focuses on the role of conscious industrialization policy as the cause of fiscal inflows to the center at the onset of development. Until the early 1950s, however,

Brazil really had no conscious policy of economic development and industrialization. Such a policy was first articulated in President Kubitschek's Target Plan, 1956-1961, during which period deliberate development policies to benefit the Northeast were also articulated. In other words, in the traditional drought-administration agencies, Brazil pursued redistributive goals prior to the initiation of its conscious industrialization, a reversal of the hypothesized sequence.[17]

PATTERNS OF INTERSTATE TRANSFERS.    Although data on the sources of federal taxation are abundant, those on regional patterns of federal expenditures are not. In table 10 taxes are allocated by point of collection without regard to patterns of shifting. In the 1930s, when a major source of federal revenues was export taxes on coffee, there was probably little interstate shifting, the tax being absorbed by Paulista planters and foreign consumers. As the country industrialized and value-added taxes became more important, an increasing share of the tax burden on Paulista manufacturing corporations was shifted to out-of-state consumers. It is noteworthy that until the period of the Target Plan the share of federal taxes raised in São Paulo was roughly proportional to the state's share of national income. In the 1956-1965 period and to a lesser extent thereafter the share of federal revenues collected in São Paulo has been considerably greater than the state's income share. This suggests that the onset of conscious industrialization policy was associated with an increase in the tax burden on the center, not on the periphery.

The federal budget reported the allocation of expenditures among states in the 1930s but not thereafter. In the mid-1960s the allocation of federal capital expenditures was reported. It is clear that São Paulo's share of federal revenues has been about one-tenth of its share of tax contributions in the earlier period. In the later period its share of capital expenditures was about one-third its contribution to tax revenues.

The rise of a comprehensive federal revenue-sharing system has reinforced this pattern. The 1946 constitution earmarked 10 percent of all federal income tax receipts to municipalities, to be equally shared, a clause that resulted in the proliferation of these entities. The 1967 constitution created special revenue-sharing funds for states and municipalities that take into account population and relative per capita income, the poorer units being

**Table 10.**  Percentage of federal taxes from and expenditures to São Paulo, 1932–1970.

| Period | Federal taxes | Federal expenditures | São Paulo share of nat'l income |
|--------|--------------|---------------------|--------------------------------|
| 1932 – 35 | 30 | 3 | — |
| 1936 – 40 | 30 | 3 | 31 |
| 1941 – 45 | 30 | — | — |
| 1946 – 50 | 35 | — | 34 |
| 1951 – 55 | 38 | — | 35 |
| 1956 – 60 | 41 | — | 35 |
| 1961 – 65 | 47 | 13 | 35 |
| 1966 – 70 | 38 | 13 | 35 |

Source: *Anuário estatístico do Brasil,* various years; *Conjuntura economica* 24 (June 1970); Ministerio de planejamento, *Balanço orçamentário consolidado do govêrno federal,* 1964 and 1965; and Ministério de planejamento, *Programa de investimento público, distribuição regional,* 1965 and 1966.

favored. Of all federal revenues shared by the states in fiscal year 1968 São Paulo received only 12 percent, considerably less than its contribution to federal revenues. At the same time these funds were responsible for about 40 percent of available state revenues in the Northeast, but only about 5 percent in São Paulo.[18] While these data are admittedly incomplete, they hardly argue that fiscal transfers have contributed to center-periphery divergence.

PATTERNS OF FISCAL FEDERALISM.     Given an essentially exploitative federal government, how was São Paulo able to finance the public investments necessary for its industrialization? In the face of such exploitation a highly decentralized federal system would have been to São Paulo's advantage. Between 1889 and 1930, when states' rights were strongest, the revenues raised by state governments equaled about one-half those raised by the federal government. After the 1930 revolution, which centralized power, the ratio of state to federal revenues increased. After the 1945 coup that decentralized power again, this ratio increased further, only to fall after the 1964 revolution, which recentralized power (table 11). Notwithstanding the changing balance of power in the federal system, states collectively have had considerable fiscal resources.

More interesting is the ratio of São Paulo state to federal revenues. This ratio rose continually since 1922, peaked in the period of the Target Plan, and diminished thereafter. This suggests

**Table 11.** Relative importance of states in Brazilian public sector, 1907 – 1970, proportions.

| Period | All states: federal revenues | São Paulo state: all state revenues | São Paulo state: federal revenues |
|---|---|---|---|
| 1907 – 10 | .46 | — | — |
| 1911 – 15 | .51 | — | — |
| 1916 – 20 | .58 | — | — |
| 1921 – 25 | .56 | .32 | .18 |
| 1926 – 30 | .63 | — | — |
| 1931 – 35 | .69 | .36 | .25 |
| 1936 – 40 | .64 | .37 | .24 |
| 1941 – 45 | .79 | .35 | .28 |
| 1946 – 50 | .74 | .36 | .27 |
| 1951 – 55 | .86 | .39 | .29 |
| 1956 – 60 | .92 | .44 | .40 |
| 1961 – 65 | .93 | .41 | .38 |
| 1966 – 70 | .80 | .46 | .37 |

Source: *Anuário estatístico do Brasil,* various years; Francisco Gusmão, *Annuaire du Bresil,* 1927, for states in years 1922-1926.

the following modification of the Hirschman hypothesis: public expenditures increase in the dynamic center at the onset of modernization and decrease relatively when regional disparities become salient. The sources of funds in the center, however, was not the national government, which continually maintained an exploitative fiscal relationship with the center, but the dynamic center itself.

Fiscal transfers aside, even the uniform application of sectoral policies can have spatially uneven consequences. This is because regions differ in industrial structure. For example, the Northeast has traditionally had a lower share of import-competing and a higher share of export-oriented industries than the Central South. Postwar exchange rate and tariff policies, which encouraged import substitution and discouraged exports, were disparity enhancing. Policy changes of the 1960s (namely, fiscal incentives, tariff reductions, export incentives, and higher labor taxes) were disparity reducing. General equilibrium simulations of the Brazilian economy suggest that the effect of sectoral policies on regional disparities is hardly decisive. For example, policy changes of the 1960s increased northeastern income by about 15 percent and decreased the Central South's income by about 5 percent.[19] In the absence of these policies, per capita income in the Northeast would have been 27 percent of that in the Southeast instead of the actual 32 percent.

Interregional capital flows, trade, and fiscal transfers are related by a set of simple accounting identities. By definition a region suffers a net capital outflow when its exports ($X$) exceed its imports ($M$) (that is, its sales exceed receipts and thus it assumes a creditor relationship to its customers). Again by definition, this occurs when its savings ($S$) exceed its investment ($I$), taxes ($T$) exceed government spending ($G$), or both. Quantitatively, the net capital outflow equals

$$X - M = S + T - (I + G).[20]$$

Unfortunately, there are no readily available data on the elements on the righthand side of this identity for the various states. As suggested above, the northeastern periphery has enjoyed net fiscal inflows while São Paulo has suffered net outflows, at least since the 1930s. Not all of these fiscal transfers can be viewed as capital inflows contributing to the productive capacity of the Northeast since much took the form of disaster relief payments. If the Northeast has also had an export deficit and São Paulo an export surplus, then one could unequivocally determine that the latter has been a net investor in the former. If the opposite were the case, then the direction of private capital flows is indeterminate without more precise information on fiscal flows.

Information on interregional trade is fragmentary. Fairly complete information on overland, coastal, and international trade for all states is available for the early 1940s and for some years in the 1960s. No data are available on invisible trade in the services, such as finance, insurance, transportation, or tourism. According to the polarization paradigm, these invisibles are a significant channel by which the center sucks surplus value from the periphery, since the center is assumed to monopolize the marketing and financing system.

A fairly complete series on the commodity trade balance of the Northeast can be constructed from the 1940s, but that for São Paulo is available for only a few years. In 1943, the first year for which complete interstate and international trade data are both available, the Northeast experienced an export deficit. São Paulo experienced a surplus of much greater magnitude. From 1948 to 1953, before any conscious import-substitution industrialization policy was adopted, the Northeast experienced years of both deficit and surplus; but for the six-year period in the aggregate trade was in balance. Between 1954 and 1961, which include the years of most vigorous industrial growth, the Northeast experienced trade surpluses and was thus a net capital exporter. With the inauguration of the fiscal incentives system in the 1960s the Northeast became a net importer (table 12).

Comparable data for São Paulo are not available. The absolute magnitude of Sao Paulo's trade surplus and deficit for the four years for which data are available are substantially greater than those for the Northeast. This suggests that the periphery was

**Table 12.** Net exports to rest of Brazil and abroad, millions of cruzeiros (1960 prices), Northeast and São Paulo, 1943-1968.

| Year | Northeast | | São Paulo | |
|---|---|---|---|---|
| | Absolute | % income | Absolute | % income |
| 1943 | − 5.8 | − | 56. | − |
| 1948 | 2.5 | 3.6 | 4.8 | 1.1 |
| 1949 | − 4.4[a] | − 0.2 | − | − |
| 1950 | − .3[a] | − 0.0 | − | − |
| 1951 | − 6.2[a] | − 4.5 | − | − |
| 1952 | 13.1 | 8.7 | − | − |
| 1953 | − 3.9[a] | − 2.7 | − | − |
| 1954 | 5.4[a] | 3.7 | − | − |
| 1955 | 9.0[a] | 5.7 | − | − |
| 1956 | 5.8[a] | 3.2 | − | − |
| 1957 | 2.6[a] | 1.3 | − | − |
| 1958 | 4.9[a] | 2.6 | − | − |
| 1959 | 9.8 | − 1.7 | − 137. | 18.3 |
| 1960 | 2.5 | .6 | − | − |
| 1961 | 10.3 | .3 | − | − |
| 1962 | − 20.4 | − 3.7 | − | − |
| 1963 | 18.2 | 5.4 | − | − |
| 1964 | − 5.9 | − 1.6 | − | − |
| 1965 | − 0.9 | − .9 | − | − |
| 1966 | − 17.2 | − 4.1 | − | − |
| 1967 | − 46.1 | − 9.6 | − | − |
| 1968 | − 96.3 | − 19.4 | 231.[b] | 20.2[b] |

Source: *Anuário estatístico do Brasil* for years 1943-1971; David E. Goodman and Roberto Cavalcanti de Albuquerque, *A industrialização do Nordeste* (*Rio: IPEA, 1971*), Relatório de pesquisa, no. 6.

a. Excluding overland trade.
b. Excluding trade with Minas Gerais.

not a substantial factor in the capital flows into and out of the center but rather that these flows were international in nature.

More direct evidence on gross interregional capital flows is suggested by deposits in the system of regional fiscal incentives. As the system has ultimately evolved, corporations and individuals can deposit up to 50 percent of their federal income tax liabilities in regional and sectoral funds, such as those under the control of SUDAM and SUDENE. While not all of these deposits were made by the taxpayers from the center, it is clear that they represent both a substantial share of regional income in the periphery and of national savings (table 13).

The import substitution policies that Brazil pursued in the 1950s and 1960s raised the cost of foreign goods relative to domestic and consequently reduced the share of national income traded internationally. One would expect interregional trade to increase as foreign competitors were eliminated. In the 1940s the share of national income exported abroad was almost as great as that of interstate trade. By the 1960s about four times as much of national income was traded across state lines as was exported abroad, a ratio that has held steadily since then. The shifting trade patterns between 1940 and 1960 did not result from a rising importance of interstate trade but from a decline in international trade. The share of national income traded across state lines has remained fairly stable at 25 percent since 1940.[21]

When Brazilian states are aggregated into macroregions, the

**Table 13.** Allocation of fiscal incentive deposits to the Northeast (SUDENE) and Amazonia (SUDAM), 1963-1969.

| Year | NCr$ thousand, current | | % regional income | | % national net private savings | |
|---|---|---|---|---|---|---|
| | SUDENE | SUDAM | SUDENE | SUDAM | SUDENE | SUDAM |
| 1963 | 19 | 1 | 1.8 | .5 | 0.1 | .0 |
| 1964 | 33 | 3 | 1.5 | .8 | 1.0 | .1 |
| 1965 | 172 | 13 | 5.2 | 2.0 | 3.3 | .3 |
| 1966 | 228 | 47 | 5.4 | 5.3 | 5.9 | 1.2 |
| 1967 | 352 | 99 | 4.0 | 8.7 | 5.7 | 1.6 |
| 1968 | 466 | 182 | 4.1 | 11.2 | 6.2 | 2.4 |
| 1969 | 627 | 230 | − | − | 4.8 | 1.4 |

Source: "Os agentes do desenvolvimento," *Perfil, supplemento do visão* 39 (Dec. 1971); *Conjuntura econômica* 24 (June 1970): 89-104.

relative importance of the foreign market looms larger. For example, foreign exports of Amazonia were 120 percent of interregional exports; of the Northeast, 180 percent; and of the Central South, 200 percent. Despite the increasing integration of the Brazilian economy, the three macroregions are still more tightly bound to the international economy than to each other, as the archipelago image suggests.

A particularly revealing indicator of integration is the degree to which interstate trade is attenuated by distance. This can be measured by means of a gravity model:

$$T_{ij} = C \frac{Y_i \, Y_j}{D_{\gamma ij}}$$

where $T_{ij}$ is the flow of goods from state $i$ to state $j$; $Y_i$ and $Y_j$ are the incomes of the exporting and importing states, respectively; and $D_{ij}$ is a measure of the distance between the two states. The parameter $\gamma$ can be interpreted as the friction of distance, which presumably falls as the road network or interstate payments system improves.

Data on value and tonnage are available to measure flows between states for 1942 and 1962 and for several commodity classes in the latter year. A log-linear regression shows that the friction of distance fell from $-2.4$ to $-1.4$ for value of trade in the intervening period. As expected, weight is more sensitive to distance than value falling from $-2.9$ to $-1.8$ in the same period; therefore the greater the distance between states, the more valuable the cargo per ton. The results for 1962 are similar for all commodity classes (live animals, food, raw materials, and manufactures).

Because the trade flow matrices cannot be duplicated for years after 1962, the friction of distance can be related to economic development in another way. To normalize for the size of each exporting state, the percentage distribution of each state's exports by destination are computed. For each importing state $j$, the log share of exports taken from each state $i$ is regressed against the log distance between the two, $D_{ij}$. This analysis is performed for all commodity classes as well as total trade.

For total trade, manufactures, and foodstuffs the magnitude of the friction of distance is inversely related to state per capita income, a proxy for level of economic development (table 14). In other words, the more developed states like São Paulo, Rio de

**Table 14.** Distance coefficients, interstate trade regressions, 1962.

| Importing state | Total trade | | Foodstuffs | | Manufactures | |
|---|---|---|---|---|---|---|
| | Value | Weight | Value | Weight | Value | Weight |
| Amazonas[a] | 1.02 | −3.97 | −3.93 | −7.56 | 2.72 | −1.48 |
| Pará[b] | .27 | .36 | .13 | 1.20 | .13 | 1.34 |
| Maranhão | −2.56[c] | −2.15[c] | −1.82[c] | −2.18[c] | −2.81[c] | −2.94[c] |
| Piauí | −2.20[c] | −2.60[c] | −2.47[c] | −2.29[c] | − .90 | −2.32[c] |
| Ceará | −1.86[c] | −2.33[c] | −1.67[c] | −2.71[c] | −1.27[c] | −1.55[c] |
| Rio Grande do Norte | −1.40[c] | −1.30[c] | −1.50[c] | − .85[c] | −1.29[c] | −1.40[c] |
| Paraíba | −1.35[c] | −1.26[c] | −1.37[c] | −1.26[c] | −1.12[c] | −1.10[c] |
| Pernambuco | −1.04[c] | −1.53[c] | −1.10[c] | −1.40[c] | − .91[c] | −1.33[c] |
| Alagoas | −1.46[c] | −1.30[c] | −1.35[c] | −1.32[c] | −1.48[c] | − .85 |
| Sergipe | −1.39[c] | −1.59[c] | − .86 | −1.08[c] | −1.40[c] | −1.55[c] |
| Bahia | −1.59[c] | −1.54[c] | −1.35[c] | −1.78[c] | −1.12[c] | − .92 |
| Minas Gerais | − .85[c] | − .99[c] | −1.19[c] | −1.29[c] | −1.24[c] | −1.36[c] |
| Espírito Santo | −1.67[c] | −1.76[c] | − .91 | −1.61[c] | −1.32[c] | −1.70[c] |
| Rio de Janeiro | − .52[c] | − .66[c] | − .98[c] | −1.08[c] | − .45 | − .66[c] |
| Guanabara | − .24 | − .38[c] | − .55[c] | − .65[c] | − .27 | − .39 |
| São Paulo | − .60[c] | − .59 | − .43 | − .83 | − .75[c] | − .60 |
| Paraná | −1.39[c] | −1.31[c] | −1.69[c] | −1.74[c] | −1.21[c] | −1.03[c] |
| Santa Catarina | −1.45[c] | −1.01 | −1.29 | −1.11 | −1.54[c] | −1.06 |
| Rio Grande do Sul | −1.33[c] | −1.43[c] | −1.48[c] | −1.88[c] | −1.29[c] | −1.42[c] |
| Mato Grosso | − .50 | − .41 | − .49 | − .21 | −2.17 | − .98 |
| Goiás | .64 | 1.19 | − .09 | 1.38 | .10 | 1.76 |
| Distrito Federal | − .28 | − .41 | −1.76 | − .79 | − .07 | .32 |
| r[d] | − .64[c] | − .48[c] | − .54[c] | − .27[c] | − .10 | − .45[c] |

Source: Raw trade data are from Brasil, *Comércio por vias internas, 1962,* various state volumes.
   a. Includes Acre, Rôndonia, and Roraima.
   b. Includes Amapá.
   c. Significance .05 (one-tail).
   d. r = Correlation between state per capita income and distance coefficient.

Janeiro, and Minas Gerais draw their imports from farther afield than do the less developed states. This is not surprising since the developed states have nodal positions on the transportation networks. As the transportation system becomes more interconnected, one would expect that the less developed states would enter into broader trading relations.

Does the export of manufactures from the center to the periphery hamper the industrialization of the latter? Those peripheral zones more open to manufactured imports presumably enjoy lower industrial growth than less accessible peripheral zones. This hypothesis is tested by two indicators of openness for each state: the friction of distance for imports of manufactures from all sources and the ratio of manufactured imports from São Paulo to state industrial production. The former indicates whether a state is well protected from manufactured imports by transportation cost barriers. Available for 1968 only, the latter indicates the relative weight of the center in supplying manufactures.

Rank-order correlations of both these indicators with state industrial growth during the 1960-1968 period are insignificantly different from 0 ($r = .15$ and $.17$, respectively).[22] In other words, states less open to industrial imports from São Paulo are not more likely to industrialize, at least for a period during which industrial growth was not disproportionately rapid in São Paulo. This is explicable by the large share of São Paulo's industrial exports during this period comprised of capital goods. These increase the productive capacity of the importing state. Whether such a finding held for an earlier period, when industry tended to concentrate more rapidly in São Paulo, cannot be tested with the available data.

The equilibrium paradigm has little to say about the political economy of the periphery, but the polarization paradigm suggests that the peripheral elites have a stake in underdevelopment (the maintenance of an economic structure based upon primary exports and manufactured imports). Evidence apropos this hypothesis is fragmentary. Leff's analysis of the attitudes of the elite focuses upon those in São Paulo and Rio, the dynamic center, rather than upon those in the periphery. Dean's study of the industrialization of São Paulo suggests that the rising industrial-urban bourgeoisie and the traditional agricultural-rural elites became ideologically amalgamated through cultural assimilation on the part of the former as well as by the diversification of investments by both groups.[23]

The tenacity of the northeastern sugar planters, who maintain their position to a great extent by the quotas administered by the Institute of Sugar and Alcohol, would be an example of an elite committed to underdevelopment from the point of view of the polarization paradigm. Their position vis-à-vis the center is competitive rather than symbiotic (if the littoral developed in the sense of producing food instead of sugar, cultivation of that crop in São Paulo would increase and a resulting broader base of demand for industrial goods would be welcomed by manufacturers in the center).

The rise of state development planning and development banking in the 1960s suggests that peripheral elites are ideologically committed to the same conception of development as their counterparts in the center. Following the lead of the national government, states are becoming engaged in comprehensive planning, whose focus is economic development. While the more backward states have created development plans to eliminate bottlenecks in energy and transportation, the more advanced states have focused on diversifying their industrial bases. The successful diffusion by the military of the ideology equating national security (from internal subversion) with development has resulted in the elimination of any significant elite opposition to industrialization.[24]

Brazilian economic development in the past several decades has been associated with the continual integration of the nation's far-flung regions, mainly as a result of the creation of an interconnected highway system. At least since 1940 the regions of Brazil have become more specialized and an increasing share of population and economic output has become concentrated in the Central South, particularly in São Paulo and the three adjacent frontier states.

States diverged markedly in per capita income in the 1940s. Interstate migration seems to have had little influence on accelerating or diminishing this pattern of income divergence. Possibly because of net fiscal inflows from the federal government, the Northeast seems to have enjoyed a net inflow of capital in the early 1940s that gave way to balanced flows around the end of the decade.

In the 1950s states converged in per capita income, nearly returning to the 1939 levels of inequality. During this decade migration accelerated and seems to have exerted a significant disparity-reducing effect, notwithstanding its selectivity in favor of the receiving areas of the Central South. It is noteworthy that such convergence occurred despite import substitution policies that favored the Central South at the expense of the Northeast and despite capital outflows from the latter region to the former in the second half of the decade.

There was no change in per capita income inequality among Brazilian regions or states in the 1960s despite massive programs aimed at developing the Northeast and Amazonia and despite sectoral policies harming the Central South. Although substantial volumes of capital flowed into the Northeast, mostly through the fiscal incentives program, income and population continued to concentrate in the Central South. While the migration rate fell somewhat to include about 4 percent of the population, migration continued to exert a converging effect on interstate per capita income differences.

It appears that migration and capital are flowing in an equilibrating direction, yet economic activity continues to concentrate in the high-income areas of the Central South. Although the interactions between the center and periphery may weigh more heavily on the latter than on the former, the growth of the center can hardly be explained by the exploitation of the periphery. Only a small proportion of the skilled labor, capital, and markets in the center originated in the Northeast. Rather the explanation for the differential growth of the regions must lie in endogenous factors, such as technology; the supply of skilled labor, savings, or fertile land; and the demand provided by internal and foreign, rather than interregional, markets.

# 7

# The Developing Center:
# Industrial Agglomeration
# in São Paulo

At the time of the first industrial census in 1907 the city of Rio de Janeiro produced 33 percent of national output; the entire state of São Paulo produced only 17 percent. During the First World War São Paulo state overtook Rio, steadily increasing its share to 56 percent by the 1960s while that of the combined city-state of Guanabara-Rio fell to 17 percent. This concentration of output is paralleled by that of industrial employment (table 15). With about 19 percent of Brazil's population and 3 percent of its land area, São Paulo state produces about as large a share of national industrial output as the entire American industrial belt from Boston to St. Louis, which comprises 43 and 8 percent of the American population and land area, respectively.[1]

The industrial growth of São Paulo was taken for granted in previous chapters since the prime concern was its impact on rural development, particularly on frontier settlement and agricultural modernization. The industrialization of Brazil is taken for granted in this chapter because the focus of attention is the concentration of industry in São Paulo, particularly in the metropolis and its satellites.

Spatial concentration of manufacturing at the onset of economic development has often been explained by agglomeration economies. This concept reduces to tautology unless these economies can be measured independently of the agglomeration itself. The two major paradigms that attempt to explain the spatial concentration of industry focus mainly on agglomeration economies external to the firm. These paradigms, the American and the French, not only differ in their explanation of the rise of primate industrial cities but generate different predictions as to the sectoral and firm size compositions of these cities and clash as to their policy prescriptions. Both of these models have been elaborated in the context of advanced capitalist economies, which vary

**Table 15.** Percentage of industrial output and employment generated by largest states, 1907-1970.

|  | 1907 | 1920 | 1939-40 | 1949-51 | 1959-61 | 1968-70 |
|---|---|---|---|---|---|---|
| A. Output |  |  |  |  |  |  |
| São Paulo | 17 | 32 | 36 | 47 | 54 | 56 |
| Guanabara[a] | 33 | 22 | 22 | 15 | 10 | 10 |
| Rio de Janeiro[b] | 7 | 6 | 5 | 6 | 7 | 7 |
| Minas Gerais | 5 | 6 | 8 | 7 | 6 | 8 |
| Rio Grande do Sul | 15 | 12 | 9 | 8 | 7 | 6 |
| Rest of Brazil | 23 | 22 | 20 | 17 | 16 | 13 |
| B. Employment |  |  |  |  |  |  |
| São Paulo | 16 | 30 | 37 | 39 | 46 | 48 |
| Guanabara | 26 | 20 | 16 | 12 | 10 | 8 |
| Rio de Janeiro | 9 | 6 | 6 | 6 | 6 | 5 |
| Minas Gerais | 7 | 7 | 9 | 8 | 7 | 8 |
| Rio Grande do Sul | 11 | 9 | 9 | 8 | 8 | 8 |
| Rest of Brazil | 31 | 28 | 23 | 27 | 23 | 23 |

Source: Brasil, *Censo industrial,* 1920, 1940, 1950, 1960, and 1970; "As contas nacionais," *Conjuntura econômica* 24 (June 1970): 89-106.

a. Containing only the city of Rio de Janeiro and formerly the Federal District, Guanabara was a state until 1974 when it merged with the surrounding state of Rio de Janeiro.

b. A state containing industrial suburbs of the city of Rio.

in certain crucial respects from Brazil at the onset of its industrialization. In particular, Brazil has a more entrepreneurial public sector, imports the bulk of its modern technology from abroad, and has a more disjointed capital market.

Implicit in both the American and French explanations of industrial agglomeration are the concepts of initial advantage and circular and cumulative causation. Specifically, if growth begins at a particular site because of some random shock, a self-perpetuating chain of investments and innovations follows. Growth induces further growth because economic processes are subject to internal and external economies of scale and because the resulting division of labor facilitates invention and innovation.[2]

There are some difficulties with models of circular and cumulative causation. First, they generally lack restraints on the concentration of all the activity in a region, a country, or even the world in a single growth pole. The deus ex machina is usually agglomeration diseconomies: rising rents and living costs, greater distance from sources of raw materials, and exhaustion of agglomeration economies. This latter is not necessarily a brake on further concentration since it merely means that at the margin costs do not decline with expanded urban output because minimum costs have been reached already.

Second, models of circular and cumulative causation are so persuasive that they have great difficulty in accounting for the rise of less developed regions, which may overtake the initial leaders. The displacement of a primate city by a parvenu is a rare event by international standards. One of the most striking facts of Brazilian urban evolution, however, has been the overtaking and surpassing of Rio de Janeiro by São Paulo as the most industrialized metropolis in the second quarter of this century. In 1890, when São Paulo was the capital of a booming coffee province, it ranked fourth in population, which was roughly one-eighth that of Rio. São Paulo surpassed Rio's population in the mid-1950s and was nearly 40 percent larger in 1970 (table 16).[3]

Rio was clearly in a position to reap the benefits of initial advantage at the onset of the industrial era. It was the largest port, the largest manufacturing center, and the hub of the rudimentary national railroad network. São Paulo was merely a provincial capital. Rio's role as a political and financial capital would seem doubly important in an economy in which industrialists as individuals and as a class have relied heavily on government patronage and regulation of the market. The rivalry between the two cities elucidates some of the mechanisms of overtaking and surpassing in urban systems.

**Table 16.** County populations (in thousands) of Rio de Janeiro and São Paulo, 1872-1970.

| Year | Rio de Janeiro | São Paulo | Ratio of SP/RJ |
|------|----------------|-----------|----------------|
| 1872 | 275  | 31   | .11  |
| 1890 | 523  | 65   | .12  |
| 1900 | 811  | 240  | .30  |
| 1920 | 1157 | 579  | .50  |
| 1940 | 1764 | 1326 | .75  |
| 1950 | 2377 | 2198 | .92  |
| 1960 | 3307 | 3825 | 1.16 |
| 1970 | 4297 | 5902 | 1.37 |

Source: Brasil, *Censo demográfico, 1970.*

According to the French school, whose spiritual founder is François Perroux, a center of rapid and self-sustaining growth tends to be a locus of a propulsive industry, which has the following essential characteristics: rapid growth in total output due to either final or intermediate demand; substantial interindustry linkages, especially backward linkages; relatively high capital intensiveness, which is associated with modernity and technological progressiveness; a large sectoral share of total industrial output; and a complex division of labor within the firm. Around the propulsive industry agglomerates those industries to which it is highly linked, which form an industrial complex. Such a complex serves as the economic base of a growth pole that foments development in its hinterland.[4]

A regional development policy based upon this paradigm has been most carefully spelled out by Albert Hirschman.[5] It includes the implantation of large, capital-intensive (conserving scarce managerial ability), technologically modern (in both product and process) firms that produce commodities weighing heavily in consumer budgets and for which there is a relatively high income-elasticity of demand. The growth of the propulsive sector will increase the demand for backward-linked industries and also for public infrastructure, which will expand in the growth pole. Such regional complexes might be steel-foundries-machine shops, petrochemicals-textiles, or automobiles.

Considerable doubt has been cast on the French paradigm as a description of the industrialization-urbanization process in advanced countries. In the contemporary United States, France, and Germany there is little relationship between the magnitude of interindustry linkages and spatial agglomeration. Most highly linked industries are not geographically associated, and most associated industries are not highly linked. A region whose industrial mix is heavily weighted toward fast-growing industries does not necessarily grow fast, for it more often than not loses its share of slower growing industries to other regions. Capital intensive and large scale are not synonymous with technologically progressive. High technology industries are often skilled-labor intensive and small in scale relative to other industries, such as the Brazilian capital goods industry.[6]

Since most of the negative evidence on the French paradigm has come from advanced countries, such does not refute the applicability of the model to developing countries. Indeed this paradigm has had considerable impact on industrialization policy for the Northeast.

In Brazil, nevertheless, the relation between São Paulo and its hinterland has historically been more complex than assumed by the French model. This hinterland can hardly be considered a stagnant backwater, for the metropolis arose as a marketing and service center for the state coffee economy. The capital to finance industry as well as the transportation and commercial infrastructure so useful in distributing manufactures all emerged from the hinterland. Finally, while the French growth pole is a source of industrial diffusion, São Paulo must be considered an important source of diffusion of agricultural modernization.

To what extent can the concentration of industry in São Paulo be explained by its ability to attract fast-growing industries? In 1920 the industrial census reported a pattern of output and employment typical of low-income countries, which was heavily weighted toward food processing, textiles, and related industries. The patterns for São Paulo state were not much different from the national ones; moreover, both the national and state industrial mixes remained relatively fixed in this traditional pattern for nearly thirty more years.

The importance of industry mix can be demonstrated quantitatively by shift-share analysis. This technique projects state employment changes on the basis of two alternative assumptions: that total state employment grows at the same rate as total national employment or that each sector in the state grows at its own national rate. Since each sector has a different growth rate nationally and since each state has a unique sectoral composition, the industry mix (or share) effect equals the difference between these two projections. The regional shift effect is the difference between actual employment change and that projected on the basis of the second assumption (that each of the state's sectors grows at its own national rate).

From 1920 to 1940 São Paulo's industrial mix was somewhat more heavily weighted toward the traditional sectors than the nation as a whole, and thus the slightly negative industry mix effect. Nevertheless, the state increased its share of these and other industries, and nearly 30 percent of its employment growth was due to this competitive regional shift (table 17).

**Table 17.** Manufacturing employment change in São Paulo state: national growth, industry mix, and regional shift effects, 1920-1970.

| Period | Employment change (thousand) | Percentage of change attributed to | | |
|---|---|---|---|---|
| | | National growth | Industry mix | Regional shift |
| 1920 – 40 | 208 | 73.3 | – 3.0 | 29.7 |
| 1940 – 50 | 218 | 82.9 | 15.4 | 1.7 |
| 1950 – 60 | 300 | 59.6 | 12.8 | 22.7 |
| 1960 – 70 | 461 | 90.4 | 8.3 | 1.3 |

Source: Brasil, *Censo industrial* for included years.

In the 1940-1950 period about 83 percent of the employment gains in São Paulo state can be attributed to the national growth effect (proportional growth of the total industrial sector). While only about 2 percent of the increase was due to a regional shift, about 15 percent can be attributed to its having a fast-growing industry mix.

From 1950 to 1960 São Paulo's employment gains were considerably greater than those projected on the basis of national growth and its own industry mix. Fully 23 percent of the employment gain represents a positive regional shift (regional growth rates in a given industry exceeding the national average for that industry). Again, the industry mix was fast, accounting for about 13 percent of the employment gain. In other words, not only did São Paulo enjoy a fast mix of industry during this period, it was also able to capture a larger share of national employment in almost all industries.

In the 1960-1970 period 90 percent of São Paulo's employment gains reflected proportional national growth and only 8 percent its fast industry mix. The regional shift effect was minimal.

In summary, the shift-share analysis indicates that the substantial increase in São Paulo's share of industrial employment (from 30 to 37 percent) in the 1920s and 1930s was due to the state's competitive advantages and hardly to its having a fast industry mix. In the 1950s, when the state's share of industrial employment again increased substantially (from 39 to 46 percent), there was also a major regional shift effect. In the 1940s and 1960s, when São Paulo's share of industrial employment increased only slightly, there were no such marked regional shift effects, although the industry mixes were fast.

To what extent have interindustry linkages encouraged the geographical association of various industrial sectors in Brazil? Examination of the 1959 thirty-sector input-output matrix for Brazil reveals several identifiable complexes, with high internal and low external linkages: metallurgy-machinery-electrical and transport equipment, chemicals-pharmaceuticals-cosmetics-plastics, agriculture-foodstuffs-textiles-clothing, and wood-furniture. In this highly decomposable matrix, no manufacturing sector has extraordinary backward linkages. Ironically, the sectors with the greatest backward linkages are paper and food products, generally thought of as traditional industries with little developmental impact. Those sectors with the highest forward linkages are metallurgical, chemical, paper, and textile sectors. If sheer size indicates the propulsive industry, then textiles and foodstuffs, the two traditional industries, would seem to qualify in terms of forward and backward linkages; but they are not fast growing, high technology, or capital intensive. If rate of growth identifies the propulsive industry, only the metallurgical and chemical seem to have important forward linkages.

One can compare the magnitude of interindustry linkages between pairs of sectors and their spatial proximity. Using indices of geographical association for thirteen sectors in 1940, 1950, and 1960, there is little relationship between the magnitude of interindustry linkages among sectors and their tendency to distribute themselves similarly across states (table 18). The state of Minas Gerais, for example, which is heavily concentrated in metallurgy and chemicals, sectors with high forward linkages, remains specialized in these activities and unable to attract final goods producing sectors.

In the view of the American school the spatial concentration of industry is largely due to agglomeration economies that are alleged to be immobile and external to the firm (a trained labor force, specialized goods and services, low-cost face-to-face communications). Few analysts have carefully specified the degree to which these factors are truly immobile and external or have

**Table 18.** Interindustry linkages and geographical associations of industrial sectors, 1940-1960.

| Degree of linkage[a] | Degree of geographical association[b] | | | | | | Total |
|---|---|---|---|---|---|---|---|
| | 1940 | | 1950 | | 1960 | | |
| | High | Low | High | Low | High | Low | |
| High | 3 | 7 | 4 | 6 | 3 | 7 | 10 |
| Low | 20 | 48 | 27 | 41 | 24 | 44 | 68 |
| Total | 23 | 55 | 31 | 47 | 27 | 51 | 78[c] |

a. After Willy van Rijckeghem, "An Intersectoral Consistency Model for Economic Planning in Brazil," in Howard S. Ellis, ed., *The Economy of Brazil* (Berkeley: University of California Press, 1969); Paulo R. Haddad, *Interdependência estructural e desenvolvimento regional* (Belo Horizonte: CEDEPLAR, 1969), monografia no. 1; an industry flow $a_{ij}$ was considered high if

$$\frac{a_{ij}}{\sum\limits_{i=1}^{13} a_{ij}} \quad \text{or} \quad \frac{a_{ij}}{\sum\limits_{j=1}^{13} a_{ij}} > 1/30 = .03$$

b. An index of dissimilarity measuring geographic association across states was considered high if it was less than .25, which is about the average index between sectors and total manufacturing. Calculated from Celsius A. Lodder, "Crescimento da ocupação regional e seus componentes," in Paulo R. Haddad, ed., *Planejamento regional* (Rio: IPEA, 1972), monografia no. 8.

c. Number of paired combinations of thirteen sectors.

quantified how important any particular externality was to particular industries. The most detailed analysis of externalities focused on New York's high fashion district, the demand for whose product varied unpredictably and whose producers required instant face-to-face communication with suppliers and comparative shoppers. Such a nonrepresentative sector can hardly illustrate the importance of externalities in the American industrial-urban system, much less in Brazil, where food and textiles remain the largest sectors.[7]

The notion of trained labor as an external economy has had long currency in the literature on development. The standard argument is that trained workers are more productive than untrained workers, an employer training workers at his own expense risks their jumping to another firm and thus losing his investment, and the risk of losing a worker is greater the more general and less specific the training, therefore firms will underinvest in training from a social point of view and will be attracted to locations where the labor force is already trained. This argument assumes that workers cannot accept a lower wage for a job offering training vis-à-vis a job that does not. While such self-financing of training is a characteristic of many European apprenticeship systems, it is essentially impossible in Brazil because of minimum wage legislation.[8]

Brazil's National Service of Industrial Apprenticeship (SENAI) subsidizes the training of workers in their employer's plants. This program reduces employers' reluctance to train workers and increases the ubiquity of skilled labor. If skilled or easily trained labor is fairly ubiquitous or mobile, there is no necessity for agglomeration. Indeed, there is a good reason for an employer of skilled labor to deglomerate. Since workers with higher levels of education are generally more mobile and sensitive to interfirm and interindustry wage differentials, a firm located far from competitors can enjoy a captive labor supply. Any pressures for agglomeration would come from the labor supply side, with workers migrating to the larger urban areas where the labor market was more competitive, more diversified, and more promising of upward mobility.

If a skilled labor force were an important agglomeration economy, one should observe skill-intensive industries locating in large metropolitan areas as opposed to small towns or rural areas and greater utilization of skilled labor in each sector within large metropolitan areas as opposed to the periphery. These hypotheses can be tested for the state of São Paulo in 1958 and 1962 for the eight most important industrial sectors by the percentage of operatives classified as skilled. From 1958 to 1962 the skill levels of industry as a whole declined; but with the striking exception of the textile sectors, the skill ranking of these sectors remained fairly stable (table 19). In both years the skill intensiveness of the various industrial sectors is not significantly related to the percentage of sectoral employment located in the capital as opposed to the rest of the state. When skill levels in the capital are compared to those in the interior (small towns and rural periphery), there are minor differences both in the aggregate and by sector. Therefore the abundance of trained labor within São Paulo state

Table 19. Percentage of skilled workers by sector and location, São Paulo state, 1958 and 1962.

| Sector | 1958 | | | 1962 | | | % workers employed in capital | |
|---|---|---|---|---|---|---|---|---|
| | Total state | Capital | Interior | Total state | Capital | Interior | 1958 | 1962 |
| Clothing | 56 | 57 | 54 | 36 | 32 | 43 | 44 | 53 |
| Textiles | 39 | 37 | 41 | 7 | 7 | 7 | 68 | 64 |
| Machinery | 29 | 35 | 22 | 28 | 26 | 31 | 54 | 57 |
| Construction | 29 | 37 | 22 | 29 | 34 | 24 | 42 | 50 |
| Paper | 26 | 26 | 30 | 24 | 25 | 22 | 63 | 64 |
| Food | 12 | 10 | 13 | 13 | 12 | 15 | 21 | 30 |
| Transportation equipment | 11 | 10 | 12 | 11 | 13 | 9 | 27 | 28 |
| Chemicals | 8 | 7 | 9 | 7 | 10 | 5 | 58 | 56 |
| Total industry | 29 | 30 | 28 | 20 | 20 | 20 | 44 | 51 |

Source: Walter Paul Krause, *O problema industrial paulista* (São Paulo: Comissão interestadual da Bacia Paraná-Uruguai, 1964).

does not appear to be an urban phenomenon and hence not a cause of urbanization.

On a national scale the situation is quite different. Skilled workers earn a substantial premium over the unskilled, a differential that has been increasing over time. As expected, a state with an abundance of skilled labor like São Paulo tends to specialize in skill-intensive industries while northeastern states, with poorly educated labor forces, tended to specialize in unskilled labor-intensive industries.[9]

Economies of scale in many industrial and service processes create potential gains to specialization.[10] While specialization permits firms to enjoy lower per unit costs of production, it increases transportation and communications costs with suppliers and customers. These transaction costs are especially high in the incipient stages of development because of the inadequacy of the transport, telephone, and postal systems. Pressures for geographic agglomeration presumably are greatest for those processes that have the highest transaction cost per unit distance (for example, service activities) and for enterprises too small to internalize all functions subject to significant economies of scale. Larger firms, which can bear the overhead of many specialized functions—such as manufacturing its own capital goods, shipping, marketing, financing, and maintenance—face much less pressure to agglomerate.

There is some evidence that small firms in Brazil do indeed benefit from external agglomeration economies. In a cross-sectional analysis of twenty-one Brazilian manufacturing sectors, Rocca related the average output of firms, stratified by number of employees, to labor and capital inputs and to statewide output. In both 1950 and 1960 statewide output had a positive impact on the output of small firms in most sectors but little impact on large firms.[11]

Following from these propositions is the hypothesis that a large industrial city is characterized by small enterprises; the French view is that the growth pole is dominated by large enterprises. If agglomeration economies were especially important for small enterprises, then rural firms should be larger than urban firms. In fact, the average urban firm has twice as many employees as the average rural firm in Brazil as a whole. When disaggregated by state, a crude method of controlling for industrial structure, the hypothesis that rural firms are larger can be rejected.

A more precise test is suggested by comparing the average size of firms in the capital with those of the interior of São Paulo state. In both 1958 and 1962 the average size of firms was larger in the capital. When controlling for sector, the same result holds except for textiles, where the interior firms are much larger.

The best Brazilian evidence calculates the average number of employees per industrial firm by city size. Consistent with the American view, the largest mean size firms were located in the smallest urban size class, twenty to fifty thousand population. The mean size of firm reaches a minimum at city size class five hundred thousand to one million and rises thereafter. Contrary to the American view, then, the largest metropolis does not seem to have the smallest firms.[12]

Averages hide the dualistic aspect of the industrial structure. The interior of São Paulo has a higher share of its labor force in both the very smallest and the very largest firms. In 1958, 15.1 percent of the interior labor force was employed in firms with fewer than ten workers and 34.8 percent was employed in firms with over five hundred workers. The corresponding figures in the capital were 10.2 and 30.1 percent. In 1962 the interior compared to the capital had 1.2 percent more of its labor force in smallest firms and 12.1 percent more of its labor force in the largest firms.[13]

During the preindustrial coffee era (1870 to 1930) the market and raw materials supply areas of metropolitan São Paulo were roughly coextensive with its agricultural hinterland, largely defined by the railroad system branching out from the city. This hinterland included São Paulo state, parts of Minas Gerais (Triangle and Zona Sul) and tangentially northern Paraná, and southern Goiás and Mato Grosso. The hinterland of Rio included the states of Rio, Espírito Santo, and part of Minas Gerais (Zona da Mata). A crude measure of the purchasing power in these market areas is suggested by their production of coffee, the major cash crop:[14]

| Millions of sacks | 1870 | 1880 | 1890 | 1900 − 10 | 1910 − 30 |
|---|---|---|---|---|---|
| RJ, MG, ES | 2.3 | 3.3 | 2.6 | 3. − 4. | 4. − 5. |
| São Paulo | .4 | 1.2 | 2.5 | 7.0 | 10.0 |

Coffee production during this period grew faster in São Paulo and resulted in a corresponding redistribution of population and income. This implies that the purchasing power in São Paulo's immediate hinterland gradually surpassed Rio's by the turn of the century. These figures, moreover, understate São Paulo's relative advantage, which lay in a better railway network and a more compact rural population.

As transportation costs fall and internal economies become realizable, national market accessibility becomes more relevant. Although the density of the road network in São Paulo state is higher than in any other, the nodality of metropolitan São Paulo is not clearly superior to that of Rio de Janeiro. New interregional highways connecting Salvador, Brasília, and Belém to the Southeast have benefited both São Paulo and Rio. It is obviously easier to reach markets throughout the country from these two cities because of the radial nature of the highway and railroad systems.

Market accessibility can be quantified by the concepts of population potential or income potential derived from the gravity model. The population potential of region $i$ is defined as

$$\sum_j \frac{P_j}{D_{ij}^\gamma}$$

where $P_j$ is the population of region $j$, $D_{ij}$ is the distance between $i$ and $j$, and $\gamma$ is a parameter reflecting the friction of distance, shown to approximate unity in table 14. Population potential is useful in measuring a region's access to mass consumer markets; income potential, which weights $P_j$ by local per capita income, is useful in measuring access to national high-income markets.

Regardless of the values of the $\gamma$ parameter or the income weights, the São Paulo-Rio axis contains the area of peak market accessibility in Brazil. Calculations of population potential of these two metropolises with respect to all other capital cities outside this axis, assuming a unitary distance parameter, indicate that Rio has had slightly worse market accessibility than São Paulo since 1920:

| Metro area | 1920 | 1940 | 1950 | 1960 | 1970 |
|---|---|---|---|---|---|
| São Paulo | 1519 | 2251 | 3583 | 6085 | 9747 |
| Rio | 1242 | 2168 | 3160 | 5546 | 9018 |
| Rio:SP | 0.82 | 0.96 | 0.88 | 0.91 | 0.93 |

São Paulo's attractiveness as the point of maximum population potential is paralleled by an even greater superiority in income potential. Weighting the one hundred largest urban centers in the nation by their levels of income results in lowering Rio's market accessibility to 0.68 relative to that of São Paulo.[15]

Two types of industry may be especially attracted to the region of greatest market accessibility: those that sell a large share of their output directly to consumers rather than to other industries and those whose value added as a percentage of sales is relatively high and whose purchase of raw materials is low.[16]

The 1959 input-output table permits calculation of the consumer orientation and value-added ratio of twenty industrial sectors. There was no significant correlation between a sector's consumer orientation or value-added ratio and its tendency to concentrate in São Paulo state in 1940, 1950, or 1960. The explanation of such lack of correlation is that national markets are not that important to São Paulo industry since the state and nearby Rio de Janeiro are the largest consumers of its output. Specifically, 65 percent of the industrial output of metropolitan São Paulo is consumed in the state; 41 percent is consumed in São Paulo county. Of the 35 percent exported to other states, less than one-quarter goes to the Northeast and Amazonia combined. The destination of total state manufactured exports follows a similar pattern, 31 percent flowing to Guanabara-Rio, 14 percent to Minas Gerais, 11 percent each to Paraná and Rio Grande do Sul, and only 33 percent to the rest of Brazil.[17]

The attractiveness of the locus of maximum market potential depends significantly upon the market structure of an industry. Central place theory predicts that those sectors with the fewest firms, whether because of especially significant internal economies of scale, low levels of demand, or monopoly power, tend to locate in the higher order (or most accessible) market centers. Indeed, the concentration of sectoral employment in São Paulo state is negatively correlated with the number of plants comprising that sector: $r = -0.50$ in 1940, $-0.75$ in 1950, $-0.68$ in 1960, and $-0.57$ in 1970.

Traditional location theory in both its French and American variants presumes that capital is highly mobile. Regional demand is presumed to create its own supply, and one alleged polarizing mechanism is the flight of capital from the periphery to the center.

Careful studies of capital markets in the early stages of industrialization have uncovered pervasive sectoral and regional immobilities. In Britain during the Industrial Revolution, for example, financial intermediaries were few and rarely utilized by individuals with large fortunes. Savings and investment tended to be embodied in the same individual or at least within a group of individuals bound by mutual trust and more often than not by kinship. During the late nineteenth-century rise of large-scale industry in the United States banks tended to invest in a few well-known lines of activity whose principals were intimates. Since capital tended to be so immobile and since large fortunes in the preindustrial era were mostly earned in the commercial centers of New York and Boston, these areas led in industrial development. For peripheral areas that may have had natural resource or labor cost advantages, the result was retarded growth.[18]

Capital immobility at the onset of industrialization surely must have been greater in Brazil than in the Anglo-Saxon countries, where the ethos places a higher value on universalism as opposed to particularism. Since the turn of the century the bulk of private investment in industry has been undertaken by people whose fortunes were linked to coffee: the planters, the brokers, and the great import-export houses.[19] Because São Paulo state has produced the great bulk of Brazilian coffee, until recently, these groups tended to reside in the state capital where civilized amenities could be enjoyed and where face-to-face contact protected one's political and economic interests.

The collapse of the world coffee market did not completely destroy the wealth of these groups, although some wealth was redistributed within them. Price support schemes reduced the losses of the coffee sector, but lack of foreign exchange meant that imported manufactures were not to be had. The unintended consequence of the foreign exchange crisis was import substitution; import-exporters manufacturing goods they formerly imported; repair shops attached to factories, manufacturing parts. These sectoral changes from services to industry involved no interpersonal or interregional capital flows, for they were changes in the behavior of enterprises.

For the lack of capital mobility per se to account for the increasing concentration of industry in São Paulo at the onset of modernization, one would have to show that a disproportion of the capital was there to begin with, that the banking system linking São Paulo savers to investors in other regions was rudimentary, and that the rate of return on capital was higher elsewhere.

In the absence of earlier evidence, one must rely on data from 1950, before the conscious import substitution policy was initiated (table 20). Compared to the important peripheral states, the banking system in São Paulo was better developed as evidenced by the lower ratio of income to bank deposits (a proxy for velocity), and by the lower reserve ratios, suggestive of less riskiness in the capital market. Again, in comparison with these states, the interest on deposits and the rate of return on bank equity were lower, suggestive of the relative capital abundance in São Paulo. The rate of return on loans, however, was not notably higher in these states, except for in the state of Rio, which comprises the hinterland of the city of the same name. In comparison to Guanabara (the city of Rio), São Paulo's capital market seems less developed by the criteria of velocity and reserve ratio. Although these data do not suggest that investment in the peripheral states was more profitable than in São Paulo, they suggest that Rio would have offered a higher rate of return on bank capital, deposits, and loans. This evidence suggests that the concentration of industry in São Paulo may have been due in part to capital immobilities between that state and Rio.

Another circular and cumulative set of forces may have been triggered by Brazil's import substitution strategy. Protective tariffs encourage foreign firms to set up local production facilities to satisfy the demand previously met by exports from the home country.

The fact that firms are foreign may introduce a locational bias in favor of the primate city. Since the policies on exchange and on the repatriation of profits were uncertain until the 1964 revolution, foreign capital goods manufacturers minimized their equity invested by bringing in used machinery, borrowing working capital on the local market, and utilizing local suppliers rather than vertically integrating their operations.[20] The attractiveness of São Paulo was the existence of an infrastructure of suppliers, commercial banks, and a trained labor force. Even if returns else-

Table 20. Characteristics of banking system, selected states, 1950.

| State | Rate of return[a] | Interest on deposits | Interest on loans | Velocity[b] of deposits | Reserve ratio | Profit margin[c] |
|---|---|---|---|---|---|---|
| São Paulo | 14.8 | 4.4 | 6.0 | 2.49 | .061 | 1.6 |
| Guanabara | 16.0 | 5.1 | 9.1 | 1.07 | .039 | 4.0 |
| Minas Gerais | .7 | 7.6 | 5.9 | 3.18 | .102 | −1.7 |
| Rio Grande do Sul | 32.4 | 5.4 | 4.8 | 4.76 | .077 | −0.6 |
| Rio de Janeiro | 2.9 | 4.3 | 6.6 | 4.79 | .073 | 2.3 |
| Pernambuco | 44.7 | 4.7 | 4.7 | 3.55 | .085 | 0.0 |
| Bahia | 25.2 | 5.1 | 6.1 | 4.36 | .074 | 1.0 |

Source: Brasil, *Censo de serviços,* 1950, Mercado de credito, tables 3, 10, 14, and 18.

a. On bank capital.

b. State income/bank deposits.

c. Interest on loans less interest on deposits.

where were higher, the necessary investment would have had to be greater.

In addition to having the basic infrastructure (as did Rio) São Paulo, as the largest industrial city, has salience as a solution to the location problem. In the absence of much information about market conditions in various production points, investors tended to copy the behavior of competitors, suppliers, and customers who tended to look for obvious location sites. Such self-fulfilling success in firm location decisions may be the mechanism by which the external economies in the growth pole are overestimated.[21]

The risk-minimizing and salience advantages of São Paulo for foreign investors are not necessarily permanent. Since it has become clear that the 1964 revolution has made Brazil safe for American capitalism, subsequent investors need not necessarily seek equity-minimizing opportunities. As possibilities in Brazil become better known, other locations may become more attractive.

It is difficult to test these hypotheses without data on flows of foreign and Brazilian investment by sector and location. As crude corroboration, the share of sectoral assets held by foreign firms in 1970 is found to be positively correlated with the share of sectoral employment located in São Paulo in 1950, 1960, and 1970.[22]

The French and American schools have traditionally explained industrial agglomeration as a result of spontaneous market forces. Such a narrow focus is clearly inadequate in a nation like Brazil where the public sector absorbs about 30 percent of the output and actively shapes the givens in market decisions. In addition to operating the nation's railroad facilities, Brazil's public sector produces the bulk of electricity, 50 percent of the steel, and 30 percent of the chemicals, or 10 percent of all manufactures. Controlling both the bulk of commercial credit and long-term financing, the public sector plays a major role in determining both the composition and location of private investment.

The channels by which the public sector's action might have favored industrial agglomeration in a particular region include the locational attractiveness of seats of political power and direct public investment.

Even prior to any industrializing drive there is a great tendency for governments to interfere with activity in the private sector. As Adam Smith aptly noted two centuries ago, governments may intervene in order to siphon wealth from business and industrial groups, who have not quite come to achieve social legitimacy and political power, in favor of traditional ruling classes. By creating gratuitous licensing requirements and excise taxes, politicians acquire the means to reward their supporters with jobs and favors and bureaucrats acquire the means to supplement their meager incomes.[23]

In order to prosper in this parasitic environment, that is, to obtain licenses, contracts, and favorable regulatory decisions, the businessman must court, cajole, persuade, and bribe the appropriate bureaucrat or politician on a face-to-face basis. Capital cities consequently become attractive locations, if for no other reason than to minimize these crucial communications costs. On a national plane these factors would favor Rio over São Paulo.

The rise of the development-oriented state has not lessened the importance of regulation, but it has enhanced its scope. Although improvements in telecommunications and the spread of impersonal bureaucratic norms may weaken the necessity of face-to-face communication, the proliferation of regulatory agencies and the increasing complexity of the economy have increased the value of political influence and intelligence. Thus the relative attractiveness of Rio, and now Brasília, should be increasing.

The importance of political influence and intelligence was recognized by Paulista coffee planters during the nineteenth century, for most of the larger ones had their homes in the state capital. As the residence of the powerful, capital cities in general have been favored by public expenditures for amenities, first electricity and gas, later telephones. In most of Brazil the state public works departments essentially limited their sphere of interest to the capital city. Many of these amenity investments, particularly in energy, spill over to industrial activity. Thus at the onset of development an industrialist requiring electricity found its availability limited to a few unused water power sites and the environs of the state capital. With the spread of electrification this locational advantage seems less important; however, it gave the capitals, especially Rio and São Paulo, an initial advantage.

Like old-style machine politicians in the United States, Brazilian politicians have used the public sector jobs to reward their followers. Over the long run an important function of government, then, has been to provide access to middle-class employment.

While the increasing complexity of the society was also a factor, employment in the public sector as a share of total employment has been rising substantially in the last century: 0.2 percent in 1872, 0.6 percent in 1900, 1.5 percent in 1920, 2.4 percent in 1940, 3.0 percent in 1950, and 3.9 percent in 1970. By 1970 the public sector had absorbed about 7 percent of the urban labor force.

The importance of access to prosperous urban markets and to political communication is evidenced by the fact that in every Brazilian state save one the capital is also the largest city. In contrast, only about one-third of American capitals are the largest cities in their respective states.

Since the 1940s the state has played a major role in the ownership and operation of basic industries, starting with steel, then moving into petrochemicals and electricity. The role of the state in the manufacturing sector is currently so large that of the top twenty firms by assets, eighteen are state enterprises. Petrobrás, the public petrochemical monopoly, is one of the largest enterprises in Latin America.[24]

In the location of its direct investments, has the public sector been biased in favor of São Paulo? In other words, if an investment in that state yielded a 10 percent rate of return while one in the Northeast yielded 12 percent, would the government favor São Paulo even though the Northeast was more profitable? Such a bias is implausible. Between 1889 and 1930 Brazil was dominated by coffee planters from São Paulo and Minas Gerais who were interested in high coffee prices and cheap manufactured imports. While tariffs were raised from time to time and domestic industry was stimulated, the purpose of these actions was balance of payments equilibrium, not industrial protection. In the wake of the world coffee crash, the revolution of 1930 signaled the dilution of power of the São Paulo-Minas axis in favor of the peripheral states.

The decline of traditional agricultural export interests did not imply that the revolution was mainly concerned with industrialization. President Vargas and his advisers were wary of any artificial industrial development, having been reared on the physiocratic notion that agriculture is the true source of wealth. The national steel and petrochemical enterprises were established in the 1940s and 1950s, respectively, for strategic military purposes rather than to promote industrialization.

Until the 1956-1961 Target Plan no Brazilian government was wholeheartedly interested in industrialization. This first development plan was executed by technocrats whose origins were in the peripheral states and whose biases were hardly in favor of São Paulo. Consequently, any concentration of federal investment in São Paulo emerged not from that state's control of the federal apparatus but from the desire to maximize national growth. If the federal government had any explicit regional biases, they were toward Amazonia, the Northeast, and Brasília.[25]

State enterprises have been organized as corporations, relatively free of bureaucratic intervention from the central administration. While the government owns most if not all of the stock in these enterprises, they depend upon sales not taxes for revenues. They consequently behave considerably like private profit-making enterprises.

Wirth's study of the federal decision during World War II to establish the first integrated steel mill in Brazil suggests that undue political factors played very little role in determining the location. While Brazil has abundant iron ore, it has inadequate, low-quality coal reserves. The alternative sites considered for the mill seem reasonable from the point of view of standard location theory: near the iron ore (Belo Horizonte), near the principal market (São Paulo), or near a secondary market that is also an excellent port (Rio de Janeiro). Volta Redonda, the site ultimately chosen, lay nearly midway between São Paulo and Rio and was inland enough to avoid the threat of naval bombardment. Other state-owned integrated steel mills were subsequently established near the original three alternative locations. The decision-making process and the results suggest that the government chose a location on the basis of principles no different from those of a private businessman, subject to the then reasonable strategic consideration.[26]

Similarly, Tendler's analysis of state power companies confirms the image of business rationality. Prior to the 1950s power generation in Rio and São Paulo was monopolized by a Canadian firm. Although Brazil was suffering chronic inflation, the populist government would not permit the power company to increase the rates for political reasons. Consequently, expansion stopped and shortages plagued the two cities throughout the 1947-1962 period. To break the impasse, states entered into the business of generation, leaving distribution to the Canadian firm. The choice of hydroelectric dam sites was determined both by kilowatt potential and demand, and Tendler concludes, "The government's power projects usually were highly commercial ventures, closely related to the market of existing utilities."[27]

In its role as manufacturer, then, the government requires no special analysis. The cases of steel and energy suggest that public enterprise reinforced the attractiveness of São Paulo as an industrial center, thus contributing to the process of circular and cumulative causation. It is unlikely that a private enterprise would have behaved much differently.

São Paulo has not grown according to the norms of the French school. At least until 1940 agglomeration was not explicable by industry mix effects because the national industrial structure had been stable for decades and because São Paulo was largely engaged in traditional food processing and textile manufacture. In the 1940s, when the national industrial structure began changing, São Paulo benefited from a fast mix; but in the 1950s industrial sectors in São Paulo grew considerably faster than their national counterparts. Throughout the 1940-1970 period those industrial sectors agglomerating in São Paulo had weak technological input-output linkages with each other.

A more reasonable explanation follows the American school: Rio de Janeiro established itself as the primate industrial city as a by-product of its being entrepôt for the largest coffee-producing hinterland. In addition, its being a national capital made it a desirable location for industrialists currying favor with government officials. Its being an affluent market was not so important at this time, since most luxuries were imported. This initial advantage provided stimulus to cumulative industrial growth; however, the economic center of gravity during the primacy of Rio was not industry but coffee production.

With the southwesterly shift of coffee production São Paulo became the entrepôt with the largest coffee-producing hinterland. Because of São Paulo's direct links to the sea, Rio was bypassed by this shift. As a result of its growing hinterland, São Paulo was able to capture an increasing share of the traditional industries, which were closely linked to agricultural raw materials and rural mass markets. The prosperity of the coffee region created a surplus for reinvestment in education, public works, and industrial machinery. Because of the poorly developed financial intermediaries in Brazil, the capital accumulated in the state tended to remain there rather than flowing to Rio, which had more highly developed external economies. Simply on the basis of the growth of its market area and the supply of capital and skilled labor, São Paulo was able to surpass Rio as an industrial center by 1920, well before the economic center of gravity began to shift toward industry.

The advantages São Paulo achieved by the 1940s and 1950s, when a conscious drive toward industrial expansion and diversification began, proved to be cumulative. Although the creation of regional development banks attenuated São Paulo's advantages as a capital market, the new primate industrial city became the most salient location for producers seeking maximum access to national markets and for foreign investors seeking minimum risks. Such cumulative advantages became more important as the economic center of gravity shifted decisively toward industry and as cities became more than service centers for agriculture.

The fact that the public sector plays such a large part in regulation and entrepreneurship does not call for any major modifications of this analysis. Although the federal government maintained a fiscal bias against São Paulo for the past fifty years or more, its directly productive investments have been supportive. Functioning like profit-making enterprises, the public steel and energy corporations have located their facilities in response to demands from this metropolis.

In summary, the overtaking of Rio by São Paulo resulted from a locational shift in the resource base during the preindustrial era. Such a phenomenon is unlikely to occur in old nations, where the best soils have been long settled. A similar shift occurred in the antebellum United States with the rise of the Midwest and decline of the Northeast in grain production. This transformation was accompanied by the rise of Chicago, which dethroned Philadelphia as the second city. Unlike Rio, New York

City was not bypassed by these events and indeed benefited as a result of the Erie Canal. Lest one write her epitaph, it should be noted that the forces of circular and cumulative causation have endowed Rio with enormous resilience. It remains the second industrial city despite its loss of raison d'être three times — becoming the national capital to claim seigniorage from the short-lived gold cycle in the late eighteenth century, losing its role as coffee entrepôt, and losing the national capital to Brasília.

# 8

# Planning for the Periphery: The Northeastern Problem

The Northeast is a political conception rather than a homogeneous or nodal region of location theory. Encompassing the hump of South America, the Northeast can be divided into three major physiographic zones connected by zones of transition. The humid littoral was the birthplace of Brazilian civilization, nurturing a latifundia-slavery complex based upon the production of sugar cane for world markets. The semiarid interior, the sertão, was settled by ranchers who provided meat and work animals for the littoral. Over the years landless workers not absorbed by the sugar economy have drifted into the sertão, eking out a seminomadic existence as sharecroppers raising cotton for market and food for subsistence. West of the sertão lies the virtually empty equatorial forest of Maranhão, which has traditionally had stronger ties to Amazonia than to other parts of the Northeast.[1]

Although the Northeast has been characterized by extraordinary disparities in the ownership of land and in income, by absolute poverty, and by stagnation relative to the Southeast, the aspect of the region that has most attracted policymakers' attention in the past one hundred years has been the social consequences of the climate. While the sertão enjoys an average of 500 to 750 millimeters of rainfall per year, there are considerable annual variations. Periodically, on an average of once every ten years, a drought devastates the sertão. Especially afflicted are the sharecroppers, who have no access to water for irrigation. Fleeing to the cities on the littoral, this class is often reduced to begging, sacking stores, and otherwise threatening the social order.[2]

A century of national efforts at dealing with the northeastern problem raises several important issues in the political economy of regional planning: What determines which regional problems acquire salience? How does the diagnosis of the problem evolve? What is the role of intellectual paradigms in formulating this diagnosis? To what extent does the diagnosis influence policy? How have institutional mechanisms and policy instruments evolved? How have these institutions and instruments been utilized in implementation? Finally, what have been the results of regional policy on the subjective level of the policymaker and on the objective level of the outside observer? How have the diagnosis, the institutions, and the instruments served the various interest groups, including the intended beneficiaries of the policy?

## The Evolution of Regional Policy

After an especially severe drought in 1877-1878 that allegedly killed half the population of the state of Ceará, the Northeast was officially recognized by the central government as a national problem. A commission of inquiry was established that led to a concept dominant until the 1950s: the problem of the Northeast rests with the climate in the interior. This diagnosis prescribed a simple remedy: the construction of reservoirs and wells for the provision of water during the droughts, which would serve the twin goals of providing employment for those thrown out of agriculture and of providing long-term protection against future calamities.[3]

Following the recommendations of the commission of inquiry, the government commenced in 1884 to build the Quixadá Dam in Ceará, the focus of the drought zone. Good weather in succeeding years weakened the urgency of dealing with the Northeast on a sustained basis and the dam was not completed until 1906. The rubber boom in Amazonia that continued until about 1910 absorbed much surplus labor from the drought-prone states.

In 1901 a National Inspectorate for Works Against the Drought (later renamed DNOCS) was created to deal with the drought problem on a sustained basis. Largely manned by engineers, this agency was charged with undertaking feasibility studies of water and transportation projects, financing these projects, and delivering relief and hiring the unemployed in time of drought. Construction projects were generally administered by states and localities, which received a 70 percent rebate from DNOCS, or by large landowners, who received a 50 percent rebate. This method of revenue sharing was understandably greeted with enormous enthusiasm by the local political and economic elites of the sertão, whose power was strengthened by this injection of outside funds.

In 1934 the constitution earmarked 4 percent of federal tax revenues in order to sustain the agency's efforts on a more consistent basis. Common in many developing countries, the device of earmarking presumably takes budgetary control out of the hands of congressmen, who are political, and gives more discretion to administrators, who are more professional. These aspirations were not easily realized. Constitutional authorizations have generally exceeded appropriations, except in years of severe drought. Required to disburse funds to state and local governments, the agency has had limited control over its expenditures. Furthermore, it could hardly be said that DNOCS had a clear set of objectives or technical criteria that would help them choose one project over another. Not surprisingly, DNOCS was accused of corruption, the use of funds for partisan ends, and inefficiency. This indictment undoubtedly contains some truth. Despite these failings, the agency did develop a set of reservoirs and a road network that palliated some of the worst social consequences of the drought. In the past many inhabitants of the interior died from thirst and were driven by hunger to eat poisonous roots in time of drought, but death from the drought is rare today. The roads make it possible for larger numbers of peasants to flee to the cities during the drought, creating a greater illusion of devastation than before. Thus, in a perverse way, the success of DNOCS led to its perceived failure.

The Depression and World War II had enormous economic and social consequences for Brazil as a whole, as well as for the northeastern region. Of most immediate consequence to the Northeast, the collapse of coffee in São Paulo led to the planting of sugar, the traditional northeastern staple. Threatened with a loss of their domestic markets, planters on the littoral pressed for the formation of the Institute of Sugar and Alcohol (IAA) in 1933, which was to protect them from unfair competition from the south.

Through the IAA the sugar planters attempted to identify their narrow interests with those of the region. The IAA initially established high minimum sugar prices; however, since São Paulo was a lower cost producer, this state increased its production even more than the Northeast. The IAA ultimately created a quota system for each sugar mill, that permits a greater intensity of cultivation in the Northeast than would occur in its absence.

The long-run consequences of the coffee crash were more important: the laissez faire view of the world, which held that natural market forces determined Brazil's role as a coffee producer, was discredited. The ensuing ideological vacuum was eventually filled by structuralism, a Latin American elaboration of the polarization paradigm. In essence the structuralist doctrine held that primary producing countries were doomed to cyclical instability, persistent poverty, and dependence because of the low income-elasticity of demand for their exports and because industrial countries created artificial barriers to the sharing of gains from international trade. The solution to this problem was import-substituting industrialization. While import substitution was not wholeheartedly espoused until the mid-1950s, structuralism created a climate conducive to programs that went beyond mere disaster relief for the Northeast.

The constitution of 1946 articulated the goal of raising living standards in problem regions like the Northeast. The hydraulic approach to the region was modified by the example of the Tennessee Valley Authority. Brazilian planners drew an analogy between the Tennessee River and the São Francisco, which winds about three thousand kilometers through the poor soils of the sertão. Not only would control of the river even out the rainfall cycles, but electrification could provide one of the prerequisites for industrial development that would ultimately eliminate poverty.

In 1948 the federal government established the São Francisco Valley Commission (CVSF), which was charged with nothing less than completely transforming the structure of the sertão economy. Although 1 percent of federal tax revenues was earmarked by the constitution for this purpose, CVSF effectively had to request appropriations on an annual basis, which weakened its independence. Because the concept of regional development was never clearly defined, CVSF had no consistent guidelines or criteria for choosing among projects. Combined with the necessity to request annual appropriations, this factor induced CVSF to succumb to a policy of undertaking small, porkbarrel projects.

The constitution envisioned the successful completion of the development program within twenty years, but it was not until

1951 that CVSF drafted its first five-year plan. In this plan (1951-1956) only 31 percent of its funds was spent on water-related projects, the rest being expended on roads, health, culture, and power projects for small towns. CVSF subsequently became more specialized in water-related projects, which absorbed about 60 percent of its funds by the third plan (1961-1966).

CVSF has been perceived as producing rather undistinguished results. Part of the perceived failure is attributed to the concurrent creation of the São Francisco Hydroelectric Company (CHESF), whose primary responsibility was the construction of the Paulo Affonso Dam and the distribution of electricity. Viewing its task as basically one of engineering, CHESF had clear but limited objectives. In building the dam and generating and distributing electricity CHESF was a tremendous success, but it failed to transform the Northeast and proved that prerequisites were not sufficient conditions for development. Nevertheless, Robock concludes that "as an affirmative resource and economic development experiment and as an effective demonstration of the ability of government to contribute to the Northeast's economic progress, CHESF represented an important transition between 'fighting the drought' and the 'New Era.'"[4]

Partly in response to a report of a joint U.S.-Brazilian mission and partly in imitation of other countries, a Northeast development bank was established in 1952, capitalized by earmarking 1 percent of federal revenue. The concept behind the development bank is that large numbers of profitable investment opportunities remain unexploited because of poorly developed capital markets, indicated by high risk premiums on loans and high equity requirements. By offering long-term loans at low rates, the Bank of Northeast Brazil (BNB) would raise the return on investor's equity and increase regional capital formation. In fact capital continued to flow from north to south during the early 1950s, and throughout this period the BNB remained a conventional commercial bank, making short- and medium-term loans to governments (in anticipation of tax collection) and to traditional businesses (for working capital).

A drought in 1958 highlighted the ineffectiveness of the piecemeal approach to the regional problem and suggested that more comprehensive planning approaches were required. To reevaluate the problem of the Northeast, the BNB realized that the engineering mode of analysis had to be replaced by the economic mode and created the Office of Economic Training for the Northeast (ETENE), which both trained economists and conducted regional analyses. From the ETENE staff President Kubitschek created the Working Group for Northeastern Development, headed by Celso Furtado, a brilliant structuralist economist.

The Furtado group redefined the northeastern problem unequivocally as one of regional disparities and the solution as nothing less than economic development that would completely transform the region. To bolster their argument the group identified the Northeast as a national problem rather than simply a regional one: "The disparity of income levels between the Northeast and the Central South of this country constitutes, beyond any doubt, the most serious problem to be faced at the present stage of Brazil's economic development." These disparities, moreover, were seen as having a tendency to increase, at least since 1948, because of the government's import substitution policy. While the fundamental cause of backwardness lay in the Northeast's climate and land tenure pattern, tariffs on imports of manufactures, overvalued exchange rates, selective application of credit, and a regressive tax system enhanced this relative backwardness.[5]

A continuation or expansion of the disaster relief strategy was seen as counterproductive, merely keeping the surplus population in the region. Export expansion was excluded as an option because of the low income- and price-elasticity of demand for the Northeast's primary products. The only viable option was seen as industrialization, which would provide jobs for the seminomadic population of the sertão, create an indigenous entrepreneurial class, and retain capital within the region.

A major obstacle to the creation of industrial employment was seen as labor costs, which reflected food costs. These were high, it was argued, because the best lands on the littoral were aggrandized by latifundia devoted to sugar rather than to food production and these latifundia were not responsive to market incentives. As Hirschman notes, the linking of land tenure on the littoral to the fundamental problems of the region was a polemical coup that broached a hitherto taboo subject. While Furtado's analysis carried some weight in the south as an argument for land reform, it overlooked the fact that labor costs were largely determined institutionally, by social legislation.

While the working group was strongly in favor of industrialization, it did not overlook the agricultural sector. To increase the drought resistance of the sertão, it looked toward irrigation. To absorb surplus rural labor, it looked toward the colonization of the humid zone of Maranhão, which had traditionally been oriented toward Amazonia.

By redefining the Northeast to include Maranhão, the working group broached a second taboo subject: emigration as a solution. This had generally been rejected by landowners, who benefited from the reserve army of labor, and by the interlocking political and cultural elites, who equated population with power, a theme that persists in Brazilian development policy.

In his monograph, Robock offers a rather devastating critique of the working group's analysis. First, through no fault of the group, the statistics on regional disparities it cited were in error. The issue of disparities came to the fore when it did because the national accounts had been developed, but subsequent revisions show that the Northeast actually gained on the industrial Southeast in per capita income during the 1950s (see table 9).

In 1952, after the long-awaited movement of Brazil toward industrialization had begun, President Vargas counseled against any premature overtures toward unsophisticated egalitarianism that would retard the growth of the dynamic Central South. President Kubitschek's 1956-1961 Target Plan set the goal of maximizing aggregate growth without mentioning the issue of regional disparities. In this context, the Furtado group never tackled head-on the question whether investment in the Northeast would retard or advance aggregate growth. If the former, then northeastern development plans would simply be a more sophisticated version of make-work relief.

A third and related criticism is that the region was viewed in an aspatial context as a separate country that should undergo its own process of import substitution. The report included no analysis of the determinants of industrial location in the Brazilian space-economy or identification of the Northeast's potential comparative advantage within this national economy.

Despite the lack of analysis, which was also a characteristic of Kubitschek's Target Plan, the egalitarian argument had considerable political appeal. Hirschman suggests that the president had to show he was doing something for the Northeast in order to maintain support for his crash program to construct Brasília.

The working group's strategy of industrial development was the creation of a Perrouxian growth pole in the Northeast from which developmental impulses would radiate to the rest of the region. Such a pole was to be created by establishing infrastructural prerequisites and basic heavy industries with backward linkages to the region's natural resource endowment and forward linkages to goods with a broad market within the region. The strategy called specifically for heavy expenditures on transportation, energy, and a steel plant.

The working group's vision of the development process was bitterly resisted by the traditional elites of the Northeast, for its analysis pinpointed the vested interests of these elites as obstacles to development. For the first time the littoral was brought into the web of the region's problems. The coastal sugar plantation complex was held responsible for the high price of foodstuffs as well as for inefficiency. Landlords in both the littoral and sertão were held responsible for the unequal income distribution, which made mass consumer goods industries unviable. While the traditional elites had a stake in regional backwardness and were well served by DNOCS and IAA, the rising industrial and agricultural groups in the Central South were not. The Northeast was seen as perpetually draining precious resources that could have been invested in the Central South. The DNOCS disaster relief strategy had to be replaced by one that would initiate self-sustaining growth, which would incidentally create a market for southern industries operating at excess capacity and facing an exhaustion of the import substitution process.

Following the recommendations of the Furtado Report, the federal government established the Superintendency for the Development of the Northeast (SUDENE), an agency with unprecedented powers. First the agency was to coordinate the activities of state and federal agencies working in the Northeast as well as to develop a comprehensive plan that orchestrated these players. Since the governors and agency directors were on the advisory board of SUDENE, it was thought that coordination would follow automatically. Although this board gave the governors some control over federal expenditures in their region for the first time, little coordination was achieved. DNOCS, which retained its own earmarked funds, was as uncooperative as other agencies, such as IAA, over which SUDENE exerted little leverage.

Second, SUDENE was allocated 2 percent of federal tax revenues for infrastructure, human services, colonization of Maranhão, and research and development. To achieve these goals, SUDENE developed a series of guiding plans that list the objectives for the period, analyze the prospects for private investment, and describe the incentives for both private investors and other government agencies to collaborate with SUDENE.

The First (1960-1962) and Second (1963-1965) Guiding Plans devoted the bulk of SUDENE's funds to transportation and energy sectors. More emphasis was placed on urban water and sewer systems and the establishment of an integrated steel mill in Bahia in the Third Guiding Plan (1966-1968). In the Fourth Guiding Plan (1969-1973) a larger share of funds was devoted to irrigation of the semiarid zones. The implementation of these plans demonstrated SUDENE's administrative flexibility. In some cases SUDENE entered a venture with private enterprise as a partner, as in the steel mill. In other cases, as in the provision of energy and sewerage, SUDENE acted as contractor with competent state or federal agencies. SUDENE was a success in its first decade in terms of effectively completing engineering projects. Per capita power consumption increased two and one-half times; road mileage doubled.

In the areas of human services delivery and agrarian reform, however, SUDENE was not as successful on its own terms. SUDENE in the 1960s had to compromise its long-term commitment for basic reform with short-term political pressures. Largely because of its fear of a Castro-type revolution in the region, the United States granted funds to help SUDENE under the Northeast Agreement, which focused on education. While SUDENE wished to devote its funds to training and curricular reform, USAID favored projects that would maximize the number of anticommunist candidates that won the 1962 elections. This meant constructing schoolhouses in the bailiwicks of candidates who were generally uninterested in reform.[6]

In the decade of the 1960s SUDENE spent only 10 percent of its budget on agriculture and was largely frustrated in implementing its programs for structurally transforming the rural areas. Although the rhetoric of land reform on the littoral acquired legitimacy, almost no land redistribution occurred. In 1966 an Executive Group to Reorganize Northeastern Sugar (GERAN) was created, comprising representatives of SUDENE, the Bank of Brazil, the national land reform agency, and the Institute of Sugar and Alcohol, which is dominated by northeastern planters. Directed by the president of IAA, GERAN expended most of its efforts on sugar mill modernization and the consolidation of minifundia.

SUDENE's greatest impact on the northeastern economy was effected through the system of fiscal incentives administered in cooperation with BNB. According to Article 34/18 (of two presidential decrees), any corporation could deduct up to 50 percent of its income tax liability for funds invested in projects approved by SUDENE. Not only was this exemption available to direct investors, but also to those who deposited funds in BNB for direct investment by others.

The formal mechanism by which funds were allocated to particular private projects has evolved to the following: a potential investor submits his project to SUDENE for approval. A lawyer verifies that the proposal fits within the spirit of Article 34/18 and that the management has performed well in the past. An engineer checks whether the proposed technology is feasible and utilizes local resources. An economist estimates the private viability of the project. In practice this review has been rather perfunctory because the amount of funds available exceeded the authorizations by a substantial amount during the 1960s. For example, the economist generally accepted the investor's market forecasts at face value and never calculated the social profitability of the project.

Approved projects were then rated according to five criteria: location within the region (sertão favored), type of good (import substitute or export good favored), absorption of labor, use of local resources, and magnitude of investment. Projects rated highly were authorized to receive up to 75 percent equity financing from SUDENE; those rated poorly received 30 percent. Since BNB normally matched an individual's equity needs, private enterprises often had to provide only 12.5 percent of the equity. In practice new private funds amounted to only about one-quarter of all SUDENE-approved investments, the rest coming largely from Article 34/18 and BNB funds.[7]

What effect did the fiscal incentives program have on industrial development of the Northeast? Hirschman estimates that the program doubled the capital stock of regional industry. Because much of this investment reflected SUDENE and BNB funds, only about 25 percent of the investment was really an influx of funds that might not have otherwise occurred.

Since BNB funds were offered at low interest rates, which were negative in real terms in the face of inflation, and labor costs included heavy surcharges for fringe benefits, the incentives were biased toward capital-intensive investment. Goodman, Sena, and Cavalcanti estimate that the maximum employment generated by the SUDENE investments by 1968 was about 112,000 jobs, which equaled 50 percent of the 1959 labor force. Half of the generated jobs were in modernization projects, which probably laid off considerably more workers than it employed. Contrary to the beliefs of Brazilian planners about the inherent capital intensity of modern industry, labor absorption of any particular project varied inversely with the share of funds coming from public sources.[8]

The drought of 1970 and the dramatic dislocation of refugees from the sertão led to a new departure in regional development policy, which joined the solution of the problem of northeastern poverty to that of populating Amazonia. The National Integration Plan (PIN), described above, proposed settling Northeasterners in colonies along a new highway linking the littoral to Amazonia. A so-called land reform program, PROTERRA was charged with improving marketing facilities, financing large-scale agroindustrial projects, and purchasing latifundia and minifundia to create optimum size farms in both regions. The purpose of these measures was to exploit empty lands, to absorb surplus labor, and to reduce food costs in the Northeast. Together these two programs were allocated 50 percent of all funds deposited in the fiscal incentive program for the 1971-1974 period. Thus a new ideology linked a previously neglected problem (Amazonia) to a privileged one (the Northeast).

### The Growth of Planning Capabilities

The style of Brazilian policy making has much in common with that of other developing societies.[9] This style is hardly synoptic — where goals are defined, the alternative means of attaining those goals are explored, and a selfless bureaucracy rationally executes the most efficient alternatives. Neither is this style characterized by muddling through, with incremental changes introduced and discredited choices abandoned, the correct solution being ultimately achieved. On the one hand the Brazilian style is highly creative: bold new programs are conceived, new "islands of rationality" are formed, and new sources of funding are invented. On the other hand there is considerable rigidity, supporting immortal institutions, immortal solutions, and immortal diagnoses.

As Robock and Hirschman have demonstrated, the salience of the Northeast in the national conscience can be predicted by the occurrence of a spectacular drought. Underlying the periodic salience of the Northeast as a problem is the potential for disorder and violence often associated with the droughts: the rebellion of Canudos, which held the army at bay in the 1890s; the reign of the mystic Padre Cicero in the interior of Ceará from around 1910 to 1930; the banditry epitomized by Lampião in the 1920s and 1930s; Prestes's "Long March," preceding Mao's, in the 1930s; and the organization of peasant leagues in the late 1950s. Although they conceded their hegemony to the more dynamic Central South over a century ago, northeastern politicians continue to use the threat of disorder effectively to obtain funds from the central government, leading Robock to conclude that the drought is more a "political phenomenon rather than a period of human suffering."[10] The president's decision to create PIN and PROTERRA after viewing the effects of the 1970 drought firsthand provides up-to-date evidence for this hypothesis.

The problem of the Northeast was originally viewed as highly localized in Ceará, the focus of the most severe droughts. The policy of earmarking funds for DNOCS created pressures from neighboring areas to be included in this zone of privileged misery. The official drought polygon was thus enlarged in 1936, then in 1947, and finally in 1951 to include half the area of the Northeast. Since the traumatic drought of 1877, the problem has evolved from simple disaster relief to making the region more drought resistant. Drought resistance was first interpreted as control of the water cycle (the hydraulic solution), then reinterpreted as economic development (the total transformation of the northeastern economy). Although the working group's conception of economic development included a transformation of agriculture, most effort was concentrated on industrialization. There are three reasons for this emphasis: conceptual, political, and eco-momic.

Conceptually, the structuralist analysis was ambivalent about the role of agriculture in economic development. On the one hand agriculture was seen at best as a reservoir of surplus labor and at worst as a drain of funds from industrial projects. On the other hand, while the modernizing ideology placed low value on increasing agricultural output, this sector was viewed as a potential bottleneck for northeastern development. In the structuralist view agriculture was composed of minifundia whose subsistence economy operated on a backward-bending supply curve and of latifundia that were irrationally committed to sugar production and to leaving the bulk of their land unutilized. Because this sector was viewed as incapable of responding rationally to price stimuli, only a massive land reform could guarantee the urban food supply.

Two points of the three-pronged agricultural plan foundered politically. While southern agriculture certainly would have benefited from the decrease of sugar production on the littoral, the latifundia have been successful in blocking any attempts to challenge their interests. Irrigation in the São Francisco River Valley would have established small proprietors on the latifundia of the sertão, raising political opposition there.

Both irrigation and the colonization of Maranhão foundered on economic grounds as well. Although PIN has recently revived the idea of irrigating a hundred thousand hectares, economic analysis has shown that the rate of return on most projects is low and that labor absorption is minimal. Similarly, the costs of colonization in Maranhão were found to be exorbitant.[11]

Why was SUDENE unable to create an alliance between modernizers in the Central South and Northeast to provide a structural solution to the agrarian problem in the Northeast? An important factor is that agriculture performed well nationally and was not actually a bottleneck. Furthermore, agricultural growth from 1948 to 1969 in the Northeast was even faster than the national average—4.7 percent per annum versus 4.2 percent. Such growth was largely extensive, mainly as a result of the road building programs of DNOCS, CVSF, and SUDENE. Although northeastern yields hardly rose, labor productivity increased about 60 percent in the two decades, as urbanization absorbed the disguised unemployed from the agricultural sector.[12]

Industrialization in the Northeast was welcomed rather than opposed by all significant groups. Thus the failures of employment generation are less political than conceptual. The structuralist conception of industrialization follows a mechanistic interpretation of input-output analysis, with fixed technological coefficients. The implantation of basic industries would automatically lead to the agglomeration of forward- and backward-linked industries. The creation of energy and transportation networks was necessary and sufficient to initiate the process.

The interindustry relationships resulting from the fiscal incentives program provide little support for the Perrouxian model of regional development. Most purchases of intermediate products, especially for heavy industry, were made in the Southeast; and only raw materials processing industries were significant utilizers of northeastern inputs. Similarly, few forward linkages were generated and the produce was generally shipped south.[13]

The greatest puzzle of the regional development policy concerns the tenacity of these structuralist assumptions about modern technology: that it is necessarily capital intensive because it was created in countries where capital was cheap and labor expensive. Industrialization then ineluctably implied low labor absorption, which in turn leads to urban marginality and social unrest. Such a view is certainly comfortable to Marxists, who view alienation and unemployment as a contradiction of capitalist industrialization; but it is not congenial to proponents of the Brazilian model of development.

Ironically, the inevitability of low labor absorption under both industrialization and agricultural modernization has been accepted in the National Integration Plan, despite mounting evidence that this need not be so. In the neoclassical paradigm, which is generally dismissed by Brazilian leftists as an apology for monopoly capitalism, labor absorption can be increased by the subsidization of labor, which would increase profits. Paradoxically, the regime has accepted the analytical assumption of its opponents while ignoring evidence that would permit the resolution of what it accepts as a contradiction in the system.

If one looks at the fiscal and financial incentives as a method of inducing corporations and individuals to declare their incomes for taxation, the puzzle is somewhat resolved. In order to offset the increasing tightness of the collections system, which would hit the regime's supporters hardest, up to half the tax liability can be deposited in several funds. These deposits are then transformed into shares in approved business ventures, the shares becoming negotiable in five years and comprising a capital subsidy to the entrepreneur in the interim. If the subsidy were for labor, the depositor would have no collateral asset, thereby destroying the attractiveness of the fiscal incentive system. While not repudiating the notion of place industrialization, the failure of people industrialization has led to an explicit view of the Amazonian frontier as a safety valve.

The evolution of regional planning institutions has several striking characteristics. First, new regional development agencies have been created at an impressive rate as part of a national process of creating islands of rationality amid the sea of bureaucratic ineptness. These new agencies rarely substitute for older ones. Although DNOCS was deemed a failure and hydraulic solutions discredited, this agency has not only survived to obtain more funds for dams and wells but was also charged with constructing the important Brasília-Fortaleza highway in the 1960s. Similarly, CVSF has been renamed and despite its undistinguished history has been given a role in the programs of the 1970s (irrigation and road building as the asphalt solution displaces the hydraulic one as a panacea).

Second, the new agencies tend to be financed less by earmarking taxes and more by issuing bonds to the public. The key to the difference between DNOCS and CVSF on the one hand and CHESF on the other seems to lie on their bases of solvency. While the former two were bureaucracies receiving earmarked funds, CHESF was a public corporation. Although most of its stock was held by the government, the power corporation had to issue balance sheets that would convince foreign bondholders of its competence and integrity.

The disadvantages to the proliferation of agencies, their overlapping jurisdictions, and their conflicting orientations are obvious. An agency like CVSF charged with coordination could not succeed in the absence of some leverage such as budgetary veto power or control of key infrastructural investments. As Robock notes, TVA would have been much less successful as a regional development agency if it had not controlled the water resources, especially electricity generation. Furthermore, the proliferation of agencies linked directly to the presidency overloads that office and effectively reduces agency accountability. While this problem was recognized by the creation of a ministry to coordinate regional programs in 1966 (now the Ministry of the Interior), the PIN and PROTERRA programs were assigned to existing agencies scattered in various ministries.

There are two justifications for this puzzling behavior. First, the implementation of development planning in the 1950s, meant that the old assistance-providing bureaucracy had to be either reformed or outflanked. Reform would not only prove costly in terms of time and energy, but the political basis of the regime, which depended upon the porkbarrel, would be jeopardized. The creation of new agencies can be interpreted as a process by which progressive groups outflank the traditional interest groups without directly challenging their power base.

Second, competition among agencies is a method of maintaining accountability to the overloaded presidency. Since no agency had exclusive jurisdiction over a function or an area, each could be judged against the others. Successful agencies are rewarded with the assumption of new functions or the acquisition of greater funding powers. The survival of even the least successful agencies maintains the competitive threat to the better managed ones.

Finally, regional development planning has shifted away from direct government spending to the utilization of incentives to influence market-oriented enterprises, epitomized by the fiscal incentive system. Under this system public funds are expended only if a private investor can be convinced to add his own resources to a given project. Publicly favored projects must thus pass the filter of private profitability. An obvious problem with this approach is that sight is lost of those activities not amenable to private profit making, such as primary education, public health, and rural extension, all of which are poorly funded in most of Brazil.

Little detailed information is available on how regional planning agencies have implemented general policy directives. Although DNOCS and CVSF undoubtedly used political criteria to distribute funds and effectively fortified the stronghold of the traditional bosses on the rural areas, there were no technical criteria that were suggested to produce better results. If the Northeast stagnated, it was not that DNOCS did not build roads but that infrastructure or multipurpose river development are insufficient to raise people's incomes.

The behavior of DNOCS was consistent with the dominant norms of government operations until World War II. After the creation of the republic in 1889 the state was largely a watchman that protected the interests of the large landowners when need be. A major function of government bureaucracy was to provide status and employment for its members, but it could hardly be guided by policy objectives. In this context DNOCS was more modern and performance oriented than the rest of the bureaucracy.

The task of BNB was more difficult: to stimulate investment in agriculture and in industry. On the one hand the bank can be faulted for functioning as a traditional commercial bank rather than a development bank during the 1950s. On the other hand there was no deluge of feasible projects that the bank could have chosen from. Once the fiscal incentives made investment projects more attractive in the Northeast, BNB began to act more like a development bank in response to the demand for investment funds. The fact that the supply of investment funds exceeded the demand for these funds by over 20 percent in the 1960s suggests that investments in the Northeast were less commercially profitable than in the Central South.

Of all the regional agencies, perhaps SUDENE is the most culpable in terms of implementation failures. The system of proposal ratings favored the largest scale and most capital intensive projects, which generated the fewest external economies or jobs. Had SUDENE rated projects according to their social rate of return based upon the social opportunity cost of labor, job creation would undoubtedly have increased.

Subjectively, policymakers have tended to denigrate the results of their predecessors, whose expectations were rarely realized. Objectively, results have not been so bad as their hindsight suggests. Although DNOCS squandered funds and strengthened the hand of the reactionary bosses of the sertão, its feasibility studies facilitated the investment decisions of succeeding agencies and built reservoirs that rendered drought less calamitous. Although the roads built by CVSF may have been counterproductive in re-

taining surplus labor in the region, they did facilitate the marketing of farm products and thus the extension of agricultural acreage in the polygon. Although the energy investments of CHESF
did not transform the region, they made the next stage of industrialization easier and provided an important amenity to consumers.

The ostensible failure of comprehensive planning and regional
import substituting industrialization is suggested by the substantial convergence in per capita income between the Northeast and
Southeast in the 1950s, before SUDENE was created, and the
lack of convergence in the 1960s. Particularly telling is the absolute stagnation and hence relative decline in the real wages of
rural farm workers, the intended beneficiaries of all development
programs, from 1959 to 1968. These disappointments notwithstanding, simulations by Rebouças suggest that in the absence of
SUDENE's production subsidies and the federal government's export promotion policies, relative conditions in the region would
have deteriorated.[14]

The Northeast has traditionally been viewed as a regional
problem rather than a bundle of sectoral problems. Analysis of
the Brazilian income distribution indicates that regional factors
directly account for little of the variance in individual incomes.
The most important factors are education, age composition, and
sector, which are all unfavorably distributed against the Northeast. In other words, the region's relatively low per capita income
is associated with its uneducated labor force, high dependency
rates, and lack of industry.

Thus far regional development policy has focused on large-
scale industrialization, has paid little attention to improving education and agricultural productivity, and has taken a pronatal-
ist position on the issue of fertility control.[15] To what extent can
these fundamental causal factors be modified within the Brazilian model of economic development?

The Perrouxian strategy has generated less self-sustaining
growth than anticipated. An alternative strategy suggested by the
American school is to make capital available to large numbers of
small firms in order to maximize the opportunities for local entrepreneurship, specialization, and learning by doing. These business projects may be too small to interest large companies and
may require SUDENE to become a venture capital corporation.

The unfavorable labor supply factors (unskilled labor and high dependency rates) are only partly explicable by selective migration of skilled, prime-age workers to the Central South. As a share of those eligible for primary education, school enrollments are considerably lower in the Northeast than in the Central South: 53 percent versus 74 percent in 1964, for example. These differences largely reflect interregional differences in urbanization, for the share of urban enrollments is similar in both regions: 79 percent versus 83 percent. Not only are rural levels of enrollment considerably lower, but interregional differences are most striking: 37 percent in the Northeast versus 65 percent in the Central South.[16] While rural enrollments are generally lower than urban throughout the world, the especially low levels in the rural Northeast are consistent with the image of a latifundia dominated society whose rulers are interested in maintaining a large pool of unskilled labor.

Interregional differences in fertility are almost completely reducible to differences in urbanization. While rural fertility is almost identical in the Northeast and Southeast, urban fertility is about one-sixth higher in the Northeast than in the Southeast. Urban-rural fertility differences partially reflect educational differences. As the urbanization of the Northeast approaches that of the Southeast, one expects educational and fertility levels, and hence per capita incomes, to converge. Public policy, however, can accelerate the process by massive support of primary education and birth-control campaigns in the rural areas.[17]

Increased labor productivity in agriculture would involve massive increases in education, credit facilities, and extension services for small farmers. Such expenditures would be of little direct benefit to the northeastern elite, whose large-scale enterprises have been defined as technologically necessary agents for modernization. Increased industrial labor absorption would require lowering the private costs of unskilled labor through public financing of social security surcharges and the elimination of capital subsidies through the fiscal incentives program, which would be of little benefit to the southern elite. Accelerated migration to cities of the Central South is unacceptable to southerners, who see the northeastern migrants as the cause of all urban ills and whose perception has been certified in PIN: thus the Central South's enthusiasm for Amazonia as an alternative safety valve.

In conclusion, a long-term solution to the northeastern problem would include massive primary education, agricultural credit and technical assistance to small farmers, and small-scale industrial loans. None of these programs would benefit the elites of the Northeast or the Southeast and would impose considerable costs upon them. That such programs would be undertaken within the Brazilian model of development is highly doubtful.

# 9

# Urbanization and Sectoral Change

In 1940 Brazil was largely a rural nation with only 25 percent of its population living in cities of more than two thousand inhabitants. By 1970 this figure had risen to 52 percent. In the intervening three decades Brazil underwent an urban revolution that was compressed into half the time within which the United States made a similar transition (approximately 1870 to 1920).[1]

Urbanization in the currently advanced countries has been a concomitant of shifts in employment from agriculture into manufacturing. In developing countries, however, only a minor proportion of the urban labor force is employed in manufacturing; and a steady stream of rural immigrants enters the city in the face of remarkably high open and disguised unemployment.

Dualistic theories, which attempt to explain urbanization as a result of sectoral shifts and institutional rigidities in the urban labor market, presume that nonagricultural employment is inherently urban. This presumption is not useful in explaining urbanization in Brazil, where the growth of cities is much greater than the growth of nonagricultural employment. What must be explained as well is the urbanization or, more properly, the deruralization of industrial and service employment.

## The Growth and Spread of Cities

The Brazilian census made no dichotomy between urban and rural populations before 1940. Consequently, any generalizations about early urbanization must perforce lack precision. One useful indicator of urbanization is the share of the total population living within the county boundaries of the state and national capitals. In 1940 these counties contained 54 percent of the total urban population; in 1970 they contained 42 percent, the decline being partially explained by their dismemberment. As to order of magnitude, then, over one-half of the urban population in Brazil lived in these counties prior to 1940.

In the fifty-year period covering the first four censuses approximately 11 percent of the total population lived in the capital counties. (This percentage showed no particular trend: 10.5 percent in 1872, 9.3 percent in 1890, 11.7 percent in 1900, and 11.4 percent in 1920.) In the subsequent fifty years this percentage rose at an accelerating pace: 13.7 percent in 1940, 15.9 percent in 1950, 18.8 percent in 1960, and 21.8 percent in 1970.

It is reasonable to infer from these data that Brazil's urban revolution began after 1920. The country's metropolitan revolution began even later, for the share of population living in cities of more than twenty thousand inhabitants remained at 15 percent from 1920 to 1940. This share rose to about 20 percent in 1950, 28 percent in 1960, and 40 percent by 1970.

Since 1940 the urban population has been growing at a rate increasingly faster than that of the rural population. For every 1 percent growth in the rural population in the 1940s the urban population grew 4.9 percent. In the 1950s the corresponding urban percentage was 5.2 and in the 1960s, 7.8 percent. Because the urban share of the population has been increasing, the ratio of urban to total growth has been declining (table 21).

The metropolitan revolution seems to be a concomitant of structural change in the economy. It is clear from the early censuses that the share of the labor force employed in manufacturing

Table 21. Urban population shares, percentage changes, and growth-elasticities, 1940-1970.

| A. Percentage urban population | 1940 | 1950 | 1960 | 1970 |
|---|---|---|---|---|
| Census definition | 31.2 | 36.2 | 45.1 | 56.0 |
| Cities, 2000 + | 25.2 | 30.8 | 40.4 | 52.0 |
| Cities, 10,000 + | 18.5 | 23.4 | 32.3 | 44.5 |
| B. Changes[a] | 1940 − 50 | 1950 − 60 | | 1960 − 70 |
| Change in percentage urban | 5.6 | 9.6 | | 11.6 |
| Ratio of urban growth rate to total growth rate | 3.12 | 2.26 | | 2.06 |
| Ratio of urban growth rate to rural growth rate | 4.92 | 5.20 | | 7.80 |

Source: Brasil, *Censo demográfico, 1970.*
a. Urban defined as living in places with population of two thousand or over.

hardly changed from 1907 to 1940, during which period the sectoral structure of manufacturing remained stable. After 1940 manufacturing employment shifted out of the traditional, natural resource-based sectors into those utilizing more capital and skilled labor, which were more easily mobilized in big cities.

The earlier discussion of regional integration and the rise of São Paulo as an industrial metropolis suggests that industrial employment has become increasingly concentrated in space. Has industrialization thereby caused a divergence among states in the distribution of the urban population?

While the industrial axis of São Paulo-Rio-Guanabara has been more heavily urbanized than other areas, all parts of the nation have taken part in the urban revolution (table 22). In 1940

Table 22. Urban population shares, states, 1940-1970.

| State | 1940 | 1950 | 1960 | 1970 |
|---|---|---|---|---|
| Amazonas | 16.8 | 20.4 | 28.2 | 38.4 |
| Pará | 25.4 | 28.2 | 38.1 | 45.0 |
| Maranhão | 10.5 | 11.7 | 14.0 | 22.7 |
| Piauí | 11.2 | 13.3 | 20.0 | 28.0 |
| Ceará | 14.5 | 18.4 | 27.6 | 34.5 |
| Rio Grande do Norte | 13.8 | 19.1 | 30.2 | 39.6 |
| Paraíba | 14.7 | 19.5 | 28.7 | 35.7 |
| Pernambuco | 23.5 | 30.0 | 41.4 | 51.4 |
| Alagoas | 19.1 | 21.1 | 28.8 | 36.0 |
| Sergipe | 24.7 | 26.7 | 32.4 | 41.2 |
| Bahia | 16.4 | 19.4 | 28.4 | 36.6 |
| Minas Gerais | 17.1 | 22.1 | 33.0 | 47.0 |
| Espírito Santo | 14.3 | 15.8 | 23.0 | 41.3 |
| Rio de Janeiro and Guanabara | 58.5 | 70.2 | 77.3 | 86.7 |
| São Paulo | 39.7 | 48.5 | 59.8 | 78.3 |
| Paraná | 18.7 | 21.1 | 26.4 | 32.1 |
| Santa Catarina | 13.7 | 16.9 | 26.2 | 37.3 |
| Rio Grande do Sul | 26.0 | 29.9 | 40.8 | 50.0 |
| Mato Grosso | 20.2 | 24.1 | 32.1 | 37.8 |
| Goiás | 7.8 | 12.0 | 26.3 | 45.5 |
| Brazil | 25.2 | 30.8 | 40.4 | 52.0 |
| $r^a$ | $0.58^b$ | $0.53^b$ | $0.52^b$ | $0.68^b$ |

Source: Brasil, *Censo demográfico*, 1940-1970.
a. r = rank-order correlation between state per capita income and percentage population urban.
b. Significance .05 (one-tail); n = 20.

about three-fifths of the population in Guanabara-Rio and two-fifths in São Paulo state were urban. No other states attained these levels by 1950, but by 1960 the latter mark was surpassed by Pernambuco in the Northeast and prosperous Rio Grande do Sul. By 1970 only half the states had reached São Paulo's urbanization level of thirty years earlier and none had reached Rio's.

Following Williamson's study of American urbanization at a comparable developmental phase, Graham and Buarque calculated the mean deviation in state urban shares within and between the Central South and the periphery. They found that in the 1940s, when per capita incomes diverged strongly, there was no comparable pattern of divergence in urban shares within the Central South or between the center and the periphery. Within the periphery, moreover, these urban shares tended to converge. After 1950, when per capita incomes began to converge, urban ratios within and between the center and the periphery tended to converge.[2] In other words, despite the continuing interstate divergence in agricultural versus nonagricultural shares of employment, urban ratios are converging. Urbanization is proceeding most rapidly in areas of initially low urban shares and conversely in areas of initially high urban shares.

Differences in urban shares are not striking among the states of the prosperous Southeast, the frontier of the Central West, the impoverished Northeast, and empty Amazonia. This does not imply that urbanization is unrelated to development level. Since 1940 there has been a direct relationship between state urban share and per capita income. The most egregious exception to this rule is Paraná, the fourth richest state and one of the least urbanized.

Brazilian cities are largely service and commercial, rather than manufacturing, centers. Aside from a few small industrial towns, like Volta Redonda and Cubatão, that have sprung up around steel mills, São Paulo is the only essentially industrial metropolis in the country. In 1940, 36 percent of São Paulo's labor force was employed in the industrial sector, in 1950 fully 44 percent, and in 1970 only 33 percent. Between 1940 and 1970 none of the remaining twenty largest cities approached 30 percent of the labor force in industry. For example, the second largest industrial city, Rio, has had only 25 percent of its labor force in industry. In the other large metropolitan areas the industrial share of the labor force has fluctuated around 20 percent throughout this period.[3]

The share of the urban labor force in manufacturing in contemporary Brazil is considerably lower than that in the United States at a comparable level of urbanization. In 1860, 32 percent of the urban population was engaged in manufacturing; in 1870, 41 percent. In 1860 over 50 percent of the urban labor force in the most industrialized region, New England, was employed in manufacturing and over 20 percent in the least industrialized region, the South. In 1870 nearly 60 percent of the urban labor force in New England and nearly 30 percent in the South were employed in manufacturing. By these standards Brazil's urban revolution is only weakly related to the nation's industrialization.[4]

### Sectoral Shifts in Employment

There is a well-established direct international correlation between the share of the labor force employed in the industrial and services sectors and the share of population residing in metropolitan areas with over one hundred thousand inhabitants. This relationship holds for time-series patterns of growth in currently advanced countries as well as in contemporary less developed nations. This relationship also holds for cross-sectional comparisons among developing nations. These normal patterns have no obvious normative implications, for it is possible that the whole sequence of urbanization may be excessive or insufficient by some criterion of efficiency.[5]

The implication of these statistical relationships is that urbanization results from the shift of employment out of the agricultural sector and into the industrial and service sectors in the course of economic development. In the past decade dualistic theories of development have emerged to explain quantitatively these well-established sectoral changes and, by implication, the urbanization in developing countries.[6]

According to these models the underlying factors leading to employment shifts out of agriculture include sectoral differences in the growth of output demand, in rates of technological change, in labor and capital intensities, in the substitutability between capital and labor, in savings propensities of workers and capitalists, and in birth rates. In addition to these behavioral and technological parameters, dualistic models generally include institutional rigidities in the urban labor market that explain the paradox of continual immigration in the face of heavy unemployment.[7] The logic of the dualistic model is briefly described as follows:

GROWTH IN OUTPUT DEMAND.    Changes in the sectoral patterns of output depend upon the income- and price-elasticities of demand. For example, Engel's Law holds that as per capita income increases, food consumption increases less than proportionately and consumption of other items more than proportionately. Although exports may generate an additional source of demand for agricultural products, as is the case in Brazil, domestic demand patterns are usually more than sufficient to cause a decline in the relative importance of agricultural output in the course of development.

TECHNOLOGICAL FACTORS.    The output of each sector is produced by a different mix of land, capital, and labor of various skills. The ease with which these production factors can be substituted among themselves also varies by sector (the service sector is generally more labor intensive than either industry or agriculture, the elasticity of substitution between capital and labor is lower in the service sector than in the other two, and technological progress seems to occur more rapidly in both industry and agriculture than in the service sector, a fairly universal phenomenon).

These factors account for the shift of labor out of agriculture and into industry and services in the following way: technological progress in the industrial and agricultural sectors implies that an expansion in output requires a smaller increase in the labor force than a similar expansion in the service sector, where progress has been nearly nil. Second, as a result of both capital accumulation and technological progress, wages tend to rise. While rising wages induce employers to substitute capital for labor in both industry and agriculture, the possibilities for such substitution in the service sector are much less. Consequently, even if the share of income expended on services remained constant, technological change in the other sectors and rising wages cause an increase in service employment.

INSTITUTIONAL FACTORS.    It is impossible to understand urbanization in developing countries without a recognition of institutional factors that were not extant when currently advanced countries were undergoing a comparable phase of growth. Most important are such labor market institutions as minimum wages and union agreements, as exemplified by the social legislation initiated by Vargas during the 1930s and elaborated thereafter. The immediate effect of these institutions is the creation of a wedge between the opportunity costs of labor (approximately average farm income) and the minimum wages for unskilled labor in the modern industrial sector, which is protected by this legislation. To the extent that legislation requires the payment of fringe benefits that are not highly valued by the employees, such as blocked savings accounts, another wedge is created between the employer's cost of labor and the worker's wage.

As a consequence of these institutions on the labor demand side, employment is constricted through the substitution of capital, which is often subsidized in developing countries, for labor, which is taxed. The degree to which employment is constricted depends upon the elasticity of substitution between capital and labor.

The most significant consequence of labor market institutions on urbanization lies on the supply side. High minimum wages in the modern industrial sector offer attractive prospects to farm laborers, who generally are not covered by this social legislation in practice. Since industrial labor absorption is not determined by the free play of supply and demand but at the point where the labor demand curve intersects the minimum wage line, rural migrants cannot automatically find jobs in the modern sector by forcing the wage down through the market. As long as the minimum wage is high enough, these migrants are willing to tolerate unemployment in the urban labor market for some prospect of entering the modern sector. The higher the minimum wage relative to the agricultural wage, the higher is the tolerable rate of urban unemployment.[8]

Let the minimum wage in the modern urban sector ($W_m$) exceed the agricultural wage ($W_a$). Migration from the countryside proceeds until the agricultural wage is equal to the expected urban wage, which is the modern sector wage ($W_m$) times the probability of obtaining employment in the modern sector ($p$). This probability in turn is the ratio of $M$, employment in the modern sector (which is determined solely by demand), and $N$, the number of urban workers, employed plus unemployed ($N = M + U$). Since rural-urban migration proceeds until

$$W_a = pW_m = M/(M + U) \, W_m,$$

the equilibrium employment rate ($p$) equals $W_a/W_m$, and the equilibrium unemployment rate is $(1 - p)$.

The implication of this model is that as employment in the modern protected sector expands, so does unemployment, at about the same rate. To the extent that the minimum wage tends to rise relative to the rural wage, as was the case in Brazil during the 1950s, unemployment may increase faster than employment. To the extent that relative minimum wages fall, as they have since 1964, urban employment can expand faster than unemployment.

How have changes in output demand and in technological supply conditions affected employment in the three sectors in Brazil? Using a dualistic model of the general type described above, Lorene Yap has been able to simulate the sectoral changes in the Brazilian economy during the years 1950 to 1965 with impressive accuracy. In her simulation nonagricultural workers were divided between the modern, presumably urban-industrial, sector and the traditional, presumably disguised unemployed, sector.[9]

The growth of employment in the agricultural sector has been relatively slow because of the low income-elasticity of demand for food. Although technological change has been slow and little capital has been substituted for labor until quite recently, there has been considerable disguised unemployment. Consequently, with an expansion of the frontier the output of Brazilian agriculture could increase with a less than proportional growth in employment. Between 1940 and 1970 national agricultural output nearly tripled, crop land area increased about 80 percent, and the labor force increased only about 35 percent. In the face of slowly growing product demand, high rural birth rates exert a severe downward pressure on farm wages.

The final and intermediate demand for skill-intensive manufactures has grown rapidly. Employment has grown considerably slower than output because of the importation of capital-intensive modern technology and because minimum wage legislation encourages the substitution of capital for unskilled labor. Attracted to the city by the prospect of high wages in the modern sector, new arrivals from the countryside enter the traditional self-employed industrial and service sectors.

In the service sector the growth of demand has been rapid and the rate of technological progress slow. As a result of these technological factors and the role of this sector as a reservoir of disguised unemployment, output per worker fell substantially in the period from 1940 to 1970, from 2.3 times to 1.4 times the average output per worker in the entire economy.[10]

## The Urbanization of Industrial Employment

The sectoral shift of employment out of agriculture is insufficient to account for Brazilian urbanization. Although the dualistic models assume that workers engaged in industry and services are urban, in the early stages of economic development nonagricultural work is largely rural. The argument that Brazilian urbanization between 1940 and 1970 cannot be explained solely by sectoral shifts rests upon three major pieces of evidence.

First, the share of total employment in the industrial and service sectors has exceeded the urban share of the population (table 23, panel A). Second, the change in the urban share has exceeded the change in the share of employment in these two sectors since 1940, but especially in the 1950s (table 23, panel B) (for every one point change in employment in these sectors the urban population increased by 1.4 points). Third, the rate of growth of the urban population is more than one and one-half times as fast as the growth of employment in these two sectors (table 23, panel C). In other words, about two-thirds of the urban population growth can be accounted for by sectoral shifts and about one-third can be accounted for by the agglomeration of existing industrial and service activities in cities.

By way of contrast, the increase in the American urban population share in the comparable period, 1870 to 1920, was similar to that of the increase in the nonagricultural labor force, 25.5 points and 26.6 points, respectively.[11] In other words, urbanization is less closely linked to the growth of employment in industry and services in Brazil than was the case in the United States.

What is the process by which industrial and service activities have become urbanized in Brazil? Prior to the onset of modern industrialization a wide range of industrial and service activities are dispersed throughout the countryside in a pattern similar to that of the rural population. Farm families undertake a plethora of nonagricultural activities: building their own homes, weaving their own clothes, milling their own grains, and transporting

Table 23. Employment shares, percentage changes, and urbanization-elasticities, 1940-1970.

| A. Shares | 1940 | 1950 | 1960 | 1970 |
|---|---|---|---|---|
| Urban percentage of population | 25.2 | 30.8 | 40.4 | 52.0 |
| Secondary percentage of labor force | 10.1 | 13.7 | 13.1 | 18.0 |
| Tertiary percentage of labor force | 25.9 | 26.4 | 33.2 | 37.4 |
| Secondary and tertiary | 36.0 | 40.1 | 46.3 | 55.4 |
| B. Change in percentages | 1940 − 50 | 1950 − 60 | 1960 − 70 | |
| Urban | 5.6 | 9.6 | 11.6 | |
| Secondary | 3.6 | − 0.6 | 4.9 | |
| Tertiary | .5 | 6.8 | 4.2 | |
| Secondary and tertiary | 4.1 | 6.2 | 9.1 | |
| C. Ratio of urban growth to sectoral employment growth | 1940 − 50 | 1950 − 60 | 1960 − 70 | |
| Secondary | 1.22 | 3.03 | .92 | |
| Tertiary | 3.25 | 1.19 | 1.37 | |
| Secondary and tertiary | 2.22 | 1.50 | 1.21 | |

Source: Brasil, *Censo demográfico,* 1940-1970.

some of their surplus to market. Other activities may be undertaken at specialized locations, such as workshops in small villages or distilleries on plantations. With the lowering of transportation costs more of these nonagricultural activities are undertaken by specialists who can undercut domestic production by greater use of machinery and a greater division of labor. If the resulting internal economies of scale are large enough, whole towns may be formed by the employees of a single industrial enterprise.[12] An increasing division of labor within the industrial and service sectors tends to result in the spin-off of specialized firms, in the creation of external economies of scale, and hence in the agglomeration of these specialized firms in fewer and fewer points. In summary, economic development results in the increasing specialization of the farm families in agricultural activities, the growth of large-scale industry at the expense of handicrafts, and the urbanization of industry and services.[13]

As the available Brazilian data do not permit direct testing of this hypothesis, one must rely instead on indirect cross-sectional evidence from the states whose per capita income is a proxy for level of economic development.

An indicator of the specialization of farm households is the share of agricultural output processed on the farm rather than shipped to off-site mills. The most meaningful evidence refers to sugar cane and manioc, which must be processed in order to be utilized and for which handicraft techniques are well known and widely diffused.

The share of sugar cane processed on farms has declined drastically, from 42 percent in 1940 to only 4 percent in 1970. The percentage of manioc processed on farms increased slightly from 1940 to 1950 and then decreased by 1970. In all years there is a negative rank-order correlation between state per capita income and the share of both sugar cane and manioc processed on the farm (table 24, panel A). Some very low income states, like Pernambuco and Alagoas, which are large-scale commercial producers, also process a low share of sugar cane on farms.

The hypothesis that employment in large-scale industry is growing at the expense of handicrafts is tested by several bits of evidence. First, the share of workers in the modern sector is measured by comparing the self-report of industrial employment in the demographic census with employer reports of the same in the

**Table 24.** Industrial specialization and modernization: levels and correlations with state per capita income for three years.

| Indicator | 1940 | 1950 | 1970 |
|---|---|---|---|
| A. Home processing of farm output | | | |
| % sugar processed | 42 | 15 | 4 |
| $r^a$ | $-.34^b$ | $-.20$ | $-.39^b$ |
| % manioc processed | 63 | 69 | 55 |
| $r^a$ | $-.47^b$ | $-.53^b$ | $-.80^b$ |
| B. Manufacturing employment Indust. census/demogr. | | | |
| census | 65 | 69 | 52 |
| $r^a$ | .24 | $.66^b$ | $.70^b$ |
| C. Artisanship | | | |
| % self-employed | 18 | 7 | 12 |
| $r^a$ | $-.76^b$ | $-.72^b$ | $-.75^b$ |

Source: Martin T. Katzman, "Urbanização e concentração industrial, 1940−70," *Pesquisa e planejamento* 4 (Dec. 1974): tables 2-4; Brasil, *Censo demográfico, Censo industrial,* and *Censo agrícola* for 1970.

a. r = rank-order correlation between indicator and state per capita income.

b. Significance .05 (one-tail); n = 20

industrial census. The latter source includes only those enterprises with more than a certain level of employment and output, so the difference should reflect employment in the handicrafts sector (table 24, panel B). By this measure the share of industrial employment in the modern sector rose slightly from 1940 to 1950 but fell markedly by 1970. Although the share of workers in the modern sector seems to have decreased from 1940 to 1970, this share is positively related to state per capita income in all years.

Second, the share of industrial workers declared as self-employed in the demographic census is a category surely comprised of artisans (table 24, panel C). By this indicator the share of industrial workers in the handicrafts sector fell considerably from 1940 to 1950 and rose somewhat from 1950 to 1970. This share is negatively related to state per capita income in all years.

Third, changes in the average size of industrial firms indicate the strength of internal economies of scale as an agglomerating force. The mean number of workers per establishment in manufacturing seems to have declined from 1920 to 1960 and risen slightly from 1960 to 1970. Disaggregated patterns are more complex, with most sectors experiencing periods of both rising and falling average size. A comparison of 1970 with 1940 finds as many sectors rising as falling. Because Brazilian industrialization has been capital intensive, the number of workers does not fully indicate the size of a firm. Nevertheless, the average Brazilian worked in increasingly smaller employment units until the 1960s (table 25).

The distribution of plant sizes confirms the persistence of small enterprises in the course of development. In the 1950s the percentage of the labor force employed in the smallest or the largest plants hardly changed in the aggregate and in sectors for which there are data (table 26). Unfortunately, data are not available to extend these trends into the 1960s.

The cross-sectional and time-series evidence conflict regarding the relationship between Brazilian economic development and the destruction of handicrafts. On the one hand, in the more developed states less farm output is processed on site, a lower share of industrial workers is self-employed, and a higher share of these workers is employed in the modern sector. On the other hand, increasing per capita income over the last thirty years has been fully consistent with the survival and indeed the expansion of small-

**Table 25.** Employees per industrial establishment, by sector, 1920 – 1970.

| Sector | 1920[a] | 1940 | 1950 | 1960 | 1970 |
|---|---|---|---|---|---|
| Nonmetallic minerals | 11.5 | 11.8 | 10.2 | 9.0 | 9.3 |
| Metallurgy | 28.7 | 42.0 | 45.3 | 35.9 | 27.6 |
| Machinery | 12.8 | 36.9 | 34.4 | 36.7 | 26.8 |
| Electrical | – | 33.8 | 46.9 | 59.0 | 36.6 |
| Transport equipment | 14.6 | 34.1 | 36.1 | 39.1 | 47.7 |
| Wood products | 10.6 | 11.8 | 11.0 | 7.8 | 9.2 |
| Furniture | 14.3 | 11.2 | 13.6 | 7.8 | 8.0 |
| Paper | 50.1 | 54.0 | 56.7 | 53.6 | 56.9 |
| Rubber | 24.6 | 69.6 | 94.9 | 61.6 | 33.7 |
| Leather | 8.7 | 8.9 | 10.0 | 10.5 | 13.0 |
| Chemicals | } 15.4 | } 22.4 | 26.9 | 43.1 | 39.6 |
| Pharmaceutical | | | 22.8 | 53.7 | 59.0 |
| Cosmetics | | | 9.1 | 13.7 | 18.1 |
| Plastics | | | 23.0 | 32.8 | 32.5 |
| Textiles | 97.4 | 105.6 | 114.3 | 76.8 | 64.6 |
| Apparel | 14.3 | 15.4 | 15.1 | 12.8 | 19.1 |
| Food processing | 10.7 | 11.6 | 7.2 | 7.5 | 8.0 |
| Beverages | 8.4 | 6.3 | 9.1 | 14.4 | 12.2 |
| Tobacco | 79.1 | 68.2 | 51.7 | 47.4 | 100.1 |
| Printing | – | 14.3 | 17.9 | 17.9 | 17.6 |
| Total Manufacturing | 20.6 | 19.9 | 16.4 | 16.1 | 16.4 |

Source: Brasil, *Censo industrial,* 1950, table 1; 1960, table 1; 1970, table 1.
a. Operatives only.

scale industry. The share of industrial workers declared as self-employed has remained fairly stable, but, more interestingly, the share employed in the modern sector has declined. In this same period both the average number of workers per firm and the share of workers in small firms in the modern sector have remained fairly stable. This evidence is consistent with an econometric analysis of internal economies, which found no striking increases in minimum optimal scales of several sectors from 1950 to 1960.[14]

The first inference from the above evidence is that the urbanization of Brazilian industry in the 1940-1970 period cannot be explained by internal economies of scale that have destroyed rural handicrafts. In this respect the Brazilian experience seems to contradict classical location theory and to diverge from the North American and European experience at a comparable level of development.[15]

**Table 26.** Percentage of employees in smallest and largest plants, by sector, 1950 and 1960.

| Sector | % employees in smallest plants | | % employees in largest plants | |
|---|---|---|---|---|
| | 1950[a] | 1960[b] | 1950[c] | 1960[d] |
| Minerals | 36 | 34 | 9 | 16 |
| Metallurgy and machinery | 7 | 7 | 24 | 29 |
| Wood and furniture | 35 | 39 | 3 | 1 |
| Chemical | 12 | 7 | 21 | 23 |
| Textiles | 2 | 3 | 59 | 51 |
| Apparel | 23 | 24 | 5 | 9 |
| Food, beverage, tobacco | 38 | 34 | 13 | 13 |
| Total Manufacturing | 20 | 18 | 25 | 25 |

Source: Brasil, *Censo industrial,* 1950, table 27; Brasil, *Censo industrial,* 1960, table 2e.
a. 0 − 10 operatives.
b. 1 − 9 operatives.
c. 501 + operatives
d. 500 + operatives.

The second inference is that rather than rural handicrafts being supplanted by large-scale urban industry, both handicraft and factory sectors are urbanizing together. An indicator of the urbanization of modern industry is the share of manufacturing employment situated in urban areas as reported in the industrial censuses of 1960 and 1970.[16] About 85 percent of all operatives in the modern industrial sector were urban in both years. The urban share is directly related to state per capita income (r = .31 and .61 in 1960 and 1970, respectively). Furthermore, this share is inversely related to the proportion of state manufacturing employment in the raw materials processing industries (r = − .52 and − .71, respectively). As the latter class of industries is generally regarded as traditional, the inference is that the more modern subsectors are more likely to be urban.

Dualistic models predict that the higher the relative wage in the modern sector, the greater the degree of open or disguised unemployment. To what extent is this the case in the Brazilian context? This hypothesis can be tested crudely by correlating the minimum wage/agricultural salary ratio with urban unemployment rates in four multistate regions of Brazil over five quarters during 1969-1970. The rank-order correlations between this ratio and overt unemployment, involuntary part-time unemployment, and the sum of these two are .43, .55, and .65, respectively.[17] These correlations suggest that the equilibrium unemployment rate in Brazilian cities is indeed related to wages in the modern sector relative to those in the surrounding countryside.

Like most developing countries, Brazil has no employment security system that guarantees the unemployed an income floor. As a result workers unable to obtain jobs in the modern industrial sector engage in self-employment, which is sectorally difficult to classify. Some examples are scavenging for old beer cans and re-fashioning them into lanterns, "guarding" automobiles, or street vending. So long as the minimum wage/rural wage ratio remains stable, any change in employment in the modern industrial sector generates a proportionate change in the self-employed sector. The expansion of the urban handicrafts sector is consequently a corollary of an expansion of the modern sector. In other words, industrial dualism, rather than being destroyed when modern factories replace handicrafts, can under certain circumstances be perpetuated. Furthermore, whereas classical location theory implies that modern and traditional manufacturing are spatially segregated into urban and rural spheres, respectively, the view developed here suggests that modern and traditional industries become increasingly agglomerated in the course of development.

What is the evidence that high wages in the modern sector create an urban handicrafts sector that is essentially a reservoir of disguised unemployment? Fragmentary evidence suggests that such is not the case. Wages in the disguised unemployed sectors are not, in fact, lower than those in corresponding modern sectors. For example, in the state of Espírito Santo the median monthly income of employees in industry, commerce, and services was about forty-five hundred cruzeiros in 1960, but among the self-employed salaries in the three sectors were five thousand, fifty-five hundred, and five thousand cruzeiros, respectively. By 1969 the median monthly wage of all nonagricultural workers was somewhat less than that of the self-employed subgroup, except in the Northeast, where wages in the modern sector relative to wages in agriculture are the highest in the nation.[18]

Adjusting employees' earnings upward about 40 percent to reflect fringe benefits and downward about 10 percent to reflect withholding taxes leaves the employee of the modern sector with 10 to 30 percent higher income than the self-employed. These comparisons, then, do not suggest that self-employment is equivalent to disguised unemployment but rather is an almost competitive alternative to employment in the modern sector.[19]

An alternative interpretation of the urbanization of handicrafts is suggested by the evolution of interfirm linkages in the course of modernization. In the initial stages of industrialization larger enterprises, particularly foreign ones, may be reluctant to produce all the components necessary for their final output; they may prefer to subcontract with smaller firms. The advantages are the foreign firm's equity investment is reduced, smaller firms pay lower wages and may thus produce at lower cost, and fluctuations in demand for the large firm's output are transmitted to the smaller firms as fluctuations in orders rather than in their own levels of employment. Forcing the smaller firms to bear the brunt of business cycles helps maintain good labor relations within the larger firm, especially important if of foreign origin. In response to these uncertainties, smaller firms may locate in the central districts of large metropolitan areas where they can maximize their access to customers as well as to their own suppliers and labor force.[20] As the foreign firms acquire increased familiarity with the Brazilian environment they may be more inclined to increase their equity position by vertical integration with their suppliers, thereby destroying the independent handicraft sector.

Dualistic models of economic development attempt to explain urbanization as a result of shifts in employment out of the agricultural sector into a modern industrial-service sector and a traditional industrial-service sector. The latter two sectors are presumed to be urban and the last to be characterized by small enterprises with low levels of capitalization, facing volatile demand as well as a rapid turnover in its labor force. The modern urban sector owes its rapid growth in employment to high income-elasticity of demand for its products and high rates of internal savings and hence of capital accumulation. Labor absorption in this sector would be somewhat higher were it not for the rapidity of labor-saving technological progress and relatively high wage rates for unskilled labor. Wage rates higher than the opportunity cost of labor serve as a magnet that attracts rural workers in quantities exceeding those demanded by the modern sector. This excess labor force continues to grow absolutely so long as wages in the modern sector remain high relative to rural wages, as has been the case in Brazil. In addition to institutional factors in the urban labor market, high rural fertility helps maintain this wage differential.

Unlike that of the currently advanced nations, Brazil's urban revolution is not simply reducible to a shift of employment out of agriculture into industry. Urbanization has been proceeding more rapidly than the growth of nonagricultural employment and especially more rapidly than growth in industrial employment. In both its rapidity and weak relationship to industrialization Brazilian urbanization is quite different from that in North America at a similar phase of economic development.

About one-third of the growth in the urban population is due to the deruralization of nonagricultural activity. While this phenomenon involves the destruction of rural handicrafts, it does not involve the complete destruction of the small firm or the artisan, which are growing and thriving in the urban areas. This spatial dislocation is due partly to external economies favoring the urban agglomeration of the handicrafts and partly to the traditional sector's role as a training ground and half-way house to the modern industrial sector.

Although the small-scale traditional urban manufacturing sector seems to have expanded at the same pace as the modern sector from 1940 to 1960, there are some indications that the latter has been expanding at the former's expense in recent years. Specifically, there has been a slight increase in the number of employees in the average manufacturing firm. One explanation for this increase may be the decline in the minimum wage that enables the larger firms to share the small traditional firms' low-cost labor and that attracts a smaller pool of disguised unemployed to the cities. A second explanation may be increasing foreign investment, which by vertical integration may result in the absorption of the market share of smaller indigenous firms. A final explanation may be the enormous range of financial incentives, especially loans at negative interest rates, that the government has been offering the larger firms.

# 10

# Hyperurbanization and the Labor Absorption Problem

The rapid growth of urban populations in developing countries has been viewed with alarm by scholars, political leaders, and international development agencies.[1] The image of tropical megalopolises with millions of beggars sleeping on the sidewalks, overburdening the municipal water and sewerage systems, creating fetid slums, congesting the streets, polluting the air, and threatening the civic order is certainly frightening.

The specter of hyperurbanization has several roots, which must be disentangled. First is the labor absorption problem. Second is the management burden placed upon municipal government as a result of the rapid rate of population growth. Third is the alleged waste of capital for sewerage, water supply, and housing that could have been spent on directly productive investment. Fourth is the threat of individual and collective violence that an urban mass that is so unemployed, so poorly served by municipal government, and hence alienated and marginalized raises against the civic order.

## The Labor Absorption Problem

In Latin America during the 1948-1961 period manufacturing employment grew only 2 percent per annum, the urban population grew 5.6 percent, and manufacturing output grew 5.7 percent. The corresponding figures in Brazil were 2.6, 7.0, and 9.2 percent.[2] Urbanization proceeded much more rapidly than the growth of both manufacturing and service employment in Brazil from 1940 to 1970. The slow growth of manufacturing employment and the rapid growth of service employment is seen as inherently problematic by some observers. Manufacturing employment is seen as truly productive and service employment is seen as unproductive, a form of disguised unemployment or, even worse, as parasitic and debilitating to the economy. The notion of service employment being unproductive dates at least as far back as Adam Smith's *The Wealth of Nations:*

> The labour of some of the most respectable orders in society is like that of menial servants, unproductive of any value . . . The sovereign, for example, with all the officers both of justice and war who serve under him, the whole army and navy, are unproductive labourers . . . In the same class must be ranked, some both of the gravest and most important, and some of the most frivolous professions: churchmen, lawyers, physicians, men of letters of all kinds; players, buffoons, musicians, opera-singers, opera-dancers, etc.[3]

Marx's adoption of this classical dichotomy between productive and unproductive labor has been incorporated in socialist income accounting, which excludes the service contribution to the national product. Even in conventional capitalist terminology operatives are called production workers and their white collar superiors are called nonproduction workers.

Within the neoclassical framework the productive-nonproductive worker dichotomy is alleged to be meaningless. In its most simplistic sense, anything people are willing to pay for has a positive marginal value. Galenson, for example, writes,

> If people are engaged in activities which enable them to support themselves, it seems difficult to argue that they are not gainfully employed, no matter what one may think of the nature or intensity of their tasks. Who is to say that seven hours spent watching a dial that controls an automated assembly line is a fuller day's work than ten hours of walking about in a hot sun seeking to sell trinkets to unwilling and elusive customers?[4]

This argument ignores any possible disparity between the private return on labor and the social return. The Smithian courtiers as well as the self-appointed car watchers in developing countries may support themselves, but their roles are largely parasitic and their rewards are based upon ultimate coercion or threat of violence. Second, irrationalities or inefficiencies in a productive system can create multitudes of jobs that are profitable for individuals but not for society (for example, the classes of expediters, intermediaries, and middlemen who thrive on the corruption and arbitrariness of the public bureaucracy).

A second line of defense of the service sector points to its size in advanced countries. In both time-series and cross-sectional comparisons among nations the service sector's share of employment (but not necessarily output) increases with per capita income. Brazil, for example, has a share of service output as high as many advanced countries (much higher than expected), but the share of employment in this sector is considerably lower than expected on the basis of its per capita income.[5]

To infer that "normal" sectoral patterns of output and employment have any normative value is to accept a best of all possible worlds view of economic systems. All economic systems could conceivably have an excess of service employment by some efficiency criterion. As Ofer has shown in his international comparisons, the institutional premises of the economy are of great influence on service employment and socialist countries have much lower shares of service employment and urban population than capitalist countries of similar per capita income.[6]

The most persuasive line of argument minimizes the real difference between service production and goods production. Breaking with the classical tradition, Alfred Marshall argued that it was difficult to distinguish, for example, a fisherman from a teamster on any productive-nonproductive dimension because they both bring a good from a place of low value to one of high value: the fisherman from the bottom of the sea to land, the teamster from the coast to the markets. In the case of manufacturing, Bauer and Yamey point out that functions of assembling raw materials and recycling wastes may be integrated in single establishments in advanced countries but are performed by independent scavengers in developing countries. While those performing these functions in factories would be considered industrial workers, those performing the same functions independently are classified as service workers. Modernization can also have an opposite effect on industrial-service classification of tasks. The earlier analysis of agglomeration economies indicated that at low levels of output a manufacturing enterprise performs a wide range of functions under one roof, all of which are therefore classified as industrial. When output expands and some of these functions are spun off into independent enterprises, many of them, such as accounting and maintenance, are reclassified as services. Finally, Galenson notes that goods production is inevitably tied to such services as repair, which is functionally almost indistinguishable from manufacturing but is statistically classified as a service.[7]

It would be worthwhile to recall some of the reasons why Adam Smith considered service employment unproductive and to relate his arguments to contemporary reality in developing countries. First, his thesis was a polemic against the mercantilist state, whose purpose was to redistribute income from its more productive subjects to the sovereign. The bureaucracy that intervened in the economy through gratuitous and arbitrary regulation not only withdrew potentially productive workers from the labor force but regulation itself reduced the productivity of this labor force. The political elite, the religious estate, and the cultural and intellectual superstructure that mutually support each other are perceived to have a basically parasitic relationship to the productive classes. Presumably, the larger the surplus income generated by the productive sector, the larger the number of retainers and other parasites that could be supported by the ruling class.

Such a classical interpretation of the public sector in developing countries is not inappropriate. In Brazil, as in parts of the United States, the public sector is viewed as an arena for obtaining personal enrichment and providing employment and favors for one's friends. The basically clientelistic nature of politics in Brazil is suggested by the necessity of the president to create independent islands of rationality in order to get anything done, for the existing bureaucracy was not performance oriented in terms of the explicit purposes of government. While the activities of the traditional bureaucracy were privately beneficial to its participants, such activities took place in the context of a basically dysfunctional set of rules from the point of view of economic development.[8]

A second line of reasoning that follows from the classical tradition is that much service output (music, dance, prostitution) was ethically undesirable. As a Scottish professor of moral philosophy, Smith was less willing than his neoclassical successors to accept the legitimacy of given preferences and was more willing to state that some preferences are better than others. This indictment, however, may extend to both goods and services.

The most graphic statement of the industrial labor absorption problem derives from a comparison of the share of national income and of employment generated by the manufacturing sector. In 1960 about 30 percent of the Brazilian gross national product originated in the industrial sector; in 1970 that figure was 33 percent. This percentage is at the same level as such advanced countries as the United States, Italy, Canada, and Argentina and higher than Mexico and Spain, which have considerably higher per capita incomes than Brazil. At the same time, the industrial sector employed about 25 percent of the American, Canadian, and Argentine labor forces but only about 13 percent and 18 percent, respectively, of the Brazilian labor force in 1960 and 1970. The ratio of employment share to output share in the industrial sector in Brazil is the world's lowest.[9]

The sources of such low industrial labor absorption in developing countries have been the focus of considerable theoretical and empirical inquiry. The theoretical arguments are divided into those that place the burden on structural-technological rigidities and those that place the burden on market imperfections.

On the structural side, Baer and Hervé have argued that in developing countries managerial ability is scarcer than any other factor of production. Capital-intensive production processes, which by definition employ few workers and which are often machine paced, conserve this ability. In many modern industries such as steel, furthermore, the only viable production processes are very capital intenstive. While on-the-job training and the breaking down of tasks has permitted some manufacturing sectors to cope somewhat with the skill bottleneck, the rate of return to higher levels of training and high supervisory salaries suggests that these skills are quite scarce indeed.[10]

Another structural argument is that Brazil's import substitution policies encouraged the importation of considerable capital equipment, which was designed for advanced labor-scarce economies and hence absorbed little unskilled labor. As direct foreign investors were attracted, they generally adopted familiar capital equipment from the home country without modification. This pattern was followed by Brazilian manufacturers, who shared the ideological belief that only capital-intensive techniques were

modern. Lacking competition, manufacturers choosing inefficient technologies could pass the costs on to consumers. On the
other side, Leff argues that a majority of capital goods has always
been produced in Brazil and that local engineers have always
adapted their designs to Brazilian labor and capital cost conditions.[11]

A third structural argument is that the excessive concentration
of income in the hands of high-income groups biases the patterns
of demand toward capital-intensive goods. While some luxuries,
like automobiles, are produced with capital-intensive technologies, others like housing and domestic service are not. In the absence of more definitive studies of consumption patterns, few
conclusions can be drawn about this factor.[12]

The market imperfections argument is that Brazilian industrialists rationally choose their factor proportions on the basis of
wage/interest rate ratios that are biased upward. Social legislation provides minimum wages and other fringe benefits at levels
considerably above the opportunity cost of labor. Santos and
Bacha have estimated these social benefits to be about 40 to 60
percent above the minimum wage, which itself is about 100 percent above the wage of unskilled farm workers. Capital, on the
other hand, has been subsidized at negative real interest rates.
These factors are exacerbated by a financial system that favors
large firms. In order to attract labor to their alienating working
conditions, large firms must offer higher wages than small firms
and thus produce at higher capital/labor and capital/output
ratios.[13]

The key to this argument is demonstrating that within the relevant range of wages and interest rates capital and labor are sub-
stitutable. Although controversial, the available cross-sectional
evidence is consistent with a nearly unitary elasticity of substitution between capital and labor in Brazilian manufacturing as a
whole. The substitutability between these factors varies from sector to sector in a pattern unrelated to the degree of foreign ownership or capital intensity of the sectors. Time-series data generate
much lower elasticities of substitution. A conservative conclusion
is that the elasticity of substitution is above 0, and probably above
0.5. The latter figure implies that a 1 percent decrease in the
wage/interest rate ratio generates a 0.5 percent increase in the
labor/capital ratio.[14]

The evidence presented above suggests that the poor labor absorption record of Brazilian industry is partly a result of high labor cost policies pursued by the government and partly a result of the nature of imported technology. While some of these costs, particularly social security expenditures, are not perceived by workers as particularly valuable, the returns to employment in the modern industrial sector are considerably higher than the earnings of unskilled rural labor. Besides reducing industrial labor absorption, this high wage policy has further consequences. As discussed above, migration from rural areas to cities depends upon the relationsip between agricultural wages and expected urban income. The growth of industrial jobs will not solve the problem, since lowering the probability of unemployment for existing urban workers raises the expected urban income, thereby attracting more immigrants from the rural areas.

The social cost of subsidizing capital and taxing labor then has two components: the industrial output lost by not absorbing sufficient industrial labor and the agricultural output lost by the excess migration from the countryside. The latter is equal to the agricultural production foregone by the urban unemployed and as such constitutes a dead loss to the society. Whether a decrease in the industrial wage leads to an increase in the urban population depends upon the elasticity of substitution between capital and labor. On the assumption of an elasticity of less than unity, say of 0.5, a 10 percent drop in the wage leads to a 5 percent increase in employment. In order to maintain an equilibrium between rural and urban opportunities, the probability of obtaining an urban job must rise by about 10 percent. In this case the actual increase in employment (5 percent) is less than that necessary to maintain this equilibrium (10 percent). As a result some of the urban unemployed drift back to the countryside until a tolerable level of unemployment is reached again. Conversely, a high wage/cheap capital policy not only leads to reduced labor absorption and a waste of resources but also to a higher level of urbanization.

## Public Management Burden

That rapid environmental change creates managerial problems is undoubtedly true. In the rural environment, where little is invested in large-scale infrastructure and congestion and pollution are less salient, the pressures created by rapid population growth on public managers may be relatively minor. In an urban environment rapid population growth creates automatic pressures on public managers as the water supply becomes contaminated, garbage piles up on the streets, conflagrations devastate neighborhoods, and traffic comes to a standstill. These pressures would seem proportional to the rate of growth rather than to the level of the urban population. Thus they would be almost as acute in small cities as in large ones and in countries with low shares of urban population as in those with high shares.[15]

An advantage of relatively small city size or urban backwardness is that public managers can learn from the experience of other cities or nations. Thus the mayor of Pôrto Alegre can draw upon the experience of his counterpart in São Paulo in dealing with the problems of a multimillion person agglomeration.

There is no obvious solution to the problem of the primate city that must break the paths in urban management. International experience may provide some lessons, but the unique political, economic, and cultural environment of each country may diminish the value of foreign solutions. The international demonstration effect nevertheless exerts a powerful hold on urban managers in developing countries, who focus attention on the most transferable aspects of that experience (the physical technology). Thus the same tendency to quick technological solutions observed in Amazonia — the importation of mining technology rather than the generation of indigenous agricultural techniques — applies to urban problems, exemplified by the headlong rush of Rio and São Paulo to construct subways. Since the growth of the urban population is tied to that of the total population, the ultimate solution to the problems of urban management may lie in the reduction of birth rates. This may result from the urbanization process itself.

### Waste of Capital

Urban public services are often distributed freely or below marginal cost because of the infeasibility of imposing a price mechanism or because the service is perceived as a merit good. Examples of these are obvious: streets, police protection, and parks. Urban growth is said to increase the demand for these services, leading to either congestion and a decline of quality or an increase in supply to bring the service up to its original level, at some out-of-pocket cost. As long as urban migrants or newborn natives, for that matter, pay less than the marginal costs of these services, either through taxes or user charges, growth creates external diseconomies.

While at first glance this simple model suggests that hyperurbanization would result, there are three implicit but dubious assumptions: the incremental urban population effectively demands and obtains these services, this population does not pay for the services it receives, and these services are in fact a net drain on economic resources.

When one envisions urban growth in developing countries, a flux of impoverished migrants into the teeming shantytowns surrounding the modern city is imagined. To some extent this image is correct. The major increment to the urban population in Latin America in general and Brazil in particular comes from net immigration rather than natural increase, and most growth in the housing stock and urban infrastructure is extensive rather than intensive (that is, building out rather than up). That migrants are not always poorer than the original urban inhabitants is ignored.[16]

The image of extensive urban growth has interesting implications for the hyperurbanization hypothesis. It is crucial to recognize that the effective demand for most municipal services is generally exerted in the neighborhoods where people live, not on the city as a whole. In a direct sense, migrants do not automatically congest the streets, sewers, and schools in the established well-to-do neighborhoods. Whether or not migrant areas are served is an explicit political decision.

Consider the spatial distribution of services in São Paulo, the most developed and one of the fastest growing Brazilian cities. A map of areas served by gas, telephone, garbage collection, postal delivery, and schools shows a complete range of services available only in the central areas, where the wealthy live. In this most advanced city only 84 percent of the households are served by water and refuse collection, 66 percent by paved streets, and 60 percent by sewerage. The availability of these services to the lower income peripheral areas is less in less advanced cities. For example, in Campina Grande, Paraíba, with one hundred thousand inhabitants, only 35 percent of the households are served by uncontaminated water and only 20 percent by sewerage. These services, as well as telephones, electricity, and paved streets, are provided only in the central business district and upper- and middle-class neighborhoods, a typical pattern in developing countries.[17]

Second, the urban population generally pays a good share of the cost of public services extended to them. Obvious examples are bus service, water, electricity, gas, and telephones, which are usually provided by profit-making, though publicly owned, enterprises. For those services where user charges are infeasible, betterment and property taxes are means of capturing some of the publicly created benefit for the state.

Bacha, Araújo, da Mata, and Modenesi have attempted to quantify the indirect urbanization costs of industrial employment creation by computing municipal budget deficits per worker. These costs amount to 20 percent of the minimum salary in Rio de Janeiro and 12 percent in Recife. In addition to these general overhead costs are additional surcharges of 16 percent for education in the former city and 10 percent in the latter.[18]

The most interesting question is to what extent urban public services provided to migrants are a gratuitous drain on resources and to what extent they increase present and future levels of welfare. Kuznets views many services as intermediate or capital goods that are necessary to maintain urban life, which is inherently more complex and requires greater coordination than rural life. Intermediate services provide no direct addition to personal well-being or national income, contrary to conventional accounting practices. In rural areas there is a greater probability than in urban areas that pigs recycle the garbage, that crime is less frequent, that people ride to work on horseback or walk, and that clean water is available in wells. Thus garbage collection, police protection, commuter bus service, and possibly water are intermediate services. Capital services, such as education and public health, add to future worker productivity and cannot be considered a total drain on resources. Finally, consumer services such as public housing, football stadiums, parks, electricity, and gas directly enhance the present welfare of the urban population.[19]

Although not inherently urban, final consumption and investment services are of higher quality in urban areas because incomes are higher there, because they may be cheaper to provide to dense populations, and because competitive urban politics prior to the 1964 revolution was more responsive to the demands of the masses than the politics of rural fiefdoms. The provision of consumption and investment services in the cities is not an argument in favor of the hyperurbanization hypothesis but rather an argument for spreading these services to rural areas as well.

In her simulation model Lorene Yap deals with the demand for urban public services in the context of the total economy. Dividing urban services into investment (education) and noninvestment (final and intermediate services), she finds that the positive effects of rural-urban migration on labor productivity overwhelm the slight urban public service costs. Her simulation suggests that if rural-urban migration were to have stopped completely between 1950 and 1965, the national growth rate would have fallen from 5.9 to 5.2 percent per year and the per capita growth rate from 3.0 to 2.3 percent.[20]

Urban growth increases land costs within the metropolitan confines and the adjacent rural areas. The conversion of agricultural land to urban uses and the growth of the urban population will increase the price of food. These pecuniary consequences of urban growth are not distortions at all since they are internalized by all urban residents.

Truly external diseconomies are pollution, congestion, and crime, which are only partially a function of urban size. For example, the growth of air pollution and traffic congestion in São Paulo can be traced to the number of automobiles, which is largely a result of rising incomes and rapidly falling prices.

In developing countries, urbanization may be related to pollution in another way. Because of the higher cost of living in larger cities, which translates into higher wages, time becomes more valuable there. As a result people may be less likely to go to the expense of collecting and recycling wastes, such as old bottles.

Against these diseconomies must be weighted the scale economies of urbanization, which are the raison d'être of cities in the first place. As suggested by the industrial-urban hypothesis, larger cities have more competitive factor and product markets, leading to greater efficiency. This may help explain why in cities of over two hundred thousand population output per worker increases with city size.[21]

## Political Costs of Urbanization

The marginalized urban masses are alleged to be a pool of dissidents easily fomented into social revolution. The social and political instability argument has been carefully analyzed and evaluated by Joan Nelson. In developing countries in general there is little evidence that migrants are potentially revolutionary or that they achieve little social mobility. Most are apolitical because of their preoccupation with getting ahead economically and most perceive that they have improved their position relative to their rural origins. The Brazilian evidence on marginality suggests that there is little difference between native and migrant urban inhabitants in terms of wage levels and unemployment. Clearly more research is needed, especially upon second generation migrants who perhaps have greater aspirations than their parents and in whom Nelson sees greater revolutionary potential.[22]

In *Political Order in Changing Societies* Samuel Huntington notes that social revolutions are more likely to occur in countries where a large percentage of the population is rural and where land is unequally distributed. He concludes that "Urban migration is, in some measure, a substitute for rural revolution. Hence contrary to common belief, the susceptibility of a country to revolution may vary inversely with its rate of urbanization." Huntington places Brazil into the highly rural-unequal land distribution category, which suggests that urbanization is a stabilizing force.[23]

The hyperurbanization hypothesis cannot be evaluated outside the context of the total resource allocation in an economy. In a theoretical sense the proper urban-rural balance results from solving the following problem: how should resources be allocated among activities and among locations in order to maximize the value of present and future income streams? It should be emphasized that a different distribution of income or institutional framework might give different results. Even holding these factors constant, the optimal spatial distribution may not be unique but may include a wide range of urban-rural balances and size distributions of cities. While in practice such a maximization cannot be performed, one can identify distortions in the economy that seem to encourage over- or even underurbanization. In other words, although the optimal urban-rural balance cannot be specified in advance, forces that lead to departures from that optimum can be identified.

Under existing conditions, Lorene Yap's simulation of the Brazilian economy suggests that if rural-urban migration were somehow reduced, for example by establishing a Soviet-type internal passport system, aggregate growth would decline. In testing for hyperurbanization, however, one is not necessarily bound by existing institutions. A reduction in social security charges against employers is likely to increase modern sector labor absorption; and because the wage remains the same, a proportional expansion in traditional sector employment and urban population follows. A reduction in the wage received toward the social opportunity cost of labor is also likely to increase modern sector labor absorption, but it will reduce the size of the traditional sector as well as the urban population.

The effects of changes in municipal finance policy are more complex. The construction of subsidized high-quality housing for the poor increases their real income and hence may encourage urbanization. On the other hand, to the extent that construction is associated with slum clearance, or the destruction of low-cost housing, living costs for large numbers of poor increase and real income falls. Increasing taxes to reflect the marginal cost of urbanization or providing schooling and health care to the rural population at levels usually enjoyed by the urban affluent is likely to make rural-urban migration less attractive.

Finally, institutional changes that increase the price of rural commodities, such as more favorable exchange rates for non-coffee exports, would increase rural income and reduce the rate of rural-urban migration whether or not there were disguised unemployment. Measures to redistribute income to unskilled rural workers, such as land reform or massive colonization of the frontier, would have a similar effect. To the extent that land reform led to a shift from crops marketed domestically to subsistence crops, agricultural prices would rise, reducing urbanization further. On the other hand, institutional changes that raised rural productivity, such as greater research and development, improved extension services and credit to smallholders, and greater subsidies to them for fertilizers and machinery, would reduce agricultural prices in the face of inelastic domestic demand for these commodities. Consequently, urbanization would increase.

Although hyperurbanization is the alleged scourge of the developing nations, little has been suggested in terms of a remedy. While Brazilian rhetoric has eulogized the frontier as a labor safety valve, actual agricultural policy has done little to encourage the formation of a rural middle class. Frontier settlement, moreover, is a potential luxury for the few land-rich countries of the world and thus little comfort to nations of the Caribbean, the Middle East, or South Asia.

# 11

# Toward a National Urban Growth Policy

A national urban growth policy connotes conscious and systematic efforts to reduce misallocations of resources that result in an improper urban-rural balance, a maldistribution of urban population within the system of cities, or disorderly metropolitan land use. In discussing urban growth policy, it is necessary to distinguish problems that are urban per se from those that happen to be played out in the urban arena or are merely more salient in big cities. The latter set of problems (for example, poverty, unemployment, and slums) is essentially aspatial and reducible to pathologies of the national socioeconomic system. Nevertheless, national urban policy, which is inherently a locational policy, has often been justified as a means of solving problems that are merely salient in the urban arena. This approach has been followed in the United States, whose potpourri Housing and Urban Development Act of 1970 could hardly be called a national urban growth policy. In contrast, British and French national urban growth policies utilize fiscal and financial incentives as well as regulation to channel investment toward peripheral cities and towns and away from the national primate cities, which are allegedly choking with congestion and pollution.[1]

Urban problems per se had little salience for Brazilian policymakers until the 1960s. Not that politicians and technocrats were unaware of the economy's poor record of industrial labor absorption, putrid slums, and other symptoms of urban marginality. Rather than conceptualizing these problems in the spatial terms that an urban growth policy implies, they viewed these problems as essentially sectoral in nature. Sectoral thinking tended to dominate all levels of planning. Inadequate labor absorption and unemployment were macroeconomic problems that could be solved by more rapid industrialization, and poor housing was the result of malfunctioning in the capital market. Regional planning basically involved scaling down national sectoral plans to the level of the state or multistate grouping, which was treated simply as a small country. Although inherently spatial in nature, urban planning was a branch of urban design, completely unrelated to the decisions made at the commanding heights of the Brazilian economy.

The urban dimension of economic development acquired greater salience in the 1960s. The urban housing problem was the first to be recognized. Later, spatial distortions — hyperurbanization, hyperconcentration in a few great metropolitan areas, and irrationalities in metropolitan land use — were acknowledged, although practically nothing has been done to deal with them. In the past decade the National Housing Bank (BNH) has become the institutional focus of national urban growth policy. Second only to the Bank of Brazil in assets by 1970, BNH has come to take a major responsibility for financing housing, urban water supply and sewerage, and urban renewal.

## Salience and Diagnosis

Urban problems were completely ignored in the national development plans that evolved out of joint U.S.-Brazilian missions charged with analyzing the economy in the 1940s. Kubitschek's Target Plan in the late 1950s was totally sectoral in orientation, except for the program to construct Brasília. This last effort hardly constituted an urban growth policy in the sense defined here but was rather an instrument of regional policy aimed at facilitating frontier settlement and the integration of the Brazilian archipelago. With the expiration of Kubitschek's mandate in 1961 national planning was effectively suspended until 1964 because of the political turmoil that climaxed with the April revolution.[2]

Despite the absence of any coherent policy direction, the 1961-1964 period was important in creating the foundations for a national urban policy. The rapid growth of the economy during the Target Plan years, 1956 to 1961, had come to an end with the easy possibilities for import substitution. The Three-Year Plan formulated for the last years of the Goulart presidency, 1963 to 1965, undertook an extensive analysis of the economy to determine the causes of stagnation and to identify remedies. Largely macroeconomic and structuralist in diagnosis, the plan singled out the constricted demand associated with a highly unequal income distribution as a major cause of stagnation.

Despite the ideological polarity of their respective goals, the Economic Action Program of the new military government almost completely adopted the analysis of the Three-Year Plan. The program focused on a short-run objective of reducing inflation, which had galloped at roughly 70 percent per annum since the Kubitschek administration. In order to dampen the recessionary effects of its policies, the program selected housing as a key labor-intensive sector whose expansion would provide jobs for those thrown out of work in other sectors of the economy. In the long run the stimulation of broad-based housing demand would permit the economy to resume its momentum. Thus for the first time an urban-oriented welfare program supplemented basic industries as a source of dynamism, and a previously neglected problem acquired the status of a privileged one. The new salience of the housing problem led to the creation of an elaborate housing finance system.

Promulgated at the departure of President Castello Branco in 1967, the Ten-Year Plan for Economic and Social Development outlined the long-term strategy of the military regime. In addition to an extensive analysis of the housing deficit, this plan contained the first official analysis of urban problems per se, which were identified as hyperurbanization, hyperconcentration of population in the great metropolises, and lack of growth poles to stimulate economic development on the periphery.

As a working document the Ten-Year Plan was soon supplanted by the Strategic Development Program of the new president, Costa e Silva. In addition to emphasizing the problems of housing and the disorganized urban network, the program introduced two new urban problems: disorderly urban land use and excessive densities in central cities. This is the first mention of intrametropolitan land use as a national concern in the formulation of an economic development strategy. Finally, the problem of comprehensive planning at the local level was raised.

The Targets and Bases for Government Action of the Médici administration (1970-1973) reiterated housing as a major sectoral problem and elaborated on the problem of integrating national sectoral planning and urban planning. The disorganized urban network was not mentioned in the plan, but Médici's administration laid the groundwork for the creation of metropolitan planning authorities in the nine largest cities.

It is clear from the analysis of these plans of the past decade that housing has dominated all consideration of urban problems. Perhaps, as in much of the world, housing is the most visible symptom of income inequality and hence the most likely target of redistributive policy. Even more importantly, the housing sector has been viewed as a lever for maintaining aggregate demand and especially employment in an economy viewed as suffering from demand constraints.

The pile up of garbage, the congestion of the streets, the fouling of the air, and the increase in crime associated with urbanization are almost automatically perceived by public officials charged with urban management. Given the rapidity of urban growth during the 1940s and especially the 1950s, it may seem somewhat surprising that urban problems did not become salient to national planners until the 1960s. One explanation is that policymakers were preoccupied with initiating the take-off toward economic development, somewhat hesitatingly until the 1950s but enthusiastically thereafter. Economic development meant industrialization, which was almost automatically urban in locus; urbanization therefore became an indicator of modernization. Under the populist regimes that intermittently dominated Brazil until 1964, slum dwellers had considerable voting strength. Profoundly aware of the improvement that migration from the countryside brought to their lives, these slum dwellers would hardly ask the various demagogues who courted their votes that fewer of their cousins be permitted to join them in the cities or that their homemade housing be replaced by "standard" housing, both more expensive and inconveniently located. If urban life was becoming unmanageable, it was probably mostly for the mayors and the upper-middle class, who recalled the days of cleaner air, more open space, less crime, and less traffic. This is not to say that the poor would not benefit from rational land-use policies, only that such issues would not seem so automatically salient to them as to other members of the urban community.[3] It is clear that Brazilian policymakers have been more fastidious in identifying the urbanization diseconomies associated with the poor, such as ugly, crime-ridden slums, than those caused by the rich, such as pollution and congestion from private automobiles.[4]

The diagnosis of Brazilian hyperurbanization basically follows the structuralist approach. Land pressure in the rural areas drives the marginal productivity of labor down toward zero so that workers flee to the cities. The modern industrial sector, however, is inherently incapable of absorbing labor as fast as the urban population grows because of technological rigidities (the productivity of labor at the extensive margin is zero in industry). The consequence of these conditions is premature tertiarization; however, the marginal product of labor in services and commerce is also close to zero.[5]

This diagnosis leads to no obvious remedy. If the marginal productivity of labor is practically zero in agriculture, industry, and services, there is no way to reallocate labor among sectors or between city and countryside to increase output. A partial solution envisioned by the Left is land reform that permits land unutilized by latifundia to be cultivated. A partial solution envisioned by the Brazilian government is frontier settlement, as discussed earlier. Since in fact neither land reform nor colonization have been given sufficient resources to absorb much labor, urban growth policy in Brazil consists of coping with the growing population within the urban context.

The strategy of coping comprises two major activities: improving the ability of municipalities and metropolitan areas to plan, finance, and administer and improving the physical infrastructure of urban areas, notably the housing stock. The public administration problem is viewed as a result of inadequate technical and managerial capacity on the part of public officials; insufficient financial resources for municipal government; and lack of institutions for horizontal coordination among local governments within metropolitan areas and vertical coordination between national, regional, state, and local planners.

The problems of the physical plant of cities were seen as institutional in origin. The Program of Economic Action of the new military government in 1964 identified the populist follies of President Vargas in the 1940s as the major cause of the housing deficit. His Tenant's Law provided renters with nearly complete protection against expulsion while the general rent freeze in the face of galloping inflation meant that landlords had little incentive to maintain their apartments and less to invest in new construction. The Usury Laws, which limited nominal interest to rates considerably lower than inflation, were an enormous disincentive for construction loans. While wealthy individuals might transfer some of their assets into housing as a hedge against inflation, even middle-income individuals with little collateral were hard pressed to obtain loans. The housing problem, then, was not seen as a consequence of poverty but as a consequence of untoward government intervention in the housing and capital markets. The remedy to the problem was to create a new financial mechanism that would channel existing savings to potential homeowners, a mechanism that would protect the lender from the erosion of his equity by inflation and that would not overburden the borrower with heavy amortization payments. With the proper mechanism, the program and its successors were to create slumless Brazilian cities by 1980.

The problems of urban infrastructure — water, sewerage, public transportation, telephones, and electricity — were also seen as a result of decades of populist folly. In order to appeal to the lower-income groups, demagogues put a ceiling on utility rates that, in the face of inflation, wiped out the ability and incentive of private purveyors of these services to expand capacity. Municipal utility companies were similarly stymied by the lack of adequate revenue. In most cases rate ceilings on utilities provided only illusory benefits to the poor as a class. Since only higher-income neighborhoods were usually served by these utilities and deficits were met by taxing the whole population, including the poor, this system in effect subsidized the rich plus a few privileged poor, who lent legitimacy to the process. Although the consequences would appear regressive, the only long-run solution to adequate supply of utilities was seen as letting rates rise to the point where expansion in capacity would be self-financing.

### Institutional Innovations

The diagnosis of hyperurbanization, hyperconcentration, and the paucity of peripheral growth poles has led to few concrete institutional innovations or programs. Rather, the federal government has created institutions for improving urban public administration and providing housing and urban infrastructure.

Since 1964 the Brazilian federal system has evolved in the di-

rection of increasingly centralized control and decentralized execution. Rather than being autonomous centers of power, states
and municipalities have become administrative arms of the
national government with appointed executives.[6] Centralized
control has taken the form of somewhat tighter administrative
linkages between levels of government, greater federal technical
assistance to municipalities, and greater dependence of lower
levels of government upon federal grants-in-aid.

The division of power between state and local governments in
Brazil is quite different from that in the United States, although
interstate differences in this division exist in both federations.
Since 1907 Brazilian states have expended about four times as
much as all municipalities, while in the United States the multiple is closer to one and one-half now and was much lower in the
past. When state and local expenditures are combined, it is clear
that the state plays a major role in the provision of what are considered municipal services in the United States. Although the
proportions vary somewhat from year to year, Brazilian states
finance roughly 90 percent of primary and secondary education,
public health, police protection, and welfare and over 60 percent
of miscellaneous urban services (sanitation, street maintainance,
and utilities). In the late 1960s, after the reforms considered below, the states' share of urban services dropped to about one-
third.[7]

In the state capitals over 40 percent of the municipal budget
goes to urban services: 10 percent each to education and public
safety, about 5 percent each to health and transportation, the
remainder to unallocated general administration and debt service.

In 1967 Brazil underwent a major fiscal reform whose ostensible purpose was to integrate and rationalize the division of taxing
powers among the three levels of government under federal control. Greater use was to be made of taxes that were easy to administer, with greater revenue-producing elasticities, and that imposed minimal distortions on economic activity. Only one level of
government was traditionally permitted to levy a particular type
of tax; the federal government reserved for itself the income and
sales taxes, leaving the value-added tax to the states and urban
property taxes to the municipalities. The reform resulted in

larger tax collections by the federal government and less by municipalities.

To redress the resulting revenue imbalance within the federal system, the method of revenue sharing was reformed. State and municipal participation funds were created, for each of which 10 percent of federal tax collections from incomes and industrial sales was earmarked. The distribution of both funds discriminated against wealthier jurisdictions. The municipal participation fund excluded the state capitals outright, although they were perceived to be the locus of the most serious urban problems. Revenues from the municipal participation fund were supposed to be devoted to broad functional areas in certain proportions (for example, 30 percent for education). In addition, states and municipalities continued to receive dedicated revenues from special taxes. Most importantly, the municipalities received 12 percent of the tax on petroleum products to be devoted to transportation.[8]

Contrary to pressures for municipal annexation in the United States, there has been a strong tendency for fragmentation of municipalities in Brazil. This tendency was accelerated by the provision in the 1946 constitution that federal revenues be shared equally by municipalities without regard to area, population, fiscal effort, or need. While fragmentation may pose no problem in rural areas, it has weakened the political unity of several metropolitan areas.

Nevertheless the problem of horizontal coordination in metropolitan areas is much less serious in Brazil than in the United States. The Brazilian municipality or *municipio* is the lowest level of government and on the average spans half the area of a North American county. Urban settlements within the municipio have no autonomous political expression and are at most administrative seats. Only the nine largest metropolitan areas include more than one municipio and the largest, São Paulo, includes merely thirty-six. In contrast, metropolitan Chicago, with a similar population, comprises eleven hundred local governments. Furthermore, a much higher proportion of the metropolitan populations lives in the Brazilian central municipio than in the North American central city.[9]

After considerable analysis by the Brazilian Institute of Geography and Statistics, the federal government officially delimited nine metropolitan areas in 1973. In each metropolitan area was to be established a coordinating council of municipal, state, and federal governments to consider functions of metropolitan interest. These functions were defined as comprehensive planning, sanitation, land use, transportation, gas, water supply, and pollution. The distinctions among comprehensive planning-land use and transportation or among sanitation and pollution are not clear and the metropolitan interest in gas distribution is not obvious. Although it is too early to judge the eventual powers and role of these councils, several problems are apparent. Since each municipio has one representative on the council, the largest municipios may find little gain in cooperating with the council. Second, as a consultive body with no powers of arbitration and no fiscal base, the metropolitan council may have no real impact on the functions of concern.[10]

Vertical coordination among different levels of government is somewhat further developed. Largely through their relatively ample financial resources SPVEA-SUDAM and SUDENE were able to encourage investment in sewerage, water supplies, and electrification in selected urban areas. Somewhat less directly the earmarked revenue funds and categorical revenue-sharing funds encourage localities to spend resources in sectors of greatest national priority (such as transportation).

In 1963 the Extraordinary Ministry for the Coordination of Regional Organizations (renamed Ministry of Interior in 1967) was established to coordinate national, regional, state, and eventually local planning efforts. In 1964 the National Housing Bank (BNH) and the Federal Service for Housing and Urbanism (SERFHAU), the first national agencies solely devoted to urban-oriented problems, were created within the new ministry. The bank was aimed at financing the housing sector and urban infrastructure; SERFHAU was aimed at providing technical assistance to local governments. It is noteworthy that efforts to coordinate planning vertically have been largely undertaken within the Ministry of Interior, which plays little role in formulating or implementing national sectoral plans. National plans are ostensibly formulated by the Ministry of Planning and General Coordination. Although planning was the most powerful ministry in the early years of the military regime, the Ministry of Finance has actually played the major role in determining public resource allocations in recent years.

Another important administrative innovation has been the establishment of fiscally autonomous public utilities. Replacing many of the private utility companies were public and mixed public-private corporations that financed their operations out of user fees and earmarked property tax revenues. The depoliticization of Brazil following the 1964 revolution removed any populist obstacles to raising these fees and taxes to a level sufficient to finance expansion of capacity. In fact, depoliticization was a more important precondition to financing the expansion of urban utilities through user fees than was the administrative change; however, nationalization of the foreign utilities companies may have made the increase in fees more palatable.

A major problem in municipal administration, particularly in rural areas and in small urban centers, was seen as a lack of managerial skills among line agency bureaucrats. To increase that capacity, the Brazilian Institute of Municipal Administration (IBAM) was established in 1953. IBAM has offered lectures, correspondence courses, and conferences for public officials upon law, administration, budgeting; technical assistance in administrative reform; research on municipal finance and administration; and the publication of a bimonthly journal and a monthly newsletter. Included in the journal is a column in which municipal officials receive answers to problems they are facing from an administrative "Dear Abby." The need for these services is indicated by the fact that the average participant in IBAM courses has only completed junior high school.[11]

A second problem was seen as lack of staff competence in drawing up comprehensive local plans that would be integrated into the national planning system. The solution to this problem goes deeper than simply publishing journals or offering training courses because of the weakness of professional city planning in Brazil. Trained as *urbanistas* or urban designers, Brazilian city planners have tended to draw aesthetically-oriented master plans that were ill suited to dealing with pollution, congestion, and low-cost housing problems of big cities. Like their architecturally-trained counterparts in the United States a generation earlier, *urbanistas* have had little impact on the major investment and regulatory decisions that have shaped urban land use. Lacking a framework for choice that took the salient economic goals into account, *urbanistas* could hardly make a strong case for good urban design. Until quite recently economists have not been trained in spatial analysis, as their major concerns have been macroeconomic issues of inflation, employment, and growth. Thus professionals conversant with the prestigious vocabulary of economics were ill equipped to analyze the problems of urban land use, transportation, or pollution. Few *urbanistas* or economists were able to relate the land-use problems of the cities to national growth despite the fact that urban investments absorbed a substantial share of national savings. For example, the Rio-Niteroi bridge is estimated to cost about twice as much as the Transamazon highway and the São Paulo subway four times as much as that bridge.[12]

Soon after the 1964 revolution the National Housing Bank (BNH) was established with the ostensible long-run purpose of reducing the housing shortage and as a byproduct to provide jobs for the unskilled. BNH was to mobilize funds for the housing market on both the supply and demand sides. Like the Federal Home Loan Bank in the United States, BNH lends to other financial intermediaries rather than directly to consumers of housing. To disburse these funds, state and local housing corporations (COHABs) were established to serve the low-income market, voluntary cooperatives to serve the middle-income market, and savings and loan associations to serve the upper-income market. On the housing supply side, BNH offers long-term and working capital to producers and distributors of building materials as well as credit to contractors for the purchase of these materials.[13]

The initial funding of BNH included a treasury loan of $910,000 plus an earmarking of 1 percent of all payrolls and 4 percent of all rents for a period of twenty years. Although BNH was also authorized to sell bonds, relatively few funds were raised this way. Its assets grew slowly until 1966, when the BNH became the repository of the new Guarantee Fund Pro Tempore Laboris (FGTS). This latest innovation epitomizes the Brazilian penchant for solving two unrelated problems at a single blow. An aspect of the Vargas social legislation was the guarantee of tenure to workers after ten years of service. Although designed to provide security to the worker, it merely hastened his firing as the decade approached. To the mutual benefit of workers and their employ-ers, tenure was replaced by a blocked indemnity fund equivalent to 8 percent of the annual salary deposited in the worker's name. As a result of the influx of these funds, BNH became the nation's second largest bank with assets of 1 billion dollars and deposits of .9 billion dollars in 1969. By 1973 the assets of BNH reached 3 bil-lion dollars, about 8 percent of the Gross National Product.

In order to attract private savings to capital markets without revoking the Usury Law, all financial transactions were subjected to "monetary correction." Approximately equal to the rate of in-flation, the monetary correction of interest on savings deposits, bonds, commercial paper, letters of credit, and other financial instruments meant that investors would be guaranteed a real rate of interest similar to the quoted nominal rate. For example, the compulsory savings of workers through FGTS received an annual rate of interest of 3 percent plus monetary correction. The instru-ment of monetary correction facilitated the creation of new insti-tutions for mobilizing private savings for the housing sector — private savings and loan associations and real estate credit socie-ties. The latter has utilized the newly created real estate letter of credit, also subject to monetary correction, to develop a second-ary mortgage market.

The complete housing finance system is self-sustaining, al-though the forced savings of the workers through FGTS is a form of subsidy. Within the system, however, there is considerable cross-subsidization, with low-income individuals paying as little as 1 percent interest per annum and high-income individuals paying as much as 10 percent, plus monetary correction.

BNH initially found that many of its housing developments located in peripheral areas were without adequate sewerage or water supply. In 1969 BNH expanded its functions to the plan-ning and financing of water and sanitary sewerage systems. Fully 60 percent of capital costs were lent to states and municipalities for this purpose. Interest rates ranged from 4 to 8 percent and varied directly with state per capita income, thereby harmonizing BNH with agencies devoted to reducing regional disparities.

In the 1970s BNH has become more directly interested in metropolitan land-use planning. Although the existence of its programs was used to justify slum clearance, BNH concentrated on construction, leaving the destruction of what the elite viewed as subhuman habitations to state and local agencies. BNH gradually became aware that many of its projects on the metropolitan periphery leapfrogged vacant land, thereby increasing the costs of providing infrastructure. Consequently, BNH proposed formulating a plan for the use of vacant land in metropolitan areas, although little was accomplished in this regard. In 1973 BNH announced a program of urban renewal of decaying sections of metropolitan areas that involved its direct participation in the acquisition, clearance, and reconstruction of large tracts. As of 1975 this program had not been implemented.

### Implementation and Results

The fiscal reform of 1967 had no perceivable impact on the municipal share of total public expenditures, which has hardly deviated from 9 percent since 1907. An obvious result of the reform was a rapid increase in the share of municipal revenues received from state and federal governments: rising from 35 percent in 1965 to 70 percent in 1970. Had the grants-in-aid statutorily due the municipalities been transferred on schedule, the municipal share of total public expenditures would have risen significantly.[14]

The implementation of programs to improve managerial and technical competence of local officials is harder to fathom. Although large numbers of municipalities availed themselves of the services of IBAM, it is not clear whether this contact has resulted in better municipal management. Federal directives for municipal program budgeting and comprehensive planning have given rise to the private planning firm. An effective device for rationing scarce planning talent, these firms generally combine the skills of engineers, economists, sociologists, as well as traditional *urbanistas*. Whether these plans have been implemented has not been systematically assessed.

Mandated to provide housing for the poorest urban classes, BNH has encountered a contradiction between this goal and its constraint to remain self-financing. The bank found that few of the poorest elements were willing or able to afford standard quality housing, even when amortization payments were spaced out to reduce monthly payments to only 20 percent of income. Consequently, BNH has shifted its loan portfolio from the low-income market to the middle- and upper-income markets. For example, in 1964 and 1965, 90 percent of the units and 80 percent of the loans were devoted to low-income housing through the various COHABs. In 1967 the share of units and loans destined for this market fell to 40 and 23 percent, respectively. By 1974, after ten years of its operation, only 20 percent of the units financed by BNH were in the low-income market.[15]

These categorical data understate the degree to which BNH has been transformed into the apex of a middle-income housing finance system. A family's eligibility for the various housing programs was determined by the multiple of its income to the official minimum salary. The Strategic Program (1968-1970) set 1.15 times the minimum salary, which is roughly $40 per month, as the ceiling for families eligible for low-income housing and 4.3 times the minimum salary as the ceiling for those eligible for the middle-income market. The Targets and Bases (1970-1973) increased the size of the "privileged" underclass by raising the low-income market ceiling to 1.6 times the minimum salary and that for the middle-income market to 5.2 times the minimum salary. In 1972 BNH found it necessary to reaffirm its commitment to low-cost housing with the promulgation of the National Plan for Popular Housing (PLANHAP). This plan offered loans to families earning 1 to 3 minimum salaries at an interest rate of 1 to 3 percent for periods of up to twenty-five years so that mortgage payments need not exceed 20 percent of income. In other words, this plan excludes from the housing finance system the 30 percent of Brazilian families whose incomes are below the minimum salary.[16]

It is exceedingly difficult to determine whether administrative reform and technical assistance have improved the capabilities of Brazilian urban management and no attempt will be made to do so here. It is clear, however, that the fiscal reforms have failed to increase the revenue base of the municipalities, largely because of delays in the transfer of funds.

The results of policies aimed at improving infrastructure and housing are only slightly easier to assess. The length of water and sewerage mains has been increasing rapidly since 1940, when the first comprehensive data were published. The mileage of water mains increased by about one-third in the 1950s and by one-half in the 1960s, a slight acceleration accompanying the creation of municipal utility corporations and BNH water supply funds. The rate of growth of sewerage, however, was no faster in the 1960s than in the 1950s. The improvement in water supply facilities is unmistakable: while one home in six had running water in 1950 and one in five had it in 1960, fully one home in three had running water by 1970. In the urban areas the share of homes with running water increased from 42 percent to 55 percent in the 1960s. Progress in sewerage facilities is less obvious, since the necessity for public sewerage depends upon city size and soil percolation among other factors. It is clear that in the 1960s the pace of sewer construction only kept pace with the growth of the urban population and the percentage of houses connected to the lines remained steady at about 30 percent.[17]

When cities are categorized by size, patterns of water supply and sewerage belie the notion that larger cities are suffering a disproportionate breakdown of public services. By 1967 about three-quarters of homes in cities with more than fifty thousand inhabitants were served by running water; only one-half were so served in cities of ten to twenty thousand inhabitants; only one-third in towns of two to ten thousand. While two-fifths of the homes were served by sewer mains in the largest cities, only one-fifth were served in cities of ten to twenty thousand.[18]

The results of the housing policies focusing on BNH are mixed. Without question the housing finance system has channeled new funds into the housing sector, but its policies are clearly a failure in terms of its stated goals of reducing the housing deficit and improving the housing conditions of the poor.

In the Ten-Year Plan the housing deficit created by the growth of the urban population alone was estimated at three hundred fifty thousand to four hundred thousand units per year. While BNH has been financing units at an accelerating rate, in no year has the number of units approached its target and by 1973 BNH had financed only one million dwellings. In the ten years of the plan's existence the total Brazilian housing stock grew by about five million units. In other words, most of the increase in the nation's housing stock was unrelated to the activities of the housing finance system.[19]

Second, the inability of BNH to finance more housing is not explicable by the lack of funds but by lack of demand for these funds on the part of low-income Brazilians, even though monthly payments cannot exceed 20 percent of a family's income. Consumer surveys indicate that the poor are reluctant to spend as much as 20 percent of their income on housing, conserving their meager resources for such essentials as food, clothing, medical care, and education. Furthermore, an analysis of a Rio COHAB project shows that hidden costs for taxes and condominium fees can amount to an additional 10 percent of a minimum salary and transportation per wage earner, up to 30 percent of a minimum salary. While the average family in the COHAB project they studied earned three times the minimum salary, the ceiling for low-income housing, they spent roughly 30 percent of their incomes on housing, taxes, condominium fees, and utilities alone. In contrast, the average family at the same income level but living in unsubsidized housing spent only 12 percent on these items. As a result, the poorest residents of COHAB projects tend to sell out to those somewhat better off and move to new squatter settlements.[20]

Third, and related to the above, the existence of the low-income housing program serves to rationalize slum clearance projects over the vigorous opposition of the residents. With the depoliticization of the slum population, "substandard" housing has been practically eliminated from the city of Rio de Janeiro. Except for one deeply entrenched and rapidly self-improving neighborhood, squatments that were sullying the pilot plan area of Brasília have been removed. Slum clearance projects in other cities are proceeding at a slower pace, possibly because the slums are located in peripheral areas or in estuaries not desired for other purposes. Not only did the slum clearance in Rio alone destroy about a hundred million dollars worth of property, the resulting relocation removed the residents from employment, educational, health care, and recreational opportunities. As in Rio, the expulsion of Brasília's squatters to satellite cities fifteen to fifty kilometers from the capital meant their spending up to 40 percent of a minimum salary on bus fare. Although one model satellite, Taguatinga, was constructed, most of the others are as squalid as traditional squatments.[21]

National urban growth policy, which by now has acquired a worldwide legitimacy, is, strictly interpreted, a conscious and systematic effort to correct distortions in the urban-rural balance, the size or spatial distribution of cities, or in metropolitan land use. Like the United States, Brazil has no conscious policy in this regard; however, it has adopted the rhetoric of urban growth policy.

As in the United States, housing has been the major instrument of urban growth policy. After a decade of operation, it would seem that the housing finance system dominated by the National Housing Bank has become an instrument for improving the welfare of the middle classes at the expense of the poor. Not that the system has neglected the poor; on the contrary, it has destroyed much of their housing on the promise of providing low-cost standard quality housing in its place and has appropriated their forced savings. Nor has the system been stymied for lack of funds, for the National Housing Bank is now the second largest in the country. Instead, there is clearly an overcommitment of funds to the National Housing Bank, for it is now investing its surplus funds in financing the national debt.

It is clear that BNH is incapable of producing housing more cheaply than squatters who value their time at levels way below the salaries and fringe benefits official housing developers must pay and who have no administrative overhead. This is not surprising because housing construction projects generally do not reap significant economies of scale that offset their higher labor and managerial costs. A finance system suited to the needs of the poor might provide working capital for the purchase of materials for self-help housing.

In a subtle manner, the policies of BNH may be having a profound impact on the urban-rural balance. As suggested in previous chapters, migration flows depend upon the relationship between rural income and expected urban income. If wages in the modern urban sector declined or urban unemployment increased, it was argued, migration would decline. An instrument for reducing migration is increasing the urban cost of living and thus reducing the real urban minimum wage. Through slum clearance BNH is decreasing the real income of the poor by forcing them to pay higher time and money costs for transportation and higher prices for standard housing. Although every migrant into the pool of urban marginality causes a slight decline in agricultural output, raising the urban cost of living gratuitously is a cruel mechanism for eliminating the social costs of disguised unemployment.

It is unlikely that the correction of sectoral distortions in the Brazilian economy would cause much change in the urban-rural balance. Rather the solution lies in reducing the private costs in the modern sector (say by subsidizing fringe benefits), which would increase labor absorption with no change in the urban share of the population. The implicit urban growth strategy of the housing finance system is pursuing quite the contrary goal.

# 12

# Conclusion

The results of this study of spatial dimensions of Brazilian economic development are now summarized and two broad issues are discussed. First, what new light has the analysis of its spatial dimensions cast upon Brazilian economic development? Second, what new light has Brazilian economic development cast upon the orthodox spatial analysis?

To answer these questions, a wide range of spatial phenomena have been investigated: frontier settlement; agricultural modernization; interregional integration; interregional per capita income disparities; and the spatial concentration of industry, urbanization, and urban rivalry. In addition, policy making and planning aimed at controlling these spatial processes have also been analyzed. Issues raised include factors that brought particular spatial problems to the attention of policymakers, the conceptual diagnosis of these problems, institutional innovations, and implementation. Successes and failures have been assessed in terms of the adequacy of conceptualization, of administrative structure, and of political support for the chosen solution.

## New Perspectives on Brazilian Economic Development

The moving frontier has been the major source of Brazilian agricultural growth in the last century or more. Not only is Brazil the major continental nation currently undergoing frontier settlement, it is the only one in the world where there are ample prospects for future expansion.

Brazilian frontier settlement has been explained by the sheer call of open space, facilitated by penetration roads, or by the exhaustion of older lands as a result of irrational, traditional farming techniques. As exemplified by the westward march of coffee from the lowlands around Rio to the Paraná plateau, this frontier has been called hollow because devastation and depopulation were left in its wake.

This study has attempted to demystify the process of Brazilian frontier settlement. While some pioneers have been lured by adventure, most settlers have sought to exploit commercial farming opportunities that became available after the mid-nineteenth century. Which frontiers are settled and at what pace are determined by availability of natural resources suitable for the production of a marketable staple, the efficiency of the marketing system, and a supply of labor.

Frontier expansion until the Depression was propelled by coffee exports, but contemporary expansion is largely conditioned by the demands of the domestic market for food and raw materials resulting from industrialization-urbanization in São Paulo. Rather than being a result of soil exhaustion and exemplar of the hollow frontier, the disappearance of coffee from the environs of metropolitan São Paulo is explicable by its being outbid for land by perishables and bulky foodstuffs. The hinterland of south central Brazil has become the agricultural supply area for the industrial cities and has become differentiated into rings of perishables, export crops, and high-value nonperishables production.

Since the 1930s the savannas of the Central West have attracted the greatest attention from policymakers as an area of planned frontier settlement. With the avowed purpose of stimulating the development of this region, two capitals (Goiânia and Brasília) were created as spearheads and the Belém-Brasília Highway as a bridge in the Brazilian archipelago. In the decade following the establishment of Brasília and the highway the Central West exhibited the most rapid growth of any region in the nation. This experience is an example of the hiding hand that has made policy appear successful when in fact positive results would have ensued in the absence of this policy. This growth was in fact a continuation of trends of the previous decades. The fundamental cause lies in the improvements of highway linkages to São Paulo and the ejection of high-value foodstuffs, such as rice and beef, from that state. Rather than serving as an autonomous influence on rural development, Goiânia owes its own growth to performing marketing and service functions for the rural areas. Despite its pretensions, Brasília remains an enclave, only weakly linked to the surrounding savanna and importing most of its manufactures and much of its food from elsewhere.

The concept of the frontier as a labor safety valve has played a major role in North American and Brazilian historiography and popular thinking. Programs to settle the Central West and Amazonia have been justified as means of reducing the flow of rural migrants to cities, where they simply increase the marginalized mass of unemployed. In practice, the Brazilian frontier has not performed this function very well. The growth of agricultural land area has not been associated with a proportionate absorption of rural labor, and rural wages have exhibited no tendency to rise in the last two decades. Moreover, the transportation improvements, which raise frontier land values, have traditionally attracted an influx of gunslingers and businessmen who with the collusion of corruptible officials have forced out small squatters and indigenes.

The major instrument of settlement policy in Amazonia has been the construction of highways, which have been endowed with astounding development powers in Brazil. To wit, the Belém-Brasília has allegedly been responsible for two million new settlers, a claim that analysis here suggests is exaggerated tenfold. The experience of the Transamazon Highway and the associated colonization schemes suggest that highways can penetrate areas that are too infertile or too distant from market to sustain high living standards. The Goiás experience indicates that mundane feeder roads in areas close to market can have greater developmental impact than more spectacular highways.

Amazonia's labor absorption potential is not too promising in the near future. First, the region's comparative advantage seems to lie in capital-intensive activities like mining, lumbering, and ranching. It is usually more economical to ship these materials by railroad than by truck. Second, its agricultural potential seems greatest on the floodplain far from the highway. With more propitious soils closer to the markets of the Central South and to the labor supply of the Northeast, Goiás and Mato Grosso are likely to remain the centers of pioneering in the near future.

The lesson of northern Paraná, the most successful example of planned settlement, has generally been ignored by Brazilian policymakers. A British company initiated a scheme that ultimately settled one million people in an area the size of Connecticut. Unlike official colonization schemes, this one was completed as planned, was self-financing, and, initially at least, created a rural middle-class society. This experience highlights the advantages of long-term comprehensive planning that is incremental and market oriented. Unconstrained by professional standards, so common in the field of housing and colonization, the Paraná planners were guided by the settlers' ability to pay. The planners helped improve this ability to pay by creating a mortgage market for farmland. The long-run failure of northern Paraná to remain a middle-class society is due less to failures of the planning process than to lack of support from institutions in the broader society (the market for small farm credits).

Mainly because of major improvements in the national highway network, the Brazilian space-economy has become more tightly integrated in the past three decades. The reduction in the friction of distance has facilitated the flow of goods and labor. Associated with this tighter integration, population and income have become redistributed away from the Northeast and toward the states of the Central South, particularly São Paulo, Guanabara-Rio, Paraná, and Goiás. There was a substantial divergence in per capita income among states in the 1940s, a substantial convergence in the 1950s, and a stable pattern of regional income inequality in the 1960s. To what extent has regional integration served as a polarizing versus an equilibrating force?

While migration has predictably been selective of more skilled prime-aged workers, the weight of the evidence suggests that interstate migration has been equilibrating, raising relative incomes in the poorer states. Similarly, with the exception of the early 1950s, capital seems to have flowed from wealthy São Paulo to the impoverished Northeast. Although private capital flows probably moved southward until the establishment of the fiscal incentives program in the early 1960s, public capital flows in the opposite direction swamped the private flows. Finally, the flow of commodity trade does not seem to have a deleterious effect on the industrialization of the peripheral states. States that imported a larger share of manufactured goods do not seem to have industrialized more slowly in the 1960s.

In the absence of polarizing commodity and factor flows, what accounts for the persistence of interregional income disparities? The answer would appear to be that the disequilibrating tendencies reflected in industrial agglomeration in São Paulo are sufficient to offset these equilibrating flows. This process of agglomeration cannot be explained by initial advantage and cumulative causation, since several other cities exceeded São Paulo as an industrial metropolis at the turn of the century when the process began. São Paulo overtaking Rio as the major industrial center is an egregious violation of the model of initial advantage-cumulative causation; this epochal event of Brazilian economic history has few international counterparts.

The simplest starting point for explaining this phenomenon lies in the fact that until recently the largest cities have served as entrepôts for rural export economies. Since the early 1880s there has been a shift of the coffee region from the hinterland of Rio to that of São Paulo. By the early part of the twentieth century São Paulo clearly had a larger commercial hinterland. The spatial pattern of industrial specialization clearly follows from central place theory — highest-order functions, in which there are the fewest establishments, are more likely to be located in the largest market center (São Paulo).

Another factor accounting for the industrial growth of São Paulo as opposed to Rio, despite the latter's initial advantage, seems to be imperfections in the capital market, which made Paulista planters reluctant to shift their capital out of state when coffee prices declined. This factor apparently offset the necessity of industrialists to cultivate close personal ties with politicians and bureaucrats, which would have favored Rio. Building upon these advantages, São Paulo became the most attractive location for foreign investors, who, initially lacking information about and faith in the Brazilian economy, sought the largest markets with the best developed network of suppliers and urban services.

In the 1920s and 1930s, before industrialization began, São Paulo increased its share of traditional output and employment. When an unconscious process of import substitution began in the 1940s, São Paulo benefited from a relatively fast industrial mix. When more conscious policies were pursued in the 1950s, the favorable industry mix effect was reinforced by more rapid growth in each industrial sector. By the 1960s São Paulo's growth resembled that of a mature region, enjoying a fast industry mix but growing largely in proportion to the national economy.

Finally, differences in development levels influence and in turn are influenced by interregional differences in labor dependency and birth rates, by levels of investment in education, and by rates of internal savings. Many of these differences are reducible to differences in urbanization.

To what extent has public policy been responsible for regional disparities? The national government can hardly be accused of favoring the regional interests of São Paulo. Removed from the seats of power since 1930, São Paulo has consistently paid more taxes than it has received in federal expenditures. Consequently, much of the state's infrastructure was financed by its own funds. Although São Paulo inadvertently benefited from import substitution policies of the 1950s because of its initial advantages, the federal objectives were sectoral not regional in nature. By the 1960s the fiscal incentive system transferred directly about 5 to 10 percent of private savings to the Northeast and Amazonia; moreover, sectoral policy increasingly favored the export-oriented interests of these regions at the expense of São Paulo. Although regional disparities remained stable in the 1960s, evidence suggests that they would have worsened in the absence of these federal policies.

In the past three decades Brazil has undergone an urban revolution compressed in half the time it took the United States to raise its urban share from 26 to 52 percent. The pattern of urbanization is weakly related to the nation's industrialization. First, the growth of the urban population far exceeds the growth of employment in industry. Second, while industry has been continually concentrating in the Rio-São Paulo axis, urbanization has been proceeding most rapidly in the least urbanized, least industrialized states. Third, the service sector accounts for the overwhelming share of employment in all major cities, with the exception of São Paulo, a share considerably higher than the United States experienced at a similar phase of urban evolution.

As in many developing countries, Brazilian policymakers feel that the nation is hyperurbanized and that the urban population is too heavily concentrated in the primate cities. This view is based upon the beliefs that the growth of the urban population should not be based on service employment, that capital that could go into directly productive investment is wasted in urban infrastructure, that municipal services are breaking down under the weight of this expanded population, and that the resulting marginalized mass is a threat to the civic order.

While the Brazilian pattern of urbanization does differ from that of currently advanced countries in its tenuous relationship to industrialization, the large service sector is not inherently problematic. Low levels of industrial labor absorption are a result of both structural factors—the importation of capital-intensive technologies, the pattern of demand distorted toward luxuries—and market factors—subsidization of capital and taxation of labor. These latter policies result in two deadweight losses to society. Not only is industrial employment and output foregone, but high wages in the protected modern sector attract productive workers from agriculture who remain somewhat marginally employed in the urban sector. Because of the near unitary elasticity of substitution between capital and labor, a reduction in private labor costs would result in nearly proportional increases in modern sector labor absorption. It is noteworthy that the resulting changes reduce expected income from migration, and hence the level of urbanization, only slightly. In other words the labor absorption problem is a sectoral problem that is played out in the spatial arena, not a spatial problem per se.

Other alleged symptoms of hyperurbanization are not easily substantiated by the evidence. Much of the capital invested in urban areas, such as in transportation facilities and water supply, are intermediate goods that provide no direct addition to welfare and in a sense are wasted. Investments like school buildings contribute to future well-being or like football stadiums contribute to present well-being and as such cannot be considered wasted. Despite the weight of these capital expenditures, there is little evidence of the deterioration in service quality. Indeed, there have been noticeable improvements in water supply, sewerage, electricity, and telephone service. Deterioration in the amenities important to the middle class, such as open space, clean air, and freedom from crime, is undeniable.

When all these factors are taken into account, general equilibrium analysis suggests that if rural-urban migration were reduced, the national growth rate would decline. This does not suggest that there are no distortions in Brazilian urbanization but that dealing with the symptom—migration—without the causes — industrial-structural, factor-price, service-price, and betterment-tax distortions — can be costly.

In Brazil, as in most of the world, national urban growth policy has inspired much encomium but little action. While the frontier has been viewed as a diversion channel for rural-urban migration flows, urban growth policy in practice revolves around improving cities' ability to cope with increasing populations. The major instrument, the housing finance system, has the avowed purpose of reducing the perceived housing deficit that is epitomized by squatter settlements. While this system has improved the ability of middle-income families to finance housing, it has not made standard housing affordable for the poor. Not unlike the American urban renewal program in the 1950s, the system justifies the destruction of substandard slum dwellings and effectively becomes an instrument of redistributing income from the poor to the middle class.

### New Perspectives on Orthodox Spatial Analysis

Orthodox spatial analysis has evolved in relatively advanced market economies, achieving much of its refinement in the United States, whose experience of laissez faire economic development is a special case in the global context. The theoretical assumptions of the orthodox approach are not totally inappropriate for this special case: perfect competition among decisionmakers, market-determined prices, and private ownership of the means of production. Within this framework there is no location theory of governmental behavior regarding investment in infrastructure and directly productive activities, the control of prices and other regulations for locational ends, or interregional fiscal transfers.

Given the geographical origins of modern spatial analysis, one is tempted to question its applicability to currently underdeveloped countries that are characterized by monopolistic competition, if not outright monopoly; by weakly articulated markets subject to enormous governmental regulation; and by public ownership of many basic industries. In repudiation of conventional economic analysis, which is viewed as an ideological justification for the exploitation of poorer nations, an indigenous analytical framework called structuralism has evolved in Latin America. In contrast to the orthodox analysis, which focuses heavily upon processes of spatial equilibration, structuralism includes a model of regional development and urbanization centered around processes of spatial polarization. This model predicts ever increasing agglomeration of wealth and power and the continual polarization in levels of welfare between rich and poor regions and between city and countryside, as the spatial epiphenomena of a hierarchical pattern of exploitation that culminates in the great metropolises of international capitalism.

As a test of the orthodox spatial analysis, the results of this study of Brazil are generally surprise-free. In other words, explaining the spatial evolution of Brazilian society does not call for any major theoretical revisions. This conclusion does not imply that this evolution can be predicted by someone completely unfamiliar with Brazilian history, politics, and institutions. Non-market institutional factors have played an important, but not decisive, role in modifying the spatial dimensions of Brazilian economic development. These factors include agricultural price regulation, land tenure, capital market subsidies, labor legislation, and governmental job provision as well as urban-regional planning and policy making itself. In conceptual terms, the effect of many of these institutional factors has been to shift the determination of prices and income distribution from the market into the political arena. Since spatial analysis generally takes prices and income distributions as given, the way in which these parameters are determined is of secondary importance.

The conclusion that the Brazilian results are surprise-free does not imply that there are no theoretical gaps or that everything has been explained. The orthodox analysis is weakest in the prediction of the spatial concentration of industry and the polarization of regional per capita income levels. Concepts such as agglomeration economies and models of circular and cumulative causation are generally poorly specified and often reduce to tautologies. The point is that one's modest ability to explain agglomeration and polarization in Brazil is not much different from one's ability to explain similar processes in the United States, France, or Italy. Any conceptual breakthroughs in understanding these processes in the advanced countries will probably also be applicable to the developing countries. Structuralists would not take issue with this conclusion because they view agglomeration and polarization as pervading the world capitalist system.

On a superficial level frontier settlement in south central Brazil is consistent with the conventional theories of agricultural land use and innovation. Increasing demand for farm products has been supplied by the incorporation of new lands, facilitated by an aggressive road-building program, especially in the past three decades. The abundance of land discourages yield-increasing inventions and innovations and thus discourages agricultural intensification.

Although conventional land-use theory views prices and costs as market determined, the state has played a major role in their determination in Brazil. A recognition of these political decisions is necessary in order to evaluate whether the present pattern of frontier expansion is efficient.

Among the factors that may have led to excessive frontier expansion in the past are coffee price supports that have resulted in an accumulation of stocks; unfavorable exchange rates for fertilizer imports; insufficient support for agricultural research, development, and extension; inadequate credit for small farmers; and the concentration of holdings in a few hands. The first three factors are self-explanatory in terms of conventional land-use theory: high coffee prices shift the gradient of land rents upward and extend the frontier; high fertilizer costs and lack of high-yield varieties result in extensive rather than intensive growth.

Some institutional factors leading to insufficient frontier expansion were more important in the past than today. The exportable surplus doctrine that inhibited noncoffee farm exports is one; the inefficient scale of the truck manufacturing industry is another. Currently the most important of these factors is the underinvestment and disorganization in the nation's railroad system. Foodstuffs are trucked as far as two thousand kilometers to market, whereas in the United States most bulky hauls over five hundred kilometers are by rail. The fact that in Brazil long line hauls by rail are cheaper than those by truck indicates that there are considerable inefficiencies in scheduling, warehousing, and intermodal transfers that hinder the railroad's ability to compete for long-distance traffic. Sugar quotas distort the pattern of frontier settlement among regions. In their absence, more land in the northeastern littoral would be devoted to foodstuffs and more land in São Paulo and Paraná would be devoted to sugar cane, thereby pushing beans and rice even farther westward into the Central West.

Conventional spatial analysis ignores the factors of tenure patterns and social relations of production. Since large holdings seem to be cultivated less intensively than small holdings, the same output could be produced on less land and at lower prices on family farms than on latifundia. Consequently, land reform is a partial substitute for frontier expansion as a technique of raising agricultural output as well as for redistributing income.

Brazilian experience also sheds light on the determinants of the social relations of production in frontier societies. Economic theories attempt to explain the rise of family farming rather than plantations by characteristics of the production function of the staple or by the endowment of land per person. Interregional comparisons of coffee culture indicate that a wide range of tenure forms coexist and that plantations predominate despite the fact that the optimal operating unit is a family tending a group of trees. In some circumstances family farming thrives in a land-abundant environment (Tomé-Açu, Mato Grosso de Goiás, and company lands in northern Paraná in the 1950s); in other cases, family farming is stifled (the Amazonian rubber frontier and southwestern Paraná). Further comparison suggests that political factors play a crucial intervening role in initiating and sustaining these relations. The Paraná experience emphasizes the importance of supportive institutions in the broader society (that is, availability of working capital) in maintaining a rural middle-class society.

The experience of northern Paraná also shows how comprehensive planning can produce a pattern of land use different from that produced by the free play of forces in a highly imperfect market. By coordinating urban, rural, and transportation investments and by providing financing, the planners were able to generate a more intensive pattern of rural land use, more closely spaced cities, and higher land values than comparable land developed by traditional subdivision.

The flows of goods and labor have been in the direction predicted by the conventional analysis. Interregional trade is most intense between larger and more proximate trading partners. Migration has been from low-income states to high-income states, with the expected pattern of selectivity. Through markets that are heavily controlled by the federal government, there have been substantial flows of capital from capital-rich to capital-poor regions.

A complete analysis of regional disparities should include a theory of public policy making. Hirschman suggests that at the onset of industrialization the center exploits the periphery and at a more mature phase the center subsidizes the periphery. In contrast to both this theory and the American experience, the center has been fiscally exploited by the periphery prior to, during, and after the onset of industrialization in Brazil. Sectoral policy seems to have benefited the center during the 1950s, but an opposite bias prevailed in the 1960s. Spatial analysis still awaits a theory to explain these international differences and changes over time.

Despite the fact that market flows have been in an equilibrating direction and that regional policy has been heavily biased in favor of the poorest regions, regional disparities failed to decrease in the 1960s. The degree of disparity in 1970 was about equivalent to that in 1940, when Brazil was one of the most regionally unequal nations in the world.

The disequilibrating force of industrial agglomeration in São Paulo presumably is sufficient to offset all the private market and public sector flows. These disequilibrating forces are poorly understood. The major conceptual schemes that account for industrial agglomeration are the French growth pole theory and the American literature on localization and urbanization economies. The former approach focuses upon the input-output linkages of propulsive industries; the latter focuses on immobile external economies and communication costs.

The empirical analysis of São Paulo found that neither approach was particularly fruitful in describing its pattern of industrial specialization or in predicting the performance of its various industrial sectors. Most of the alleged external agglomeration economies were not found to be particularly urban in character.

A factor that merits more careful attention is the role of capital market imperfections in encouraging the industrialization of the capital surplus region. Experience indicates that New England owes it primacy as the cradle of American industrialization not to its superior market, abundant labor, or access to raw materials, but to its surplus capital accumulated in an earlier stage of devel-

opment. The extent to which capital immobilities elsewhere play
a role favoring the industrialization of one location over another
and the degree to which the government can attenuate this as a
locational factor by the creation of a network of regional and
state development banks merits further attention.

Most studies of industrialization-urbanization focus on cases
where initial advantages proved cumulative. As alluded to earlier, the overtaking of Rio by São Paulo as the primate industrial
center is a rare event. It was hypothesized that the shift of the
coffee frontier from the hinterland of Rio to that of São Paulo in
the preindustrial era offset the former's initial advantages. Research focusing on other counterexamples to the law of cumulative and circular causation is needed to elucidate the nature of
agglomerating forces.

It was hypothesized earlier that in a nation where the public
sector absorbs such a high level of the national product and
where public enterprises control the bulk of the basic industries
like steel, petroleum, and electricity, conventional locational analysis is inapplicable. In fact, it was found that public industrial
enterprises in Brazil behaved very much like their private counterparts and require no special locational analysis. This experience does not necessarily imply that a location theory for public
enterprise is unnecessary. In many ways Brazilian public enterprises are internationally atypical. In many countries managers of
public enterprises are bureaucrats, products of humanistic training with inadequate business experience, political sense, or both.
In Brazil the Escola Superior de Guerra, an institute of strategic
studies, has played a major role in creating a common ideology
among the military, government technocrats, and businessmen
regarding the relationship between internal security and economic development. The universities are increasingly emphasizing
analytical and managerial skills. Most important, there has been
considerable flow of personnel among these three sectors. It is
highly unlikely that the manager of a Brazilian public enterprise
would have the litterateur's contempt for cost accounting. Because of these unusual conditions, generalization about the behavior of public enterprises from the Brazilian experience is hazardous.

Conventional spatial analysis generally explains urbanization by sectoral shifts in employment out of agriculture and into industry and commerce. More sophisticated dualistic models are necessary in developing countries because urbanization has mirrored not only sectoral shifts in employment but also the growth of unemployment. Only about two-thirds of urbanization in Brazil can be explained by sectoral shifts; one-third can be explained by the deruralization of industrial and service activities.

While conventional location theory explains the destruction of rural handicrafts by internal economies of scale enjoyed by modern urban industry, the Brazilian experience contradicts this. The average firm size has not increased in the past fifty years and the handicraft sector continues to thrive. It was hypothesized that the handicraft sector in developing countries shifts to urban areas, where artisans can benefit from external economies, one of which is the opportunity to enter the modern industrial sector. This hypothesis awaits further verification.

The creation of urban growth poles to stimulate regional development has been adopted in many developing countries. Growth pole policy in fact has tended to follow the analysis and prescriptions of the French school. Brazilian experience is similar to that in the rest of the world: the implantation of high-technology, capital-intensive, large-scale industry generally results in the creation of an enclave with little linkage to the surrounding area. The American school, which eulogizes the development consequences of small-scale, labor-intensive, and low-technology industry, has not yet spelled out an alternative policy prescription. The generation of an alternative policy framework for the creation of growth poles in developing countries would seem of utmost urgency.

The hypothesis that industrialization-urbanization stimulates modernization and economic development in the surrounding hinterland has been tested with mixed results in the American context. The results are most favorable to the hypothesis in labor-surplus regions like the American Southeast. The frontier state of Goiás provides verification of this hypothesis in a developing country context. While agricultural modernization is more intense near the regional entrepôt, as suggested by the neoclassical theory of rents, localized industrialization-urbanization seems to improve agricultural efficiency.

## The Evolution of Spatial Policymaking Capacity

Brazil has expended proportionately more time, energy, and resources on urban and regional policymaking and planning than most developing and many advanced countries. Urban and regional planning does not occur in a vacuum but as part of an ongoing governmental system with a particular configuration of political interests, conceptual paradigms, and administrative institutions with their own inertia. Clearly such planning is an expression of this broader system of decision making and administration within which the choices are severely constrained. This is not to say that the interests of the dominant political group are unambiguous or coherent and that the Brazilian policymaking and planning system has reached the limits of rationality in pursuing these interests.

The Brazilian model of economic development has the following basic characteristics. First, the federal government actively directs macroeconomic activity through monetary and fiscal policy, sets minimum wages and certain prices, invests heavily in infrastructure, and operates industries in several basic sectors. Second, decentralized execution of federal priorities is implemented by control of credit and fiscal incentives for the private sector and by revenue sharing with lower levels of government. Third, the economy is open to direct foreign investment and importation of technology. Fourth, a co-optive policy of paternalism is espoused and privileged members of the working class are protected by minimum wages, social security legislation, and subsidized housing. But in practice the strategy of growth before redistribution is pursued. Fifth, authoritarianism has eliminated competitive politics and the right to strike, among other things, and has cut short the trend toward greater enfranchisement of the population. It is important to emphasize that only the last of these characteristics is truly a creation of the post-1964 revolutionary regime. The rest, with the possible exception of the open door to foreign investment, are a continuation of past trends.

In the past three decades of urban and regional planning and policymaking improvements in technical capacity are apparent. These improvements are based upon superior conceptual understanding, more flexible administrative structures, and the enlargement of the financial base.

On a conceptual level the most notable event has been the decline of geography and structuralist economics and the rise of neoclassical economics as the dominant intellectual paradigm and its diffusion from federal to state and local technocrats. Although an essentially leftist nationalist doctrine, structuralism is part of the intellectual baggage of much of the Brazilian elite. The grounds for its decline are both scientific and political.

As a scientific doctrine, structuralism holds that economic development, defined as industrialization, was almost impossible without major structural changes in the Brazilian economy, notably land reform, income redistribution, and shifts in traditional patterns of international specialization. While import-substituting industrialization was clearly responsible for the increase in the industrial share of output, practically as small a share of the labor force was employed in the industrial sector in 1960 as in 1940. Second, the industrialization occurred without any major structural reforms in the countryside, which performed remarkably well, and despite an increasing concentration of income.

A political reason for the decline of structuralism has been the consolidation of a regime committed to strengthening Brazil's ties to the international capitalist system, notably by the encouragement of foreign investment. As a doctrine of self-reliance or even autarchy, structuralist policy was basically incompatible with these goals. A counterpart of the opening up of Brazil has been a sustained interest of American foundations and government agencies in the training of intellectuals and technicians at the university level in both Brazil and the United States.

The displacement of structuralist thinking has been most pronounced in those problem areas that have been of greatest interest to economic policymakers (macroeconomic issues of inflation, agricultural development, and export expansion). Structuralist thinking still dominates urban and regional policymaking, where there are few Brazilians trained in neoclassical economics. With the rising interest in these fields this structuralist bastion may also fall. Interestingly both the populist and authoritarian regimes have eagerly adopted policies that encourage the importation of technology from advanced countries rather than developing indigenous technologies. This headlong rush toward a "technological fix" to the problem of industrialization reflects a residual structuralist belief that there are few choices within the spectrum of modern technology and that capital intensity is indicative of modernity. The adoption of modern capital-intensive technology in manufacturing, mining, agriculture, and animal husbandry is acknowledged as producing a contradiction within the system — the inevitable marginalization of the urban and rural working classes.

A more important source of improvement in urban and regional planning capability has resulted from administrative trends pervading the federal bureaucracy. An increasing proportion of planning and executive activities is undertaken by public and mixed public-private corporations and agencies that function outside the normal bureaucracy. Central control over sectoral and regional priorities is exercised by shifting resources among these competing corporations and agencies.

In the past centrally allocated resources took the form of earmarked tax revenues, but greater weight is currently placed upon the allocation of fiscal incentive deposits and compulsory savings. The shift from dedicated revenues to fiscal incentives and compulsory savings has effectively resulted in an increase of funds available for urban and regional development. In order for SUDENE or SUDAM to utilize the deposited fiscal incentives or BNH to utilize the pension funds, private counterpart investment must be attracted. Thus one constraint is that these agencies' projects must be privately profitable. Because the funds of these corporations comprise the equity of their depositors or shareholders, a second constraint is to remain self-financing. While the private market filter may discourage blatantly irrational uses of funds, a resulting bias of these constraints is that non-self-financing investments, say in education or public health, are excluded from consideration.

The improvement in technical planning capacity has occurred in the context of depoliticization and the establishment of an authoritarian rightist regime. To what extent has this depoliticization had an impact on urban and regional planning? Speculation on this matter turns on the types of conceptual paradigms and institutional innovations that might have occurred under the continuation of the pre-1964 political system.

To a great extent the policy directions of the military government in the arena of regional planning are a continuation of the pre-1964 strategy. Sharing the basically structuralist view of industrial development in the Northeast, the military government has continued its predecessors' fiscal incentives program. The improvement of the agricultural marketing system as a stimulus to frontier settlement is also a continuation of prior policies.

The government's capacity to undertake whimsical regional development programs does not confine itself to authoritarian regimes. The Transamazon Highway and Perimeter Road have their counterpart in the construction of Brasília, which was considerably more costly and of no more obvious benefit.

However, authoritarianism made a difference in both urban and rural spatial structure. By suppressing minimum wages, industrial labor absorption was stimulated but expected urban income of potential migrants reduced. This factor, as well as the increase in utility rates and destruction of slums, probably discouraged rural-urban migration. Rising utility rates and earmarked taxes have increased the pace of investment in water supply and telephone facilities, which may encourage a more decentralized urban form. The squelching of the movement toward land reform on the northeastern littoral probably resulted in a less intensive agriculture as well as in higher food costs and less rural labor absorption in that region. This in turn translates into lower rural incomes and perhaps greater rural-urban migration.

The regime's commitment to large-scale enterprises, also shared by Stalinists and populists, resulted in few financial innovations to fill the small-scale credit gap. On the agricultural front this gap facilitated the demise of the rural middle class in northern Paraná, which was apparent by 1960, well before the 1964 revolution. On the industrial front this commitment inhibited the creation of an American school growth pole based upon small enterprises in the Northeast.

Brazil has proven a rich testing ground for the hypotheses of orthodox spatial analysis. The conventional conceptual schemes have stood up well against the evidence of this developing country with its unique institutions. In turn, these schemes have shed considerable light on neglected or misunderstood dimensions of economic development.

The Brazilian experience nevertheless highlights several important conceptual gaps. First, there is no coherent theory of the location of government enterprises. While this did not prove to be a major difficulty in analyzing Brazil, given the profit orientation of its public corporations, this is not generally the case. Second, there is no theory of regional policymaking and planning that would explain which regions suffer and benefit, and when, from fiscal transfers, infrastructure investment, and sectoral policy. Third, although equilibrating forces are well understood, the forces of disequilibrium, particularly industrial agglomeration, are not. Many of the alleged external urbanization economies that have explained industrial agglomeration did not invariably prove to be external or urban in the Brazilian case. Fourth, the limits to the initial advantage-cumulative causation paradigm need to be spelled out carefully. Brazil provided a counterexample in the rise of São Paulo, for which an ad hoc explanation was adduced, but a more coherent framework is necessary. Finally, economics, geography, and regional science have not generated a technology of urban and regional planning that is transferrable to developing countries. Other than disseminating formalistic programming models, little attention has been devoted to issues of innovation in administrative and financial institutions or to substantive issues of elaborating an American school growth pole strategy. These conceptual gaps suggest that a complete spatial analysis of advanced countries, like the United States, is not yet possible.

# Appendix
# Notes
# Index

# Appendix

The theory of agricultural rents provides a framework for understanding the complex interactions between natural resources, production costs, demand, and marketing costs on the one hand and frontier expansion on the other. While the theory can handle such complications as spatial variations in soil quality or geographical dispersion of markets, it is simpler to assume that a single market center absorbs all the produce of a region that is physiographically homogeneous. This assumption is not unrealistic in the Brazilian context, where metropolitan São Paulo is the largest food distribution center in Latin America and is flanked by large homogeneous regions like the Paulista plateau and the savanna of the Central West. In addition it is simpler to assume that each crop is produced by a unique traditional technique that does not vary with respect to location.

To begin with consider an economy that has only one commercial staple. At any distance $k$ from the market the rent offered for agricultural land equals the value of the output per acre at the market price less the direct production costs (capital, labor, and intermediate inputs) less the costs of shipping the output to market. Arithmetically, rent at any distance $k$ from the market equals

$$R_k = Y(p - a) - Yfk$$

where $Y$ = yield, in tons per hectare
$p$ = price per ton, at the market center
$a$ = direct production costs
$f$ = marketing costs per ton-kilometer
$k$ = kilometers between farm and market

Simple algebraic manipulation shows that at any given site the more fertile the land, and hence the higher the yield, the greater is the rent and the greater the market demand, and hence the higher the price, the greater is the rent. A rent-bid gradient relates the rent offered per hectare to distance from the market. Rents are highest at the market itself and fall with distance from it. The limit of commercial cultivation ($K$) is that distance from the market at which rents equal zero, or

$$Y(p - a) = YfK$$
$$\text{and hence } K = (p - a)/f$$

From this it follows that the greater the demand and the lower the marketing costs per ton-kilometer, the more extensive the frontier.

Each crop $i$ has its own characteristic yield $(Y_i)$, direct production cost $(a_i)$, and marketing cost per ton-kilometer $(f_i)$. Marketing costs tend to vary directly with bulk, perishability, and the necessity for special handling. Consequently, each crop has its own rent-bid gradient with a unique slope and limit of feasible commercial cultivation. As before,

$$R_{ik} = Y_i(p_i - a_i) - Y_i f_i k_i$$
$$K_i = (p_i - a_i)/f_i$$

Other things being equal, crops with higher value per ton and lesser direct production costs per hectare (lower $a_i$), both relative to marketing costs $(f_i)$, have more distant limits of commercial cultivation $(K_i)$. The slope of the rent-bid gradient is greater for commodities with higher yields and marketing costs per ton-kilometer $(\partial R_i/\partial k_i = -Y_i f_i)$.

At any distance from the market the crop that bids the most for the land is cultivated. Together these results imply that crops commanding low prices, that have high yields, and that are costly to market are produced closer to market.

Where do the various Brazilian crops fit into this picture? Evidence for the 1948-1970 period indicates that coffee commands a market price per ton that is two to four times higher than perishables like milk or tomatoes. Coffee yields are considerably lower than those of perishables and somewhat higher than those of nonperishable foodstuffs like milled rice and beans. Compared to perishables and coffee, beef cattle have the lowest yield and highest price.[1]

The spatial structure of São Paulo agriculture can be represented graphically by a trio of rent-bid gradients (figure 4). Since the dominant activity at any point is determined by the highest gradient, three zones of commercial agriculture surrounding the market center emerge: a greenbelt of perishables, bulky foodstuffs like potatoes, and some bulky staples, like sugar; an intermediate coffee zone; and a frontier zone of high-value food production, like beef cattle, rice, and beans. Beyond the commercial frontier lies a zone of diversified subsistence farming.

The absolute and relative size of the three zones is determined by the level of demand for their respective outputs. When the level of industrialization-urbanization was low, so was the rent-bid gradient for

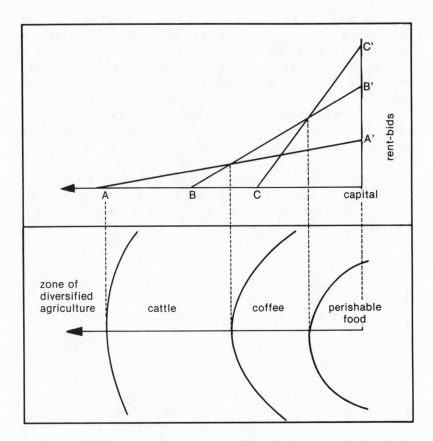

**Figure 4.** Rent-bid curves for cattle (AA'), coffee (BB'), and perishables (CC') and zones of specialized production derived from rent-bid curves

perishables. Urbanization raises this gradient, pushing the circle of its production outward at the expense of coffee. Similarly, growth in demand for beef and rice pushes the limits of coffee cultivation inward and the frontier outward. Other things being equal, total acreage devoted to coffee culture declines. Because in fact São Paulo is such a large supplier, any contraction in its coffee output would raise world prices. As a result, the coffee rent-bid gradient rises also. After further adjustments in the innermost and outermost rings, the ultimate result of the growth of domestic demand is an increase in prices and an extension of all cultivation zones (figure 5).

The above changes represent the expansion of output along the supply curve as a result of increasing prices. This is clearly not the mechanism by which Brazilian frontier expansion has taken place because agricultural prices have not increased relative to industrial prices. The major mechanism has been improvements in marketing (decreases in $f_i$) and a consequent flattening of the rent-bid gradients. The resulting shift in the supply curve permits prices to remain stable and leads to the outward expansion of all production rings (figure 6).

The above argument suggests that agricultural zones are completely specialized in a single commercial crop. In fact a given zone may diversify somewhat because of the possibility for sequential cropping, the necessity for crop rotation when little fertilizer is used, the advantage of portfolio diversification to reduce risk, and the subsistence demands of the farm family. Brazilian experience shows that a reduction in marketing costs, however, enhances the tendency toward complete specialization in the suggested direction.

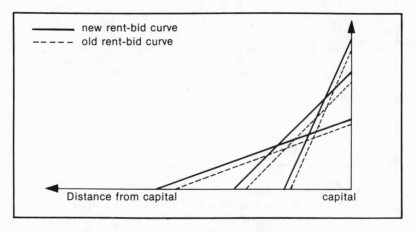

**Figure 5.** Impact of increased demand on rent-bid curves and extension of zones of production

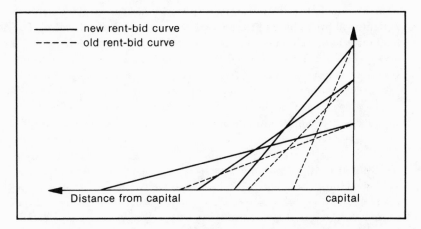

**Figure 6.** Impact of transportation improvement on rent-bid curves and extension of zones of specialized production

# Notes

## 1. Introduction

1. John Friedmann, *Regional Development Policy: A Case Study of Venezuela* (Cambridge: MIT Press, 1966), chap. 1; William Alonso, "Urban and Regional Imbalances in Economic Development," *Economic Development and Cultural Change* 17 (Oct. 1968): 1-14. For an international perspective on spatial imbalances see E. A. G. Robinson, ed., *Backward Regions in Advanced Countries* (London: Macmillan, 1969); Lloyd Rodwin, *Nations and Cities: A Comparison of Strategies of Urban Growth* (Boston: Houghton Mifflin, 1970).

2. Dietrich Gerhard, "The Frontier in Comparative View," *Comparative Studies in Society and History* 1 (Mar. 1959): 205-229; Marvin Mikesell, "Comparative Studies of Frontier History," *Annals of the American Association of Geographers* 50 (Mar. 1960): 62-74; Martin T. Katzman, "The Brazilian Frontier in Comparative Perspective," *Comparative Studies in Society and History* 17 (July 1975): 266-285.

3. Frederick Jackson Turner's classic, "The Significance of the Frontier in American History," was first published in 1893 and was republished with other essays in Turner, *The Frontier in American History* (New York: Henry Holt, 1920), reissued by Holt, Rinehart and Winston in 1962. A useful compendium of critique and revisionist defense of Turner's work is Ray Allen Billington, ed., *The Frontier Thesis: Valid Interpretation of American History?* (New York: Holt, Rinehart and Winston, 1966). On the symbolism of frontiers see Henry Nash Smith, *Virgin Land: The American West as Symbol and Myth* (Cambridge: Harvard University Press, 1950 and 1970). On new capital cities see Rodwin, *Nations and Cities*, chaps. 3 and 4; Preston E. James and Speridião Faissol, "The Problem of Brazil's Capital City," *Geographical Review* 46 (July 1956): 301-317.

4. Jeffrey Williamson, "Regional Inequality and the Process of National Development," *Economic Development and Cultural Change* 13 (July 1965): 3-45.

5. For some evidence of the overurbanization and labor absorption problems see Werner Baer and Michel Hervé, "Employment and Industrialization in Underdeveloped Countries," *Quarterly Journal of Economics* 80 (Feb. 1966): 88-107; David Turnham, *The Employment Problem in the Less Developed Countries* (Paris: Organization for Economic Cooperation and Development, 1971). For a focus on Brazil's labor absorbtion problem see Edmar Bacha "El subempleo, el costo social de la mano de obra, y la estrategia brasileña de crecimiento," *El trimestre económico* 33 (Oct.-Dec. 1971): 1069-1079.

## 2. The Brazilian Frontier in Comparative Perspective

1. In Canada, for example, between 1901 and 1951 the Prairie Provinces increased their acreage from 15 to 120 million; the Maritimes decreased their acreage from 11 to 8 million. The westward movement of agriculture in the United States had led to the reduction of farmland in New England from 5 million acres in 1880 to 3.8 million in 1945. See George V. Haythorne, *Labor in Canadian Agriculture,* Harvard Studies in Labor Agriculture, 1960; John D. Black, *The Rural Economy of New England* (Cambridge: Harvard University Press, 1950), p. 149.

2. On the northern Chinese frontier see Owen Lattimore, *Inner Asian Frontiers of China* (New York: American Geographical Society, 1951); Dwight Perkins, *Agricultural Development in China, 1368-1968* (Chicago: Aldine, 1969), especially pp. 15-18.

3. William H. Nicholls, "Agriculture and the Economic Development of Brazil," in John Saunders, ed., *Modern Brazil: New Patterns of Development* (Gainesville: University of Florida Press, 1971), pp. 215-245.

4. Clifton R. Wharton, Jr., "Recent Trends of Output and Efficiency in the Agricultural Production of Brazil, Minas Gerais, and São Paulo," *Inter-American Economic Affairs* 13 (Autumn 1959): 60-68; Clarence Moore, "Recent Developments in Brazilian Agriculture," *Journal of Political Economy* 64 (Aug. 1956): 341-346; Paul I. Mandell, "The Development of the Southern Goiás-Brasília Region: Development in a Land-Rich Economy," unpublished doctoral dissertation, Columbia University, 1969, chap. 2.

5. On French Canada see Horace Miner, *St. Denis, a French-Canadian Parish* (Chicago: University of Chicago Press, 1939), pp. 1-19; Marcel Rioux and Yves Martin, *French Canadian Society,* vol. 1 (Toronto: McClelland and Stewart, 1969), pp. 1-31; W. J. Eccles, *The Canadian Frontier, 1534-1760* (New York: Holt, Rinehart and Winston, 1969). Compare Herold J. Wien, *China's March Toward the Tropics* (Hamden, Conn.: Shoestring Press, 1954); S. Daniel Neumark, *The South African Frontier: Economic Influences, 1652-1836* (Stanford, Calif.: Stanford University Press, 1957); W. K. Hancock, "Trek," *Economic History Review* 10 (Apr. 1958): 331-339.

6. Gerald K. Helleiner, "Typology in Development Theory: The Land Surplus Economy (Nigeria)," *Food Research Institute Studies* 6, no. 2 (1966): 181-194; Ester Boserup, *The Conditions of Agricultural Growth* (Chicago: Aldine, 1963).

7. Emilio Willems, *A aculturação dos alemães no Brasil* (São Paulo: Editora nacional, 1946); Jean Roché, *Le colonisation allemande et le Rio Grande do Sul* (Paris: Institute des hautes études de l'Amerique Latine, 1959). For a discussion of the impact of land abundance on French Canadian fertility see Rioux and Martin, *French Canadian Society,* pp. 204-216.

8. Leo Waibel, "European Colonization in Southern Brazil," *Geographical Review* 40 (Oct. 1950): 529-547; Setor de geografia urbana, "Cidade e região no sudoeste paranaense," *Revista brasileira de geografia* 32 (Apr.-June 1970): 3-156; Solon Barraclough and Arthur Domike, "Agrarian Structure in Seven Latin American Countries," *Land Economics* 42 (Nov. 1960): 408.

9. Larry Sjaastad, "The Costs and Returns on Human Migration," *Journal of Political Economy* 70 (supplement, Oct. 1962): 77-94; Martin Primack, "Land Clearing Costs and 19th Century Techniques," *Journal of Economic History* 22 (Dec. 1962): 484-497.

10. William N. Parker, "Productivity Growth in American Grain Farming: An Analysis of its 19th Century Sources," in Robert W. Fogel and Stanley L. Engerman, eds., *Reinterpretations of American Economic History* (New York: Harper Row, 1971), pp. 175-186; Robert E. Gallman, "Changes in Total U.S. Agricultural Factor Productivity," *Agricultural History* 47 (Jan. 1972): 191-210.

11. See Donald Treadgold, *The Great Siberian Migration: Government and Peasant Resettlement from Emancipation to the First World War* (Princeton, N.J.: Princeton University Press, 1957); Fred Shannon, "A Post-Mortem on the Labor Safety-Valve Doctrine," *Agricultural History* 19 (Jan. 1945): 31-37; cf. Nathaniel Leff, "Economic Development and Regional Inequality: Origins of the Brazilian Case," *Quarterly Journal of Economics* 86 (May 1972): 243-262; Nathaniel Leff, "Tropical Exports and Nineteenth Century Economic Development," *Journal of Political Economy* 81 (May-June 1973): 678-696.

12. Barraclough and Domike, "Agrarian Structure," p. 408.

13. Marshall Harris, *Origin of the Land Tenure System in the United States* (Ames: Iowa State College Press, 1953); A. Whitney Griswold, *Farming and Democracy* (New York: Harcourt, 1948).

14. Fred Shannon, "The Homestead Act and the Labor Surplus," *American Historical Review* 41 (July 1936): 637-651; Paul W. Gates, "The Homestead Act in an Incongruous Land System," *American Historical Review* 41 (July 1936): 651-681; Allen Bogue, "Profits and the Frontier Land Speculator," *Journal of Economic History* 17 (Mar. 1957): 1-24.

15. Robert Baldwin, "Patterns of Development in Newly Settled Regions," *Manchester School of Economics and Social Studies* 24 (May 1956): 161-179; Antônio de Barros Castro, "Modêlo histórico latinoamericano," in Antônio de Barros Castro, *Sete ensaios sôbre a economia brasileira* (São Paulo: Forense, 1972).

16. William Cline, *The Economic Consequences of a Land Reform in Brazil* (Amsterdam: North Holland Publishing Co., 1970).

17. Evsey Domar, "The Causes of Slavery or Serfdom," *Journal of Economic History* 30 (Mar. 1970): 18-32.

18. A. V. Chayanov, *The Theory of the Peasant Economy,* Daniel Thorner, Basïle Kerblay, and R. E. F. Smith, eds. (Homewood, Ill.: Richard D. Irwin, 1966); Michael Sund, "Land Tenure and Economic Performance of Agricultural Establishments in Northeast Brazil," University of Wisconsin, Land Tenure Center, research paper no. 17, April 1965; Cline, *The Economic Consequences.* These effects are consistent with the maximizing model of the farm household; see Amartya K. Sen, "Peasants and Dualism with or without Surplus Labor," *Journal of Political Economy* 74 (Oct. 1966): 425-449.

19. James L. Scobie, *Revolution on the Pampas: A Social History of Argentine Wheat, 1860-1910* (Austin: University of Texas Press, 1964); Allen W. Johnson, *Sharecroppers of the Sertão: Economics and Dependence on a Brazilian Plantation* (Stanford, Calif.: Stanford University Press, 1971). Two inter-

esting papers on the evolution of the social relations of production in Argentina's wheat frontier by Roberto Cortés Conde are "Algunos rasgos de la expansión territorial en Argentina en la segunda mitad del siglo XIX," *Desarrollo económico* 8 (Apr.-June 1968): 3-30 and "Patrones de asientamento y explotación agropecuaria en los nuevos territorios Argentinos, 1890-1910," in Alvaro Jara, ed., *Tierras nuevas: Expansión territorial y ocupación del suelo en America, siglos XVI-XIX* (Mexico, D. F.: Colegio de Mexico, 1968), pp. 77-120.

20.  Richard Morse, ed., *The Bandeirantes* (New York: Alfred Knopf, 1967) presents documents of the seventeenth-century explorations. On the geopolitical impact of explorations, see David M. Davidson, "Rivers and Empire: The Madeira Route and the Incorporation of the Brazilian Far West, 1737-1808," unpublished doctoral dissertation, Yale University, 1975. Works that consider the early mining and cattle frontiers are Roberto Simonsen, *História econômica do Brasil, 1500-1820,* 6th ed. (São Paulo: Companhia editora nacional, 1969); Caio Prado Júnior, *The Colonial Background of Modern Brazil,* trans. Suzette Macedo (Berkeley: University of California Press, 1967); Sérgio Buarque de Hollanda, *Raízes do Brasil* (Rio: José Olympio, 1968); Celso Furtado, *The Economic Growth of Brazil,* trans. Ricardo W. de Aguiar and Eric C. Drysdale (Berkeley: University of California Press, 1968), which is drawn to a major extent from the works of Prado and Buarque. Comparative works include Clodomir Vianna Moog, *Bandeirantes and Pioneers,* trans. L. L. Barrett (New York: George Braziller, 1966), which attempts to relate the geographical and sociocultural conditions of pioneering to the subsequent development of Brazil and the United States in a highly speculative manner, and Otávio Guilherme Velho, *Capitalismo autoritário e campesinato* (São Paulo: Difusão européia, 1976), which attempts to synthesize the Turnerian and Marxist views of frontier settlement in Brazil, Russia, and the United States.

21.  The best discussions of the coffee frontier are Sérgio Milliet, *O roteiro do café* (São Paulo: Estudos paulistas, 1938); Pierre Monbeig, *Pionniers et planteurs de São Paulo,* Cahiers de la fondation nationale de sciences politiques 28 (1952); Richard Graham, *Britain and the Onset of Modernization in Brazil, 1850-1914* (Cambridge, England: Cambridge University Press, 1968); Stanley J. Stein, *Vassouras: A Brazilian Coffee County, 1850-1900* (Cambridge: Harvard University Press, 1957); J. F. Normano, *Brazil: A Study of Economic Types* (Chapel Hill: University of North Carolina Press, 1935), chap. 4; Antônio Delfim Neto, *O problema do café no Brasil,* Universidade de São Paulo, faculdade de ciências econômicas e administrativas, boletim no. 5, 1970.

22.  Preston James, "Coffee Lands in Southeastern Brazil," *Geographical Review* 22 (Apr. 1932): 225-245; Brasil, Ministério de planejamento, *Programa estratégico de desenvolvimento, 1968-1970, estudo especial, zoneamento agrícola e pecuário do Brasil,* February 1969; Normano, *Brazil,* chap. 4.

23.  Brian Fitzpatrick, "The Big Man's Frontier and Australian Farming," *Agricultural History* 21 (Jan. 1947): 8-12; H. C. Allen, *Bush and Backwoods: A Comparison of the Frontier in Australia and the U.S.* (East Lansing: Michigan State University Press, 1959). On the use of influence and force to acquire land see Warren Dean, "Latifundia and Land Policy in Nineteenth-Century Brazil,"

*Hispanic American Historical Review* 51 (Nov. 1971): 606-626; Stein, *Vassouras;* Emília Viotti da Costa, *De senzala à colônia* (São Paulo: Difusão européia, 1966), chaps. 1 and 2.

24. On the role of coffee planters in the abolition of slavery see Richard Graham, "Causes for the Abolition of Slavery in Brazil," *Hispanic American Historical Review* 46 (May 1966): 123-137; Robert Conrad, *The Destruction of Brazilian Slavery, 1850-1888* (Berkeley: University of California Press, 1972).

25. Viotti da Costa, *De senzala.* Cf. J. H. Gallaway, "The Last Years of Slavery on the Sugar Plantations of Northeast Brazil," *Hispanic American Historical Review* 52 (Nov. 1972): 580-597.

26. Leff, "Economic Development and Regional Inequality"; Florestan Fernandes, *The Negro in Brazilian Society* (New York: Columbia University Press, 1969); Thomas Skidmore, *Black into White: Race and Nationality in Brazilian Thought* (New York: Oxford University Press, 1974).

27. Warren Dean, *The Industrialization of São Paulo, 1880-1945* (Austin: University of Texas Press, 1969), suggests that the purchase of urban land by rural interests and rural land by urban interests may have helped to form a homogeneous outlook among planter, merchant, and industrialist. This sense of common interest may have saved the country from the necessity of a bloody bourgeois revolution, which might have broken the hierarchical class structure in the rural areas.

28. For example, Monbeig, *Pionniers et planteurs;* Robert Platt, "Coffee Plantations of Brazil," *Geographical Review* 25 (Apr. 1935): 231-239; Annibal Villanova Villela and Wilson Suzigan, *Política do govêrno e crescimento da economia brasileira, 1889-1945* (Rio: Instituto de pesquisas econômicas aplicadas [IPEA], 1973), série monográfica no. 10, pp. 58-67, 110-113, 144, 159-165, 179-219, 225-228.

29. *Conjuntura econômica* 24 (June 1970): 89-106; Villela and Suzigan, *Política do govêrno,* chap. 1.

30. *VIII recenseamento geral do Brasil, censo preliminar, 1970, São Paulo* (Rio: Instituto brasileira de geografia e estatística [IBGE]). Although the census defines any county seat regardless of size as urban, I count those agglomerations of two thousand people or more, which gives a minutely lower estimate. The figures on the growth of the city of São Paulo are underestimates since they refer only to the county in which the capital is located. Not only has this county been gradually dismembered but urban growth has been spilling over its original boundaries. By 1970 at least an additional 40 percent of the state population lived beyond the capital county but within the metropolitan area.

31. Trends in land use are reviewed in Martin T. Katzman, "Industrialization, Agricultural Specialization and Frontier Settlement in South-Central Brazil, 1940-70," *Development and Change* 6 (Oct. 1975): 25-50.

32. Harry Ayer, "The Costs, Returns, and Effects of Agricultural Research in a Developing Country: The Case of Cotton Seed Research in São Paulo, Brazil," unpublished doctoral dissertation, Purdue University, 1970; Stanley Stein, *The Brazilian Cotton Manufacture* (Cambridge: Harvard University Press, 1957). The substitution of coffee by cotton during the Depression in São Paulo is

analyzed by Villela and Suzigan, *Política do govêrno,* pp. 179-218; Carlos M. Peláez, *História de industrialização brasileira* (Rio: APEC editora, 1972), pp. 109-140.

33. For a discussion of stockpiling schemes see Delfim Neto, "O problema do café no Brasil"; Villela and Suzigan, *Política do govêrno,* pp. 61-67, 113-122, 191-200; Peláez, *História de industrialização,* pp. 33-108; Furtado, *The Economic Growth of Brazil,* pp. 193-212. On the policy of exchange confiscation see Nathaniel Leff, *Economic Policy-Making and Development in Brazil, 1947-1964* (New York: John Wiley, 1968), chap. 2. On the exportable surplus see Nathaniel Leff, "Export Stagnation and Autarkic Development in Brazil," *Quarterly Journal of Economics* 81 (May 1967): 286-301; G. Edward Schuh, *The Agricultural Development of Brazil* (New York: Praeger, 1971), chaps. 3 and 6. On minimum prices and fertilizer subsidies see Gordon Smith, "Brazilian Agricultural Policy, 1950-1967," in Howard S. Ellis, ed., *The Economy of Brazil* (Berkeley: University of California Press, 1969), pp. 213-265. On marketing see Gordon W. Smith, "Agriculture Marketing and Economic Development: A Brazilian Case Study," unpublished doctoral dissertation, Harvard University, 1965; cf. George Wilson, ed., *The Impact of Highway Investment on Development* (Washington,)D.C.: Brookings Institution, 1966), chaps. 1 and 7. Trade statistics are found in Brasil, Ministério de fazenda, *Comércio exterior,* various years.

34. Preston E. James, "Brazil: Agricultural Development," in Simon K. Kuznets, Wilbert E. Moore, and Joseph J. Spengler, eds., *Economic Growth: Brazil, India, Japan* (Durham, N.C.: Duke University Press, 1956), pp. 78-102; Nicholls, "Agriculture and Economic Development"; William H. Nicholls and Ruy Miller Paiva, "Estrutura e produtividade de agricultura brasileira," *Revista brasileira de economia* 19 (June 1965): 27-63; Ruy Miller Paiva, "Bases de uma política para a melhoria técnica da agricultura brasileira," *Revista brasileira de economia* 21 (July 1967): 5-38; Ruy Miller Paiva, "Modernização e dualismo tecnológico na agricultura," *Pesquisa e planejamento* 1 (Dec. 1971): 171-234.

35. Yujiro Hayami and Vernon W. Ruttan, *Agricultural Development: An International Perspective* (Baltimore: Johns Hopkins Press, 1971); cf. Alain de Janvry, "A Socioeconomic Model of Induced Innovations for Argentine Agricultural Development," *Quarterly Journal of Economics* 87 (Aug. 1973): 410-435.

36. For a pessimistic view of the environmental dangers see William Denevan, "Development and the Imminent Demise of the Amazon Rain Forest," *The Professional Geographer* 25 (May 1973): 130-135. For an opposing view see P. A. Sanchez and S. W. Buol, "Soils of the Tropics and the World Food Crisis," *Science* 188 (9 May 1975): 598-603. Data on agriculture in Vassouras are from *Divisão do Brasil: em micro-regiões homogêneas, 1968* (Rio: IBGE, 1970), pp. 363-364.

## 3. Growth Poles and Developmental Highways in Goiás

1. Douglas H. Graham, "Divergent and Convergent Regional Economic Growth and Internal Migration in Brazil, 1940-60," *Economic Development and Cultural Change* 18 (Apr. 1970): 268-285. Revised and updated per capita income figures can be found in *Conjuntura econômica* 24 (June 1970): 89-106.

2. The historical picture is gleaned from the following secondary sources: *Enciclopédia dos municipios brasileiros, vol. 2, Região Centro-Oeste* and *vol. 36, Goiás* (Rio de Janeiro: IBGE, 1958); Speridião Faissol, *O Mato Grosso de Goiás,* série A, no. 9 (Rio de Janeiro: IBGE, 1952); Speridião Faissol, "O problema do desenvolvimento agrícola do sudeste do planalto central do Brasil," *Revista brasileira de geografia* 19, no. 1 (1957): 3-66; Marília Velloso Galvão, ed., *Geografia do Brasil, vol. 2, Grande Região Centro-Oeste,* Publication no. 16, (Rio de Janeiro: IBGE, 1960); Campanhia Nacional do Aperfeiçoamento de Pessoal da Nivel Superior [CAPES], *Estudos do desenvolvimento regional—Goiás,* série levantamento e análise, no. 21 (Rio de Janeiro: CAPES, 1959). The best presentation of the history of Goiás in English is Paul I. Mandell, "The Development of the Southern Goiás-Brasília Region: Development in a Land-Rich Economy," unpublished doctoral dissertation, Columbia University, 1969, chaps. 3 and 4. For a quantitative analysis of recent policy see Martin T. Katzman, "Regional Development Policy in Brazil: The Role of Growth Poles and Development Highways in Goiás," *Economic Development and Cultural Change* 24 (Oct. 1975): 75-107.

3. Brasil, *Comércio por vias internas, Goiás,* various years.

4. Moacir Silva, *Geografia dos transportes no Brasil,* série A, no. 7, (Rio de Janeiro: IBGE, 1949); *Anuário estatístico do Brasil,* various years; Ney Rodrigues Inocêncio, "As vias de transporte," in Galvão, *Geografia,* pp. 379-418; CAPES, *Estudos de desenvolvimento regional—Goiás; Censo preliminar, 1970, Goiás.*

5. For the view that Brazilian farmers are irrationally traditional see Celso Furtado, *The Economic Growth of Brazil,* trans. Ricardo W. de Aguiar and Eric C. Drysdale (Berkeley: University of California Press, 1968), chap. 36; Preston E. James, "Brazil: Agricultural Development," in Simon K. Kuznets, Wilbert E. Moore, and Joseph J. Spengler, eds., *Economic Growth: Brazil, India, Japan* (Durham, N.C.: Duke University Press, 1956). For evidence to the contrary see Affonso Celso Pastore, *A resposta da produção agrícola aos preços no Brasil,* Universidade de São Paulo, faculdade de ciências econômicas e administrativas, boletim no. 55, 1968.

6. Martin T. Katzman, "The Von Thuenen Paradigm, the Industrial-Urban Hypothesis, and the Spatial Structure of Agriculture," *American Journal of Agricultural Economics* 56 (Nov. 1974): 683-696.

7. In this period real wages for spade workers fell from 930 to 786 in Paraná, from 750 to 574 in Mato Grosso, and from 570 to 525 in Goiás. In the shorter period 1950-1959 wages in São Paulo fell from 840 to 655. All figures are in 1950 cruzeiros, adapted from Raouf Kahil, *Inflation and Economic Development in Brazil, 1946-1963* (Oxford, England: Clarendon Press, 1973), p. 98; George Patrick, *Desenvolvimento agrícola no nordeste* (Rio: IPEA, 1972), relatório de pesquisa, no.11, tables 5.5 and 5.6.

8. Theodore Schultz, "A Framework for Land Economics—the Long View," *Journal of Farm Economics* 33 (May 1951): 205-215; Theodore Schultz, *The Economic Organization of Agriculture* (New York: McGraw-Hill, 1953), chaps. 9, 10, 12, and 18. The seminal empirical works include Vernon W. Ruttan, "The Impact of Urban-Industrial Development on Agriculture in the Ten-

nessee Valley and the Southeast," *Journal of Farm Economics* 37 (Feb. 1955): 38-56; Anthony M. Tang, *Economic Development in the Southern Piedmont, 1860-1950: Its Impact on Agriculture* (Chapel Hill: University of North Carolina Press, 1958); William H. Nicholls, "Industrialization, Factor Markets, and Agricultural Development," *Journal of Political Economy* 69 (Aug. 1961): 319-340. For a test of the hypothesis in São Paulo see William H. Nicholls, "The Transformation of Agriculture in a Semi-industrialized Country: The Case of Brazil," in Eric Thorbecke, ed., *The Role of Agriculture in Economic Development* (New York: National Bureau for Economic Research, 1970), pp. 339-378; also comments by G. Edward Schuh in ibid., pp. 379-385. The hypothesis has much in common with central place theory; see Walter Christaller, *Central Places in Southern Germany* (Englewood Cliffs, N.J.: Prentice-Hall, 1967). That the number of functions and the number of firms per function increases with the size of the market center was observed in São Paulo state by Rui Aguiar Leme, *Contribuições à teoria de localização industrial,* Universidade de São Paulo, faculdade de ciências econômicas e administrativas, boletim no. 39, 1965.

9. The extension of protective labor legislation to farm workers and agitation to grant land to the tiller in the early 1960s resulted in the expulsion of most resident plantation workers. Many of these workers have drifted into nearby towns, which have become markets for casual farm labor.

10. Celso Lafer, "The Planning Process and the Political System in Brazil: A Study of Kubitschek's Target Plan, 1956-1961," unpublished doctoral dissertation, Cornell University, 1970, p. 210.

11. Ibid., chap. 3; "Public Expenses in Brasília," *Conjuntura econômica* 9 (Dec. 1962): 47-54. The cost estimates for Brasília include interregional highways that would enable the city to bridge the archipelago.

12. For a technical discussion of the impact of urbanization on the production of food for export and for local consumption see Richard Muth, "Economic Change and Rural-Urban Land Conversions," *Econometrica* 29 (Jan. 1961): 1-22.

13. Paul I. Mandell, "The Rise of the Modern Brazilian Rice Industry: Demand Expansion in a Dynamic Economy," *Food Research Institute Studies* 10, no. 2 (1971): 161-219.

14. CODEPLAN, *Diagnóstico de abastecimento de produtos alimentícios do Distrito Federal,* 4 vols. (Brasília: Govêrno do Distrito Federal, 1965), vol. 1, tables 8 and 23; vol. 3, tables 72, 73, 87-93, 107-109; vol. 4, tables 32-36.

15. *Anuário estatístico do Brasil* (Rio: IBGE), table 3.5.2 "Comércio Interior," various years.

16. Mario de Barros Cavalcanti, *Da SPVEA à SUDAM* (Belém: Universidade Federal de Pará, 1967).

17. The stability of the state's population dispersion can be expressed by two summary statistics: correlation coefficients and indices of dissimilarity. The correlations of county densities (logarithms) from successive censuses since 1920 are all over .90; and the correlation between 1920 and 1970 is .68, which means that about half the variance in county densities in 1970 is explained by the 1920 population distribution. Indices of dissimilarity indicate that about 11 to 16

percent of the state's population is redistributed between successive censuses and that about 40 percent of the 1970 population would have to be redistributed to reproduce the 1920 county dispersion.

18. For example, P. A. Sanchez and S. W. Buol, "Soils in the Tropics and the World Food Crisis," *Science* 188 (9 May 1975): 602.

19. Commissão interestadual da bacia Paraná-Uruguai, *Plano de industrialização regional, Goiás* (São Paulo: Commissão interestadual, 1964), p. 73 on per capita income by microregions. Per capita income by state is calculated from *Conjuntura econômica* 24 (June 1970): 89-106.

## 4. Colonization and Rural Democracy in Northern Paraná

1. Craig L. Dozier, *Land Development and Colonization in Latin America* (New York: Praeger, 1969); Vania Pörto Tavares, Claudio M. Considera, and Maria Thereza de Castro e Silva, *Colonização dirigida no Brasil* (Rio: IPEA, 1972), relatório de pesquisa, no. 8; Michael Nelson, *The Development of Tropical Lands* (Baltimore: Johns Hopkins Press, 1974).

2. Warren Dean, "Latifundia and Land Policy in Nineteenth-century Brazil," *Hispanic American Historical Review* 51 (Nov. 1971): 606-626; Emília Viotti da Costa, *De senzala à colônia* (São Paulo: Difusão européia, 1966), chaps. 1 and 2.

3. Pierre Monbeig, *Pionniers et planteurs de São Paulo*, Cahiers de la fondation nationale de sciences politiques, 23 (1952); Ariadne Souto Maior, "Povoamento," in Aluizio Capdeville Duarte, ed., *Grande Região Sul*, 2 vols. (Rio: IBGE, 1968), vol. 2, pp. 3-45.

4. Leo Waibel, "As zonas pioneiras do Brasil," *Revista brasileira de geografia* 17 (Oct. 1955): 389-423; Speridião Faissol, *O Mato Grosso de Goiás,* série A, no. 9 (Rio de Janeiro: IBGE, 1952); Otto Vergara, "Análise socio-econômica das migrações inter-rurais: Ceres e Rubiataba — Goiás," unpublished master's thesis, Universidade Rural, Viçosa, M.G. 1968.

5. Lysia Bernardes, "O problema das frentes pioneiras no estado do Paraná," *Revista brasileira de geografia* 15 (July 1953): 335-385; Craig L. Dozier, "Northern Paraná, Brazil: Settlement and Development of a Recent Frontier Zone," unpublished doctoral dissertation, Johns Hopkins University, 1954; Craig L. Dozier, "Northern Paraná, Brazil: An Example of Organized Regional Development," *Geographical Review* 46 (July 1956): 218-233; Pedro Calil Pades, "Formação de uma economia periférica: O caso paranaense," unpublished doctoral dissertation, Pontifical Universidade Católica, São Paulo, 1970; William H. Nicholls, "The Agricultural Frontier in Modern Brazilian History: The State of Paraná, 1920-1965," *Revista brasileira de economia* 24 (Oct-Dec. 1970): 64-92; Emilio Willems, "The Rise of a Rural Middle Class in a Frontier Society," in Riordan Roett, ed., *Brazil in the Sixties* (Nashville: Vanderbilt University Press, 1972), pp. 325-344.

6. Monbeig, *Pionniers et planteurs;* William Cline, *The Economic Consequences of a Land Reform in Brazil* (Amsterdam: North Holland Publishing Co., 1970).

7. The short amortization period of the mortgages may reflect the time horizon with which farmers practicing slash-and-burn agriculture view the land.

Since the time horizon of coffee planters is considerably longer (a tree bears for roughly twenty years), a lengthier amortization period would seem appropriate.

8. Bernardes, "O problema."

9. Monbeig, *Pionniers et planteurs;* Nicholls, "The Agricultural Frontier."

10. Nicholls, "The Agricultural Frontier."

11. Dozier, "Northern Paraná, Brazil: An Example." Brazil, *Censo agrícola, Paraná,* 1940, 1950, and 1960. Cruzeiros are inflated to 1960 prices using the index in *Conjuntura econômica* 25 (Feb. 1971): 160.

12. Gordon Smith, "Brazilian Agricultural Policy, 1950-1967," in Howard Ellis, ed., *The Economy of Brazil* (Berkeley: University of California Press, 1970), pp. 213-265.

13. Maxine L. Margolis, *The Moving Frontier: Social and Economic Change in a Southern Brazilian Community,* Latin American Monographs, 2nd series, no. 11 (Gainesville: University of Florida Press, 1973), chap. 4.

14. Very few people from the poorest region of Brazil, the Northeast, have migrated to Paraná, mainly because of the distance involved. Of all individuals living in Paraná who were born elsewhere, 53 percent were from São Paulo and only 5 percent were from the Northeast in both 1940 and 1950. By 1970 the share born in São Paulo fell to 33 percent and the share born in the Northeast rose to 15 percent.

15. Nicholls, "The Agricultural Frontier."

16. These events were reported in *Estado do São Paulo* in the period 1964-1965.

17. Albert O. Hirschman, *Journeys Toward Progress* (New York: Twentieth Century Fund, 1963), chap. 1.

### 5. Planning for a Demographic Vacuum: Amazonia

1. On the geography of the Amazon see Hilgard O'Reilly Sternberg, *The Amazon River of Brazil,* Erdkundliches Wissen, vol. 4 (Wiesbaden: Franz Steiner Verlag, 1975). For a discussion of the Brazilian ideology of population, resources, and national power, see Herman Daly, "The Population Question in Northeast Brazil: Its Economic and Ideological Dimensions," *Economic Development and Cultural Change* 18 (July 1970): 536-574. For a somewhat paranoid view of foreign greed for Amazonia see Arthur Cezar Ferreira Reis, *A Amazônia e a cobiça internacional* (Rio: Gráfica record editora, 1968); for a slightly more balanced view see Osny Duarte Pereira, *Transamazônica: prós e contras* (Rio: Civilização brasileira, 1970); for a study of a quixotic antebellum project to resettle American slaves in the basin, see Nícia Villela Luz, *A Amazônia para os negros americanos* (Rio: Editora saga, 1968).

2. Good sketches of the rubber cycle are Celso Furtado, *The Economic Growth of Brazil,* trans. Ricardo W. de Aguiar and Eric C. Drysdale (Berkeley: University of California Press, 1968), pp. 141-148; Charles Wagley, *Amazon Town: A Study of Man in the Tropics* (New York: Alfred Knopf, 1964); Speridião Faissol, "Amazônia," in Marília Velloso Galvão, ed., *Panorama regional do Brasil* (Rio: IBGE, 1969), pp. 3-29; for a moving literary account see Richard Collier, *The River that God Forgot: The Story of the Amazon Rubber Boom* (London: Collins, 1968).

3. Brasil, *Sinopse preliminar do censo demográfico,* 1970, table 2.

4. For a description of the Amazonian ecosystems see Antônio Teixeira Guerra, ed., *Grande Região Norte* (Rio: IBGE, 1959); Betty J. Meggers, *Amazonia: Man and Culture in a Counterfeit Paradise* (Chicago: Aldine, 1971).

5. Socrates Bonfim, "Valorização da Amazônia e sua comissão de planejamento," superintêndencia de plano de valorização econômica de Amazônia, *Coleção Araújo Lima* 6 (1958): 13-15.

6. For a discussion of Fordlandia see Wagley, *Amazon Town,* pp. 89-90; Harald Sioli, "Recent Human Activities in the Brazilian Amazon Region and Their Ecological Effects," in Betty J. Meggers, Edward S. Ayensu, and W. Donald Duckworth, eds., *Tropical Forest Ecosystems in Africa and South America* (Washington, D.C.: Smithsonian Institution Press, 1973), pp. 321-334.

7. For these crude computations Brazilian Amazonia is defined as the states of Acre, Amazonas, and Pará and the territories of Amapá, Rondônia, and Roraima. Income estimates are drawn from "As contas nacionais," *Conjuntura econômica* 24 (June 1970): 89-106; population estimates, from Brasil, *Sinopse preliminar,* table 2. It should be noted that physiographically, Brazilian Amazonia extends beyond the above states to include about one-half of Mato Grosso, Goiás, and Maranhão.

8. The hierarchical distribution system has been described by Wagley, *Amazon Town,* pp. 81-101; Roberto Santos, "O equilíbrio da firma aviadora e a significação econômico-institucional do aviamento," *Pará desenvolvimento* 3 (June 1968): 9-30.

9. Phillip Staniford, *Pioneers in the Tropics: The Political Organization of Japanese in an Immigrant Community in Brazil* (New York: Humanities Press, 1973); Orlando Valverde and Catharina V. Dias, *A rodovia Belém-Brasília* (Rio: IBGE, 1967), pp. 90-111. The anthropologist Staniford notes that overseas Japanese descend from sons excluded from inheriting land through the primogeniture system in Japan proper. Such sons, he argues, tend to be highly self-reliant, perseverant, and innovative.

10. Ferreira Reis, *A Amazônia,* pp. 184-234.

11. Jorge Gustavo Costa, *Planejamento governamental: a experiência brasileira* (Rio: Fundação Getúlio Vargas, 1971), chap. 8; Mario de Barros Cavalcanti, *Da SPVEA à SUDAM* (Belém: Universidade federal de Pará, 1967). The ambit of SPVEA and its successor SUDAM corresponds closely to the Brazilian portion of the basin, defined physiographically.

12. Superintendência de plano de valorização, *A SPVEA num visão do conjunto* (Belém, 1955), for a description of the strategy. For a critique of the performance see Cavalcanti, *Da SPVEA à SUDAM;* Costa, *Planejamento governamental,* chap. 8.

13. On the supply and demand for fiscal incentive funds see *Anuário estatístico do Brasil* (Rio: IBGE, 1970 and 1972). On project analysis see Edmar Bacha et al., *Análise governamental de projetos de investimento no Brasil: procedimentos e recomendações* (Rio: IPEA, 1972), relatório de pesquisa, no. 1.

14. *SUDAM em revista* 2 (Aug.-Sept. 1971): 17-18, reviews the projects. On investment per worker see Vania Pôrto Tavares, Claudio Considera, and Maria

Thereza de Castro e Silva, *Colonização dirigida no Brasil: possibilidades na re gião Amazônica* (Rio: IPEA, 1972), relatório de pesquisa, no. 8.

15. The figures on modernization projects in the Northeast are from David Goodman, "Industrial Development in the Brazilian Northeast: An Interim Assessment of the Tax Credit Scheme of Article 34/18," in Riordan Roett, ed., *Brazil in the Sixties* (Nashville: Vanderbilt University Press, 1972), pp. 231-272. Figures for Amazonia are from Annibal Villela and José Almeida, "Obstaculos ao desenvolvimento da Amazônia," *Revista brasileira de economia* 20 (June-Sept. 1966): 177-199.

16. Villela and Almeida, "Obstaculos"; Jonathan Levin, *Export Economies* (Cambridge: Harvard University Press, 1960), part 1; Harvey S. Perloff et al., *Regions, Resources, and Economic Growth* (Lincoln, Neb.: University of Ne- braska Press, 1960), part 2.

17. Pôrto Tavares, Considera, and de Castro e Silva, *Colonização dirigida,* pp. 110-114 and 158-162; Alberto Tamer, *Transamazônica: solução para 2001* (São Paulo: APEC, 1970) pp. 212-218; Pereira, *Transamazônica,* pp. 260-262, for a description of the failure of the Maranhão colonization scheme.

18. Pereira, *Transamazônica,* p. 116.

19. Instituto Nacional de Colonização e Reforma Agraria (INCRA), "A col- onização no Brasil: situação atual, projecções e tendências," Nov.-Dec. 1970; INCRA "Transamazônica—colonização e reforma agraria," June 1971.

20. For a critique on the Right by a former minister of planning, see Roberto de Oliveira Campos, "La rage du vouloir conclure," in Fernando Morais, ed., *Transamazônica* (São Paulo: Editora brasiliense, 1970). The military doctrine of national security through territorial integration is considered in the special issue of *Revista brasileira de estudos políticos* 21 (July 1966). For a defense of the highway see appendix by Eliseu Rezende, in Tamer, *Transamazônica.* The leftist critique of the Transamazon is similar to that of their Russian counter- parts regarding the 1868-1917 colonization of Siberia. In other words both the Right and Left accept the notion of the frontier as a safety value from revo- lutionary pressures.

21. *Visão,* August 13, 1973.

22. Shelton H. Davis, *Victims of the Miracle: Development against the In- dians of Brazil* (Cambridge, England: Cambridge University Press, 1977). In June-July 1972 the São Paulo newspapers carried several stories about the bloody conflict between a cattle company and peasants who squatted on the "compa- ny's" land for forty years prior to the company's establishment. The peasant co- operative was effectively dissolved and the members scattered. For example, see *Estado do São Paulo,* June 27, 1972.

23. Paul I. Mandell, "The Rise and Decline of Geography in Brazilian Devel- opment Planning," paper presented at Conference of Latin American Geogra- phers, Syracuse University, December 2-4, 1971. See Valverde and Dias, *A ro- dovia,* p. 109, on how the Japanese pepper achievements defied prediction. For an intelligently pessimistic view of Amazonia's prospects see William N. Dene- van, "Development and the Imminent Demise of the Amazon Rain Forest," *The Professional Geographer* 25 (May 1973): 130-135.

24. See Sioli, "Recent Human Activities," for a simple scheme. Yield esti-

mates are from Meggers, *Amazonia*, p. 22. Consumption patterns refer to a middle-income urban family in Maranhão, where rice prices are low; from Paul I. Mandell, "The Rise of the Modern Brazilian Rice Industry," *Food Research Institute Studies* 10, no. 2 (1971): 161-219. Note that milled rice has about half the weight of the unmilled.

25. Albert O. Hirschman, *Development Projects Observed* (Washington, D.C.: Brookings Institution, 1967), pp. 39-44 ff.

## 6. The Process of Regional Integration

1. On fiscal barriers see Aloísio Barboza de Araújo, Maria Helena Taques Horta, and Claudio M. Considera, *Transferências de impôstos aos estados e municípios* (Rio: IPEA, 1973), relatório de pesquisa, no. 16, pp. 20-29; on development banks see "Os agentes do desenvolvimento," *Perfil, supplemento de visão* 39 (Dec. 1971).

2. Gordon Smith, "Agricultural Marketing and Economic Development: A Brazilian Case Study," unpublished doctoral dissertation, Harvard University, 1965; Gordon Smith, "Brazilian Agricultural Policy, 1950-1967," in Howard Ellis, ed., *The Economy of Brazil* (Berkeley: University of California Press, 1969), pp. 213-265; Howard Gauthier, "Transportation and the Growth of the São Paulo Economy," *Journal of Regional Science* 8 (Summer 1968): 77-94; Paul I. Mandell, "The Development of the Southern Goiás-Brasília Region: Development in a Land-Rich Economy," unpublished doctoral dissertation, Columbia University, 1969.

3. Werner Baer, Isaac Kerstenetzky, and Mario H. Simonsen, "Transportation and Inflation: A Study of Irrational Policy Making in Brazil," *Economic Development and Cultural Change* 13 (Jan. 1965): 188-202; Alan Abouchar, "Inflation and Transportation Policy in Brazil," *Economic Development and Cultural Change* 18 (Oct. 1968): 92-109; Pedro Cipollari, *O problema ferroviário no Brasil*, Universidade de São Paulo, faculdade de ciências econômicas e administrativas, boletim no. 52, 1969; "Transportes no Brasil: estudo especial," *Conjuntura econômica* 28 (May 1974): 53-94.

4. Since orthodox neoclassical analysis is so heavily biased toward equilibrating or negative feedback processes, no specific citations are warranted. The opposing view, which may have originated from such a notorious Marxist as Lenin himself as the Law of Uneven Capitalist Development was revived by Gunnar Myrdal, *Economic Theory and Underdeveloped Regions* (London: Duckworth, 1959) and Albert O. Hirschman, "Interregional and International Transmission of Economic Growth" in Albert O. Hirschman, *The Strategy of Economic Development* (New Haven: Yale University Press, 1958), pp. 183-201. The dynamic concept of cumulative and circular causation is an elaboration of the vicious circle from Myrdal's earlier study of race relations, *The American Dilemma: The Negro Problem and American Democracy* (New York: Harper and Brothers, 1944), especially pp. 1065-1070. Applications of the polarization approach to Latin America come from the structuralists, whose seminal paper is Raul Prebisch, "Economic Development of Latin America and its Problems," United Nations, 1950, and reprinted in *Economic Bulletin for Latin America* 7 (Feb. 1962): 1-22. For a most recent statement of this view see Anibal Pinto and

Jan Knakel, "The Center-Periphery System Twenty Years Later," *Social and Economic Studies* 22 (Mar. 1973): 34-89. For a neo-Marxist restatement see Andre Gunder Frank, *Capitalism and Underdevelopment in Latin America* (New York: Monthly Review Press, 1967).

5. The terms of trade effect are the major mechanisms by which the gains of integration are said to be transferred to the center. See Hans Singer, "The Distribution of Gains between Investing and Borrowing Countries," *American Economic Review* 40 (May 1950): 473-485; Ragner Nurkse, *The Problems of Capital Formation in Underdeveloped Countries* (London: Oxford University Press, 1957); Jagdish Bhagwati, "Immiserizing Growth," *Review of Economic Studies* 25 (1958): 201-205.

6. Hirschman, *Strategy,* pp. 183-201.

7. Frank, *Capitalism and Underdevelopment;* Jonathan Falk, "Regional Inequality and Rural Development: The Case of the Maine Paper Industry," unpublished honors thesis, Harvard College, 1973.

8. Jeffrey G. Williamson, "Regional Inequality and the Process of National Development," *Economic Development and Cultural Change* 13 (July 1965): 3-45.

9. The value of the index is 0 when the distribution of employment is identical in all states; the maximal value of the index is unity. Income figures are from *Conjuntura econômica* 24 (June 1970): 89-106; employment figures from Celsius A. Lodder, "Crescimento da ocupação regional e seus componentes," in Paulo Haddad, ed., *Planejamento regional: métodos e aplicação ao caso brasileiro* (Rio: IPEA, 1972), série monográfica, no. 8, pp. 53-110.

10. Sergio Boisier, Martin O. Smolka, and Aluizio A. de Barros, *Desenvolvimento regional e urbano: diferenciais de produtividade e salários industriais* (Rio: IPEA, 1973), relatório de pesquisa, no. 15.

11. Albert Fishlow, "Brazilian Size Distribution of Income," *American Economic Review* 62 (May 1972): 391-402.

12. Douglas Graham and Sérgio Buarque de Hollanda Filho, *Migration, Regional and Urban Growth and Development in Brazil: A Selective Analysis of the Historical Record—1872-1970,* Instituto de pesquisas econômicas, Universidade de São Paulo, 1971. The internal migration rates for intercensal periods greater than ten years are adjusted to reflect ten-year rates. Data on migrant stocks are from Alberto Cataldi and Manoel A. Costa, "Análise demográfico regional," Rio, IPEA, August 1969, chap. 7; Milton da Mata, Eduardo de Carvalho, and Maria Thereza de Castro e Silva, *Migrações internas no Brasil: aspectos econômicos e demográficos* (Rio: IPEA, 1973), relatório de pesquisa, no. 19, pp. 57-61.

13. Lorene Yap, "Internal Migration and Economic Development in Brazil," unpublished doctoral dissertation, Harvard University, 1972, pp. 50-59; Mata et al., *Migrações internas,* chap. 4.

14. Douglas Graham, "Divergent and Convergent Regional Economic Growth and Internal Migration in Brazil, 1940-1960," *Economic Development and Cultural Change* 18 (Apr. 1970): 268-285; Graham and Buarque, *Migration,* chap.4; Mata et al., *Migrações internas.*

15. Gian Sahota, "An Analysis of Internal Migration in Brazil," *Journal of Political Economy* 76 (Mar. 1968): 218-245.

16. Hirschman, *Strategy,* pp. 183-201; Albert O. Hirschman, *Journeys Toward Progress* (New York: Twentieth Century Fund, 1963), chap. 1. A study of fiscal transfers in the nineteenth-century United States suggests that the industrial center, in this case New England and the Middle Atlantic states, received net inflows from the Midwestern frontier states; see Lance E. Davis and John Legler, "The Government in the American Economy, 1815-1902," *Journal of Economic History* 26 (Dec. 1966): 514-552.

17. Some of these changes are reviewed in Araújo, Taques Horta, and Considera, *Transferências;* Thomas E. Skidmore, *Politics in Brazil, 1930-1964* (London: Oxford University Press, 1967); Nathaniel H. Leff, *Economic Policy-Making and Development in Brazil, 1947-1964* (New York: John Wiley, 1968); Celso Lafer, "The Planning Process and the Political System in Brazil: A Study of Kubitschek's Target Plan, 1956-1961," unpublished doctoral dissertation, Cornell University, 1970.

18. Araújo, Taques Horta, and Considera, *Transferências;* Hans Schellenberg and José C. de Souza Lima, *Um aspecto da reforma tributaria: o fundo de participação,* Instituto de pesquisas econômicas, Universidade de São Paulo, 1971.

19. Werner Baer, "Regional Inequality and Economic Growth in Brazil," *Economic Development and Cultural Change* 12 (Apr. 1964): 268-285, was the first to consider the effects of import substitution policies on regional disparities. For an analysis of policies in the 1960s see Osmundo E. Rebouças, "Interregional Effects of Economic Policies: Multisectoral General Equilibrium Estimates for Brazil," unpublished doctoral dissertation, Harvard University, 1974, especially chap. 5.

20. The methodology in this section is from J. Thomas Romans, *Capital Exports and Growth Among U.S. Regions* (Middletown, Conn.: Wesleyan University Press, 1965).

21. Martin T. Katzman, "The Influence of Transportation Improvements on Interregional Trade in Brazil," *Transportation,* in press.

22. All correlations referred to henceforth are Spearman's rank order. Since all are based on $n = 20 \pm 1$, one-tail statistical significance at the .05 level is achieved when $r = \pm 0.38$.

23. Leff, *Economic Policy-Making;* Warren Dean, *The Industrialization of São Paulo, 1880-1945* (Austin: University of Texas Press, 1969).

24. Maria de Conceição Tavares and Antônio Castro, "Economic Planning in Brazil at the Level of the States," *Economic Bulletin for Latin America* 11 (Oct. 1966); Jorge Gustavo Costa, *Planejamento governamental* (Rio: Fundação Getúlio Vargas, 1971), chap. 9. On the role of the Higher War College see Stefan Robock, *Brazil: A Study in Development Progress* (Lexington, Mass.: D.C. Heath, 1975), pp. 189-195.

### 7. The Developing Center: Industrial Agglomeration in São Paulo

1. Edward Ullman, "Regional Development and the Geography of Concentration," *Papers and Proceedings, Regional Science Association* 4 (1958): 179-198.

2. For recent applications of these concepts see Allen Pred, *The Spatial Dynamics of U.S. Urban-Industrial Growth* (Cambridge: MIT Press, 1966),

chap. 3; Allen Pred, *Urban Growth and the Circulation of Information: The U.S. System of Cities 1790-1840* (Cambridge: Harvard University Press, 1973).

3. While American cities have tended to grow areally by annexations, Brazilian counties have tended to be dismembered. Thus, the populations in both Rio and São Paulo would have become progressively larger than indicated if the original boundries were reconstituted. On a metropolitan basis the São Paulo population probably exceeded that of Rio in the early 1950s and was 16 percent larger, 8.4 million versus 7.2 million in 1970. Even if we add the population of Brasília to that of Rio to compensate for the transference of the capital, these results still hold.

4. François Perroux, "Note sur la notion de 'pôle de croissance,' " *Economie appliquée* 8 (Jan.-June 1955): 307-320, translated in David L. McKee, Robert D. Dean, and William H. Leahy, eds., *Regional Economics* (New York: Free Press, 1970), pp. 93-104.

5. Albert O. Hirschman, *The Strategy of Economic Development* (New Haven: Yale University Press, 1958), pp. 183-201.

6. Charles E. Richter, "The Impact of Industrial Linkages on Geographic Association," *Journal of Regional Science* 9 (Apr. 1969): 19-27; M. E. Streit, "Spatial Associations and Economic Linkages Between Industries," *Journal of Regional Science* 9 (Aug. 1969): 177-188; Stan Czamanski, "Some Empirical Evidence of the Strength of Linkages Between Groups of Related Industries in Urban-Regional Complexes," *Papers and Proceedings, Regional Science Association* 21 (1971): 137-150; Wilbur Thompson, "Internal and External Factors in the Development of Urban Economies," in Harvey S. Perloff and Lowdon Wingo, eds., *Issues in Urban Economics* (Baltimore: Johns Hopkins Press, 1969): 43-62; Nathaniel Leff, *The Brazilian Capital Goods Industry, 1929-1964* (Cambridge: Harvard University Press, 1968); cf. Edward Ames and Nathan Rosenberg, "The Progressive Division of Labor and Specialization of Industries," *Journal of Development Studies* 1 (July 1965): 363-383.

7. The American school has been developed by several luminaries. The best syntheses are Eric E. Lampard, "The History of Cities in the Economically Advanced Areas," *Economic Development and Cultural Change* 3 (Jan. 1955): 81-102; Walter Isard, *Location and Space-Economy* (Cambridge: MIT Press, 1956), pp. 172-187; Robert M. Lichtenberg, *One-Tenth of a Nation* (Cambridge: Harvard University Press, 1960); Edgar Hoover and Raymond Vernon, *Anatomy of a Metropolis* (Cambridge: Harvard University Press, 1959), chaps. 1-5; Benjamin Chinitz, "Contrasts in Agglomeration: New York and Pittsburgh," *American Economic Review* 51 (May 1961): 279-289; Wilbur Thompson, "Internal and External Factors," in Perloff and Wingo, eds., *Issues;* Jane Jacobs, *The Economy of Cities* (New York: Random House, 1969), chaps. 3-6.

8. A clear analysis of the external economies of education is Gary Becker, *Human Capital: A Theoretical and Empirical Analysis* (New York: Columbia University Press, 1964), chap. 2.

9. On rates of return to education see Carlos Geraldo Langoni, "A Study in Economic Growth: The Brazilian Case," unpublished doctoral dissertation, University of Chicago, 1970, chap. 4. On specialization in skill-intensive industries

see Martin T. Katzman, "Some Developing Region Tests of the Heckscher-Ohlin Theory," *Review of Regional Studies* 5 (Jan. 1976): 92-98.

10. George Stigler, "The Division of Labor is Limited by the Extent of the Market," *Journal of Political Economy* 59 (June 1951): 185-193.

11. Carlos Antônio Rocca, "Economias de escala na função produção," unpublished doctoral dissertation, Universidade de São Paulo, faculdade de ciências econômicas e adminstrativas, 1967, summarized in Joel Bergsman, *Brazil: Industrialization and Trade Policies* (New York: Oxford University Press, 1970), appendix 2.

12. Martin O. Smolka and Celsius A. Lodder, "Concentração, tamanho urbano e estrutura industrial," *Pesquisa e planejamento econômico* 3 (June 1973): 447-468.

13. Walter Paul Krause, *O problema industrial paulista* (São Paulo: Comissão interestadual da bacia Paraná-Uruguai, 1964), p. 28.

14. From Paul Singer, *Desenvolvimento econômico e evolução urbana* (São Paulo: Universidade de São Paulo, 1970), chap. 2.

15. Ivo Babarovic, "Polos de desarollo y superación de la marginalidad rural: elementos para la definición de una política regional," Brasil, ministério de planejamento, IPEA (mimeo, 1970, 4 vols.).

16. Chauncy D. Harris, "The Market as a Factor in the Localization of Industry in the United States," *Annals of the Association of American Geographers* 44 (Dec. 1954): 315-331 and 341-348; Edward Ullman, "Regional Development"; Alan Pred, "The Concentration of High Valued-Added Manufacturing," *Economic Geography* 41 (Apr. 1965): 108-132.

17. Exports of metropolitan São Paulo were estimated in a special survey, in Govêrno do estado de São Paulo, secretária de economia e planejamento, *Pesquisa do setor industrial de grande São Paulo,* 3 vols., 1969, vol. 1, pp. 191-192 and vol. 3, pp. 42, 157.

18. Lance E. Davis, "Capital Markets and Industrial Concentration: The U.S. and the U.K., A Comparative Study," *Economic History Review* 19, no. 2 (1966): 255-272; Lance E. Davis, "Capital Immobilities and Finance Capitalism: A Study of Economic Evolution in the U.S. 1820-1920," *Explorations in Economic History,* 2nd series, 1 (Fall 1963): 88-105.

19. Nícia Villela Luz, *A luta pela industrialização brasileira* (São Paulo: Difusão européia, 1961); Warren Dean, *The Industrialization of São Paulo* (Austin: University of Texas Press, 1969); Fernando Henrique Cardoso, *O empresário industrial e desenvolvimento econômico* (São Paulo: Difusão européia, 1964).

20. Samuel Morley and Gordon Smith, "Import Substitution and Foreign Investment in Brazil," *Oxford Economic Papers* 23 (Mar. 1971): 120-135; Leff, *The Brazilian Capital Goods Industry.*

21. On the salience of the center as an investment opportunity see Hirschman, *Strategy of Economic Development,* pp. 183-201; Michael J. Webber, *The Influence of Uncertainty on Location* (Cambridge: MIT Press, 1973).

22. Sectoral patterns of foreign investment are from Stefan H. Robock, *Brazil: A Study in Development Progress* (Lexington, Mass: D.C. Heath, 1975),

pp. 62-65. Correlations are 0.76 in 1950, 0.71 in 1960, and 0.76 in 1970.

23. Fred W. Riggs, *Administration in Developing Countries: The Theory of Prismatic Society* (Boston: Houghton Mifflin, 1964); Celso Lafer, "The Planning Process and the Political System in Brazil: A Study of Kubitscheck's Target Plan, 1956-1961," unpublished doctoral dissertation, Cornell University, 1970; John Friedmann, "The Spatial Organization of Power in the Development of Urban Systems," *Development and Change* 4, no. 3 (1972-1973): 12-50.

24. "Atividades empresarial dos govêrnos federal e estaduais," *Conjuntura econômica* 27 (June 1973): 66-95.

25. Nathaniel Leff, *Economic Policy-Making and Development in Brazil, 1947-1964* (New York: John Wiley, 1968).

26. John Wirth, *The Politics of Brazilian Development, 1930-1954* (Stanford: Stanford University Press, 1970).

27. Judith Tendler, *Electric Power in Brazil: Entrepreneurship in the Public Sector* (Cambridge: Harvard University Press, 1968).

### 8. Planning for the Periphery: The Northeastern Problem

1. Caio Prado Júnior, *The Colonial Background of Modern Brazil*, trans. Suzette Macedo (Berkeley: University of California Press, 1967), pp. 35-85.

2. Friedrich Freise, "The Drought Region of Northeastern Brazil," *Geographical Review* 28 (July 1938): 363-378.

3. This discussion draws heavily upon Stefan H. Robock, *Brazil's Developing Northeast* (Washington, D.C.: Brookings Institution, 1963); Albert O. Hirschman, *Journeys Toward Progress* (New York: Twentieth Century Fund, 1963), chap. 1; Jorge Gustavo Costa, *Planejamento governamental: a experiência brasileira* (Rio: Forense, 1972), vol. 2, chap. 6.

4. Robock, *Brazil's Developing Northeast*, p. 80.

5. Conselho de Desenvolvimento de Nordeste (CODENO), *A Policy for the Development of the Northeast*, Doc. no. 1, 1959. Nathaniel Leff argues that the overvaluation of the exchange rate in the nineteenth century initiated the Northeast-Southeast disparity. Undertaken to maximize Brazil's advantage as a coffee monopolist, this policy resulted in pricing sugar and cotton, northeastern staples in which Brazil had no monopoly, out of world markets. See his "Economic Development and Regional Inequality: The Origins of the Brazilian Case," *Quarterly Journal of Economics* 86 (May 1972): 243-262.

6. See the discussion in Riordan Roett, *The Politics of Foreign Aid in the Brazilian Northeast* (Nashville: Vanderbilt University Press, 1972).

7. David E. Goodman, Júlio Sena, and Roberto Cavalcanti de Albuquerque, "Os incentivos financeiros à industrialização do Nordeste, e a escolha de tecnologias," *Pesquisa e planejamento* 1 (Dec. 1971): 329-365; Albert O. Hirschman, "Industrial Development in the Brazilian Northeast and the Tax Incentive Scheme of Article 34/18," *Journal of Development Studies* 5 (Oct. 1968): 5-28; Edmar Bacha et al., *Análise governamental de projetos do investimento no Brasil: procedimentos e recomendações* (Rio: IPEA, 1971), relatório de pesquisa, no. 3.

8. David Goodman, "Industrial Development in the Brazilian Northeast:

An Interim Assessment of the Tax Credit Scheme of Article 34/18," in Riordan Roett, ed., *Brazil in the Sixties* (Nashville: Vanderbilt University Press, 1972); Goodman et al., "Os incentivos financeiros."

9. This section draws very heavily on Hirschman, *Journeys,* chap. 1; Fred Riggs, *Administration in Developing Countries: The Theory of Prismatic Society* (Boston: Houghton Mifflin, 1964); Albert Waterston, *Development Planning* (Baltimore: Johns Hopkins Press, 1965).

10. Robock, *Brazil's Developing Northeast,* p. 86.

11. William R. Cline, "Cost-Benefit Analysis of Irrigation in Northeast Brazil," *American Journal of Agricultural Economics* 55 (Nov. 1973): 622-627; Vania Pôrto Tavares, Claudio M. Considera, and Maria Thereza de Castro e Silva, *Colonização dirigida no Brasil* (Rio: IPEA, 1972), relatório de pesquisa, no. 8.

12. The structuralist view of nonadaptive northeastern agriculture is reiterated by Francisco Sá, "O desenvolvimento da agricultura nordestina e a função das atividades de subsistência," *Estudos CEBRAP* 3 (Jan. 1973): 87-147. While the price-elasticity of the supply of foodstuffs in the Northeast is somewhat less than in São Paulo, it is clearly positive. Surprisingly, the supply curves for the two northeastern export staples seem to be backward bending, according to Affonso Celso Pastore, *A resposta de produção agrícola aos preços,* Universidade de São Paulo, faculdade de ciências econômicas e administrativas, boletim no. 55, 1968. Michael Sund, "Land Tenure and Economic Performance of Agricultural Establishments in Northeast Brazil," Land Tenure Center, University of Wisconsin, RP-17, April 1965, suggests that latifundia lands are only slightly less intensively used than lands on middle-sized farms. For an exhaustive review of the performance of northeastern agriculture see George Patrick, *Desenvolvimento agrícola do Nordeste* (Rio: IPEA, 1972), relatório de pesquisa, no. 11.

13. David E. Goodman and Roberto Cavalcanti de Albuquerque, *A industrialização do Nordeste, vol. 1, a economia regional* (Rio: IPEA, 1971), relatório de pesquisa, no. 6; Osmundo E. Rebouças, "Interregional Effects of Economic Policies: Multi-sectoral General Equilibrium Estimates for Brazil," unpublished doctoral dissertation, Harvard University, 1974, chaps. 4 and 5.

14. Patrick, *Desenvolvimento agrícola,* pp. 158-163; Rebouças, "Interregional Effects," chap. 5.

15. Herman Daly, "The Population Question in Northeast Brazil: Its Economic and Ideological Dimensions," *Economic Development and Cultural Change* 18 (July 1970): 536-574.

16. Richard and Francine Weisskopf, "The Political Economy of the Educational System," in H. Jon Rosenbaum and William G. Tyler, eds., *Contemporary Brazil: Issues in Economic and Political Development* (New York: Praeger, 1972), pp. 371-398.

17. José Francisco Camargo, *Êxodo rural no Brasil,* Universidade de São Paulo, faculdade de ciências econômicas e administrativas, boletim no. 1, 1957, pp. 50-64; C. Procópio Camargo and Elza Berquo, eds., *Diferenciais de fertilidade* (São Paulo: CEBRAP, 1971), caderno no. 1.

## 9. Urbanization and Sectoral Change

1. The share of American population in cities of over twenty-five hundred inhabitants rose from 25.7 to 51.2 percent between 1870 and 1920. See Eric E. Lampard, "The Evolving System of Cities in the United States," in Harvey S. Perloff and Lowdon Wingo, eds., *Issues in Urban Economics* (Baltimore: Johns Hopkins Press, 1968), pp. 107-108.

2. Jeffrey G. Williamson, "Urbanization in the American Northeast, 1820-1870," in Robert Fogel and Stanley Engerman, eds., *Reinterpretation of American Economic History* (New York: Harper and Row, 1971), pp. 426-436; Douglas H. Graham and Sérgio Buarque de Hollanda Filho, "Interregional and Urban Migration and Economic Growth in Brazil," paper presented at a Symposium on Internal Migration, CEDEPLAR, Belo Horizonte, April 1972.

3. Brasil, *Censo demográfico,* 1940, 1950, 1960, and 1970, various state volumes. Inferences on the industrial labor force are drawn from self-reports in the demographic census, which covers the entire labor force. Because this census was incomplete for 1960, few conclusions can be drawn for this year.

4. Williamson, "Urbanization in the American Northeast."

5. Thomas O. Wilkinson, "Urban Structure and Industrialization," *American Sociological Review* 25 (June 1960): 356-363; N. V. Sovani, "An Analysis of Overurbanization," *Economic Development and Cultural Change* 12 (Jan. 1964): 113-122; Gur Ofer, "Industrial Structure, Urbanization, and the Growth Strategy of Socialist Countries," *Quarterly Journal of Economics* 90 (May 1976): 197-218.

6. Hollis B. Chenery, "Patterns of Industrial Growth," *American Economic Review* 50 (Sept. 1960): 624-654; Simon Kuznets, *Modern Economic Growth* (New Haven: Yale University Press, 1966); Simon Kuznets, *Economic Growth of Nations* (Cambridge: Harvard University Press, 1971).

7. A clear textbook presentation of dualistic models is Paul Zarembka, *Toward a Theory of Economic Development* (San Francisco: Holden-Day, 1972).

8. From Michael Todaro, "A Model of Labor Migration," *American Economic Review* 59 (Mar. 1969): 138-148; John Harris and Michael Todaro, "Migration and Unemployment," *American Economic Review* 60 (Mar. 1970): 126-142.

9. Lorene Yap, "Internal Migration and Economic Development in Brazil," unpublished doctoral dissertation, Harvard University, 1972.

10. Graham and Buarque, "Interregional and Urban Migration."

11. Lampard, "The Evolving System," pp. 107-108.

12. On the urbanization of nonagricultural activities see T. S. Ashton, *The Industrial Revolution* (New York: Oxford University Press, 1948), pp. 24-26, 109-118; Stephen Hymer and Stephen Resnick, "A Model of an Agrarian Economy with Nonagricultural Activities," *American Economic Review* 59 (Sept. 1969): 493-506; Stephen Resnick, "The Decline of Rural Industry under Export Expansion," *Journal of Economic History* 30 (Mar. 1970): 51-73; Thomas J. Weiss, "Urbanization and the Growth of the Service Workforce," *Explorations in Economic History* 8 (Spring 1971): 241-258.

13. This argument assumes infinitely increasing internal economies and transport costs that are born by the customer. The derivation is spelled out in more detail in a classic article on central place theory by August Loesch, "The Nature of Economic Regions," *Southern Economic Journal* 5 (July 1938): 71-78. For a numerical demonstration of the trade-off between internal economies and transportation costs see William R. Henry and James A. Seagrave, "Economic Aspects of Broiler Density Production," *Journal of Farm Economics* 42 (Feb. 1960): 1-17.

14. Carlos Antônio Rocca, "Economias de escala na função produção," unpublished doctoral dissertation, Universidade de São Paulo, faculdade de ciências econômicas e administrativas, 1967, summarized in Joel Bergsman, *Brazil: Industrialization and Trade Policies* (New York: Oxford University Press, 1970), appendix 2.

15. Allan Pred, "The External Relations of Cities During 'Industrial Revolution,'" University of Chicago, department of geography, research paper no. 76, 1962; and Allan Pred, *The Spatial Dynamics of U.S. Urban-Industrial Growth* (Cambridge: MIT Press, 1966), chap. 3.

16. Since the industrial census only includes modern industry, it clearly undercounts rural handicrafts and cottage industries. We are here assuming that modern rural industry is midway on a spectrum between workshops and urban factories.

17. Four regions multiplied by five quarters yields twenty observations; therefore, all correlations are significant at the .05 level. Source: IBGE, *Pesquisa nacional de amostragem domiciliar,* first quarter 1970. The four regions for which this relationship was calculated were South, São Paulo, Minas Gerais-Espírito Santo, and Northeast. Guanabara-Rio was excluded for lack of significant rural population.

18. Brasil, *Censo demográfico,* 1960, part 1, table 15, various states; and IBGE, *Pesquisa nacional.*

19. Among their fringe benefits, employees are entitled to a paid "thirteenth month" Christmas bonus, tenure after ten years, and pensions upon retirement. On the other hand, employees must pay income and social security taxes, which many marginally employed avoid.

20. Ignes Costa Barbosa, Lourdes de Mattos Strauch, and Maria de Glória Campos Hereda, "Atividades industriais," in Aluizio Capdeville Duarte, ed., *Geografia do Brasil: Grande Região Sul,* vol 4, part 2 (Rio: IBGE, 1968), pp. 189-236.

## 10. Hyperurbanization and the Labor Absorption Problem

1. Bert Hoselitz, "Parasitic and Generative Cities," in Bert Hoselitz, *Sociological Aspects of Economic Growth* (Glencoe, Ill.: Free Press, 1960); Janet Abu-Lughod, "Hyperurbanization in Egypt," *Economic Development and Cultural Change* 13 (Apr. 1965): 313-343; Werner Baer and Michel Hervé, "Employment and Industrialization in Underdeveloped Countries," *Quarterly Journal of Economics* 80 (Feb. 1966): 88-107; "Structural Changes in Employment within the Context of Latin America's Economic Development," *Economic Bulletin for Latin America* 10 (Oct. 1965): 163-187; Lúcio Kowarick, *Capital-*

*ismo e marginalidade na América Latina* (Rio: Paz e terra, 1975); Joseph Ramos, *Labor and Development in Latin America* (New York: Columbia University Press, 1970).

2. Baer and Hervé, "Employment and Industrialization."

3. Adam Smith, *The Wealth of Nations,* Modern Library Edition (New York: Random House, 1937), p. 315; see discussion in Harry Greenfield, *Manpower and the Growth of Producer Services* (New York: Columbia University Press, 1966).

4. Walter Galenson, "Economic Development and the Sectoral Expansion of Employment," *International Labor Review* 88 (June 1963): p. 516.

5. Simon Kuznets, *Modern Economic Growth* (New Haven: Yale University Press, 1966), pp. 86-127; Simon Kuznets, *The Economic Growth of Nations* (Cambridge: Harvard University Press, 1971), pp. 99-208; Wanderly de Almeida and Maria de Conceição Silva, *Dinâmica do setor serviços no Brasil: emprego e produto* (Rio: IPEA, 1973), relatório de pesquisa, no. 18.

6. Gur Ofer, *The Service Sector in Soviet Economic Growth* (Cambridge: Harvard University Press, 1973); Gur Ofer, "Industrial Structure, Urbanization, and the Growth Strategy of Socialist Countries," *Quarterly Journal of Economics* 90 (May 1976): 219-244.

7. Peter Bauer and Basil S. Yamey, "Economic Progress and the Occupational Distribution," *Economic Journal* 61 (Dec. 1951): 741-755 and "Further Notes on Economic Progress and the Occupational Distribution," *Economic Journal* 64 (Mar. 1954): 98-101; M. A. Katouzian, "The Development of the Service Sector: A New Approach," *Oxford Economic Papers* 22 (Nov. 1970): 362-382.

8. Fred W. Riggs, *Administration in Developing Countries: The Theory of Prismatic Society* (Boston: Houghton Mifflin, 1964); Celso Lafer, "The Planning Process and the Political System in Brazil," unpublished doctoral dissertation, Cornell University, 1970,

9. Edmar Bacha, "El subempleo, el costo social de la mano de obra, y la estrategia brasileña de crecimiento," *El trimestre económico* 33 (Oct.-Dec. 1971): 1069-1079; Joel Bergsman and Arthur Candal, "Industrialization: Past Success and Future Problems," in Howard Ellis, ed., *The Economy of Brazil* (Berkeley: University of California Press, 1971), pp. 29-73.

10. Baer and Hervé, "Employment and Industrialization"; Werner Baer, *The Development of the Brazilian Steel Industry* (Nashville: Vanderbilt University Press, 1969). For an examination of the Stalinist justification of capital-intensive development see Peter J. D. Wiles, *The Political Economy of Communism* (Cambridge: Harvard University Press, 1964), chap. 16; Joseph Berliner, "The Economics of Overtaking and Surpassing," in Henry Rosovsky, ed., *Industrialization in Two Systems* (New York: John Wiley, 1966), pp. 159-185. For a discussion of managerial salaries see José Pastore, Archibald O. Haller, and Hernando Gomez-Buendia, "Wage Differentials in São Paulo's Labor Force," *Industrial Relations* 14 (Oct. 1975): 345-357.

11. For this argument about imported technology see Bergsman and Candal, "Industrialization"; Gordon Smith and Samuel Morley, "Managerial Discretion and the Choice of Technology by Multinational Firms in Brazil," Rice Univer-

sity, Program in Development Studies, Paper no. 56, 1976. For a rebuttal see Nathaniel Leff, *The Brazilian Capital Goods Industry, 1929-1964* (Cambridge: Harvard University Press, 1968); Kent Hughes, "Factor Prices, Capital Intensity and Technological Adaptation," in H. Jon Rosenbaum and William G. Tyler, *Contemporary Brazil: Issues in Economic and Political Development* (New York: Praeger, 1972), pp. 125-138.

12. For a general analysis of labor absorption and discussion of demand see David Morawetz, "Employment Implications of Industrialization in Developing Countries: A Survey," *Economic Journal* 84 (Sept. 1974): 491-542; for an analytical model of a Brazilian-type economy see Lance Taylor and Edmar L. Bacha, "The Unequalizing Spiral: A First Growth Model for Belindia," *Quarterly Journal of Economics* 90 (May 1976): 197-218; for some empirical estimates see William R. Cline, *Potential Effects of Income Redistribution on Economic Growth: Latin American Cases* (New York: Praeger, 1972).

13. Roberto Santos, *Leis sociais e custo da mão-de-obra no Brasil* (São Paulo: Universidade de São Paulo and Editora LTr, 1973); Edmar Bacha, Milton da Mata, and Rui L. Modenesi, *Encargos trabalhistas e absorção de mão-de-obra: uma interpretação do problema e seu debate* (Rio: IPEA, 1972), relatório de pesquisa, no. 12.

14. Carlos Antônio Rocca, "Economias de escala na função produção," unpublished doctoral dissertation, Universidade de São Paulo, faculdade de ciências econômicas e administrativas, 1967; William G. Tyler, "Labor Absorption with Import-substituting Industrialization: An Examination of Elasticities of Substitution in the Brazilian Manufacturing Sector," Kiel Institute of World Economics, Discussion paper no. 24 (Oct. 1972); David Goodman, Júlio Ferreira Sena, and Roberto Cavalcanti de Albuquerque, "Os incentivos financeiros à industrialização do Nordeste e a escolha de technologias," *Pesquisa e planejamento* 1 (Dec. 1971): 329-365. For a methodological criticism of these studies that arrives at similar conclusions about the elasticity of substitution see Roberto Macedo, "Models of the Demand for Labor and the Problem of Labor Absorption in the Brazilian Manufacturing Sector," unpublished doctoral dissertation, Harvard Universiy, 1974. On labor absorption during the 1960s by sector see Bacha et al., *Encargos trabalhistas*.

15. Cf. Mancur Olson, Jr., "Rapid Growth as a Destabilizing Force," *Journal of Economic History* 23 (Dec. 1963): 529-552; Wilbur Thompson, *Preface to Urban Economics* (Baltimore: Johns Hopkins Press, 1968), chap. 1.

16. Eduardo Arriaga, "Components of City Growth in Selected Latin American Countries," *Milbank Memorial Fund Quarterly* 46 (Apr. 1968); Douglas H. Graham and Sérgio Buarque de Hollanda Filho, "Interregional and Urban Migration and Economic Growth in Brazil," paper presented to the Symposium on Internal Migration at CEDEPLAR, Belo Horizonte, April 1972; Milton da Mata, "Urbanização e migrações internas," *Pesquisa e planejamento* 3 (Oct. 1973): 715-746.

17. Prefeitura de São Paulo, *Metrô: sistema integrado de transporte rapido coletivo da cidade de São Paulo* (Hochtief-Montreal-Deconsult, 1968), vol. 1, p. 36 ff.; Prefeitura de São Paulo, *Plano urbanistico basico*, 6 vols. (Asplan-Leo A. Daly-Wilbur Smith, 1969), vol. 2, pp. 42-44, vol. 3, p. 24; Arthur Rios, "The

Growth of Cities and Urban Development," in John Saunders, ed., *Modern Brazil* (Gainesville: University of Florida Press, 1971), pp. 269-288. For international evidence see International Bank for Reconstruction and Development, "The Task Ahead for the Cities of the Developing Countries," Staff working paper no. 209, July 1975, pp. 57-66.

18. Edmar Bacha et al., "Análise de rentabilidade macroeconômica de projectos de investimento no Brasil," *Pesquisa e planejamento* 1 (Jun.-Nov. 1971): 35-82.

19. Kuznets, *The Economic Growth of Nations.*

20. Lorene Yap, "Internal Migration and Economic Development in Brazil," unpublished doctoral dissertation, Harvard University, 1972.

21. Sergio Boisier, Martin Smolka, and Aluizio de Barros, *Desenvolvimento regional e urbano: diferenciais de produtividade e salários industriais* (Rio: IPEA, 1973), relatório de pesquisa, no. 15. This study did not control for capital per worker, which also influences output per worker. A better measure of worker efficiency, salary, was found to be invariant with city size, except for higher levels in São Paulo and Rio, where living costs and minimum wages are higher.

22. Joan M. Nelson, *Urban Poverty and Instability in Developing Countries,* Occasional paper no. 22, Harvard Center for International Affairs; Yap, "Internal Migration."

23. Samuel Huntington, *Political Order in Changing Societies* (New Haven: Yale University Press, 1968), pp. 229 and 382.

### 11. Toward a National Urban Growth Policy

1. A key official document that justifies the urban growth policy in the United States is Advisory Commission on Intergovernmental Relations, *Urban and Rural America: Policies for Growth* (Washington, D.C.: U.S. Government Printing Office, Apr. 1963). For an analysis of the political source of the growth policy, see Lowdon Wingo, Jr. "Issues in a National Urban Development Strategy for the United States," *Urban Studies* 9 (Feb. 1972): 3-28. For an analysis of British and French policies see Lloyd Rodwin, *Nations and Cities: A Comparison of Strategies for Urban Growth* (Boston: Houghton Mifflin, 1970).

2. A review of the major national plans can be found in Robert Daland, *Brazilian Planning: Development, Politics, and Administration* (Chapel Hill: University of North Carolina Press, 1967); Betty M. Lafer, ed., *Planejamento no Brasil* (São Paulo: Editora perspectiva, 1970); Jorge Gustavo Costa, *Planejamento governamental: a experiência brasileira* (Rio: Fundação Getúlio Vargas, 1971).

3. This analysis of the perception of urban problems is similar to Raymond Vernon, *The Myth and Reality of Our Urban Problems* (Cambridge: Harvard University Press, 1966); James Q. Wilson, "Urban Problems in Perspective," in James Q. Wilson, ed., *The Metropolitan Enigma* (Cambridge: Harvard University Press, 1968), chap. 12.

4. Rubens Vaz Costa, "Demographic Growth and Environmental Pollution," Rio: National Housing Bank, 1973.

5. For a summary of the structuralist diagnosis see Joseph Ramos, *Labor and Development in Latin America* (New York: Columbia University Press, 1970).

6. In the 1889-1930 and 1945-1964 periods Brazil was probably the Latin American nation in which subnational units had the most autonomy. The present centralization is reminiscent of the Vargas dictatorship from 1930 to 1945. For a full inter-American comparison see Francine Rabinovitz and Felicity Trueblood, "Introduction," in Francine Rabinovitz and Felicity Trueblood, eds., *Latin American Urban Research,* vol. 3 (Beverly Hills, Calif: Sage, 1973).

7. A breakdown of state and municipal expenditures is available for selected years since 1944 from *Anuário estatístico do Brasil,* various years. Comparable American data are from Oliver Oldman and Ferdinand Schoettle, *State and Local Taxes and Expenditures* (New York: Humanities Press, 1974), pp. 1-51.

8. The Brazilian tax reform and fiscal federalism are described in Hans Schellenberg and José de Souza Lima, *Um aspecto da reforma tributária: o fundo de participação,* Instituto de pesquisas econômicas, Universidade de São Paulo, 1971; Aloisio Araújo, Maria Helena Taques Horta, and Claudio Considera, *Transferências de impostos aos municipios e estados* (Rio: IPEA, 1973), relatório de pesquisa, no. 16, 1973; Harley H. Hinrichs and Dennis J. Mahar, "Fiscal Change as National Policy: Anatomy of a Tax Reform," in H. Jon Rosenbaum and William G. Tyler, eds., *Contemporary Brazil: Issues in Economic and Political Development* (New York: Praeger, 1972), pp. 191-212.

9. Oldman and Schoettle, *State and Local Taxes,* pp. 1-51.

10. Instituto brasileiro de geografia e estatistica, *Divisão do Brasil em regiões funcionais metropolitanas* (Rio: IBGE, 1972); Cleuler de Barros Loyola, "Urbanização e funções metropolitanas," *Revista de administração municipal,* no. 122 (Jan.-Feb. 1974): 40-48.

11. Instituto brasileiro de administração municipal, *Relatório das atividades, 1973* (Rio: IBAM, 1974).

12. Mario D. Andreazza, "A ponte Rio-Niteroi: dados e previsões," *Revista de administração municipal,* no. 119 (July-Aug. 1973): 55-65; "Metrô de São Paulo—aspectos financeiros," *Conjuntura econômica* 23 (May 1969): 83-93.

13. This discussion of BNH draws from *National Housing Bank: A Brazilian Solution to a Brazilian Problem* (Rio: BNH, 1973); Rubens Vaz Costa, *Urban Development Strategy and Programs: The Brazilian Case* (Rio: BNH, 1973); "Sistema financeira habitacional," *Conjuntura econômica* 28 (Mar. 1974): 45-49, 62-99; *Anuário estatístico do Brasil,* 1969 and 1970, table 4.1.1.1.

14. Hinrichs and Mahar, "Fiscal Change as National Policy"; Kenneth Cann, "Federal Revenue Sharing in Brazil, 1946-1966," *Bulletin for International Fiscal Documentation* 24 (Jan. 1970): 12-27.

15. *Anuário estatistico do Brasil, 1969,* table 4.1.1.1; Brasil, Ministério de planejamento, *Programa estratégico de desenvolvimento, 1968-1970,* 2 vols., Rio, 1967, vol. 2; Brasil, Presidência da república, *Metas e bases para a ação do govêrno, 1970-1973,* Brasília, 1970, pp. 215-220; "Sistema financeira habitacional," *Conjuntura econômica.*

16. "Sistema financeira," *Conjuntura Econômica;* Albert Fishlow, "The Brazilian Size Distribution of Income," *American Economic Review* 62 (May 1972): 391-402.

17. *Anuário estatístico do Brasil,* various years, tables 4.2.1.1 and 4.2.1.2.

18. *Anuário estatístico do Brasil, 1969,* tables 4.2.1.1b and 4.2.1.2b.

19. *Anuário estatístico do Brasil, 1968* and *1969,* table 4.1.1; Vaz Costa, *Urban Development Strategy.*

20. Affonso Fortuna, Márcio R. Villaça, e Wilma M.A. Couto e Silva, "Valores urbanos e habitação popular," *Revista de administração municipal,* no. 122 (Jan.-Feb. 1974): 49-78; Anthony Leeds, "Political, Economic, and Social Effects of Producer and Consumer Orientations Toward Housing in Brazil and Peru," in Rabinovitz and Trueblood, *Latin American Urban Research,* pp. 181-215; *Conjuntura econômica* 29 (July 1975): 72-83.

21. Lawrence Salmen, "Urbanization and Development," in Rosenbaum and Tyler, *Contemporary Brazil,* pp. 415-438; Govêrno do Distrito Federal, *Diagnóstico do setor transporte* (Brasília: CODEPLAN, 1971); David Epstein, *Brasilia: The Plan and the Reality* (Berkeley: University of California Press, 1973).

**Appendix. A Simplified Exposition of the Theory of Rents and Land Use**

1. Martin T. Katzman, "Industrialization, Agricultural Specialization, and Frontier Settlement in South-Central Brazil, 1940-1970," *Development and Change* 6 (Oct. 1975): 25-50.

# Index